SPALDING.

WINNING
DEFENSE

Del Harris

MASTERS PRESS

A Division of Howard W. Sams & Co.

Published by Masters Press
(A Division of Howard W. Sams)
2647 Waterfront Parkway E. Dr., Suite 300
Indianapolis, IN 46214

Published 1993.
Printed in the United States of America.

Library of Congress Cataloging-in-Publication Data

Harris, Del, 1937–

    Winning with defense: an advanced guide to man-to-man defense for players
and coaches / Del Harris.
    p. cm. — (Spalding sports library)
    ISBN 0-940279-76-2
    1. Basketball — Defense. I. Title. II. Series.
GV888.H36   1993   93-27102
796.323'6—dc20   CIP

Credits:
Front cover photo by Brian Spurlock.
Back cover photo by John Bievers.
Cover design by Christy Pierce.
Diagrams by Julie Biddle and Lisa Barnett.

Table of Contents

ACKNOWLEDGMENTS

It has been almost 20 years since I wrote my last book on basketball, *Coaching Basketball's Zone Offenses*, and more than that since I wrote *Multiple Defenses for Winning Basketball*. Professional basketball in Europe, the ABA and the NBA has consumed my time and more since then.

Over the years, I was always thrilled to encounter a coach who would tell me that one of my books had been a help to him or her. When I started, I read all the books that were out. I know that I could have never achieved any success without the help of books by Garland Pinholster, Adolph Rupp, John Wooden, Clair Bee, Glenn Wilkes, Ed Jucker, Joel Eaves, Doggie Julian, and many others.

The basketball community as an entity is indebted to people like Red Holzman, Jack Ramsay, Dick Motta, Cotton Fitzsimmons, John MacLeod, Bill Fitch, Chuck Daly, Hubie Brown, Pat Riley, Doug Moe, Larry Brown, Lenny Wilkens, Alex Hannum, Gene Shue, Larry Costello, Kevin Loughery, Stan Albeck, Billy Cunningham and many more who have given so much to the game as coaches. I would like to mention especially Don Nelson and Tom Nissalke as two successful professional coaches (four NBA/ABA league Coach of the Year honors between them) under whom I worked as an assistant coach. They both added to my understanding of the game and the NBA. Without that, any success I may have had would be less and so would the information found in this book.

I am also indebted to my loyal and able assistant coaches and the outstanding players that I have been associated with over the years: Frank Hamblen, Scotty Robertson, Carroll Dawson, Mike Dunleavy, Rudy Tomjanovich, Mack Calvin, Herb Brown, Mike and Larry Riley, Butch Carter, Al Hawkins, Mike Henry, and Chevy Rodriguez. Thank you, Moses Malone.

The urging of Al Menendez, long-time coach and NBA scout, and the interest of Manhattan coach Fran Fraschilla and Buck's scout Hal Wissel stimulated my interest in writing again. Therefore, this book is to fill in the blanks left in the *Multiple Defenses* book relative to man-to-man defense. The first book dealt with man-to-man on a basic level only. The strength of the book was that it was the first to explain in detail the match-up zones at half and full court and gave a good overview of how to use different zones and combination defenses in the context of game strategy. This book is the result of having lived with man-to-man defense for nearly 2000 games since then.

A special thanks to those coaches who read the book to give me their opinions prior to the final printing — Jody Conradt, Pat Summit, Gary Colson, Rick Majerus Gerald Myers, Sonny Smith, and Glenn Wilkes.

I would also like to thank a very special group of coaches that it has been my privilege to have been involved with one of the best clinic experiments ever conceived. Since the late 1970's, a group of coaches have met annually to compare basketball notes and to invite a few guest coaches each year to share the experience. That core group of coaches includes some great coaches/teachers, and I am indebted to them and proud to have been associated with them. Thanks to Glenn Wilkes for forming the group, Sonny Smith, George Raveling, Gary Colson, Bill Foster, Bobby Hussey, Murray Arnold, Rick Majerus, and Jim Calhoun.

Thanks to Baseball Canada, their players and coaches and especially Ken Shields, Dan Malemet, and all for their interest and support. And thanks to the Puerto Rico Basketball Federation for the opportunity to coach in Puerto Rico early in my career. Thanks to Milligan and Earlham colleges, and Jerry Pimm for my year at Utah.

Finally, thanks to my family and friends who have been of great support for so many years through the many ups and downs of all the games.

FOREWORD

I would like to preface my comments about Del Harris' book with some remarks about the man himself. Other than my own father, Del Harris is the finest man I've ever known. He's a wonderful father, a terrific husband, and a great role model. He is a person that I would like to emulate as a parent, and someone that I would want my children to have as a coach.

As a coach, the respect I bear for Del is immeasurable. I feel that he is the best X's and O's man in the game today. It has been my privilege to copy and employ many of his techniques in the years subsequent to our work together with the Milwaukee Bucks. As a result of his influence, I feel that I am a better coach, which is reflected by my winning percentage of nearly 80 percent at Ball State and the University of Utah.

Del Harris is an innovator. He is a fantastic clinician, but more importantly, he is an excellent teacher. Those of you who use this book will be privileged to "inside information" from one of the finest coaches in the game. Del gives his readers explicit and detailed explanations of his man-to-man defensive strategies, and I am sure that if you use them you will find the success that I have enjoyed.

In this invaluable reference tool, Del has addressed virtually every defensive situation and how to execute it. The book will challenge coaches at all levels to think about basketball defense in a new way, and thereby enable them to be become better coaches. If you were only able to purchase one book on defense, I would urge you to spend your money on this one.

I wish you much success and hope that you will one day have the privilege of working with or learning from this man. This book is a great way to start.

RICK MAJERUS
Head Coach, University of Utah

Basketball is basketball! For over thirty years I have coached this great game and have been privileged to have had championship teams at every level. Yes, I am talking about the 1981 Western Conference Champion Houston Rockets, the three Superior League of Puerto Rico Champion Bayamon teams, the Central American Games (with the Puerto Rico National team), the Earlham College (Indiana) teams that won 19 championships in 9 years, and teams at Spencer and Dale high schools (Indiana) that won Sectional and/or conference titles. In fact, the first team I coached, King Springs Elementary of Johnson City, Tennessee won its conference championship and was renowned for having scored over 100 points on four occasions back in the 1950's. I also coached the girl's team at King Springs.

If it can be taught, it can be learned. Simple enough, since without learning no teaching is taking place. But the point is that the depth of knowledge of man-to-man defense that I gained as a coach from my peers and the players in professional basketball over an eighteen year period is something that a high school/college coach and player can use. I have directed the text more to the coach, yet have purposely put in specific points of execution on the major issues of defense to help any young player who is really serious about understanding how to play man-to-man defense.

Though the pronouns used in the text are masculine, the game of basketball certainly crosses gender lines without need for elaboration. My wife, Ann, coached basketball for ten years and my daughter, Carey, played at Marquette University. A coach or player of either gender will find the text that follows of equal value in my opinion.

There are other books that can get a beginner started on the basics, but this one will take a coach or player deep into the trenches. After reading this book, watch an NBA game a little closer, and you will see a lot more defense going on than you have imagined, regardless of where you have worked.

It is great pitching that keeps major leaguers from batting .500, and without strong defense, NBA players are so good that they would score 150 points every night, even with all the travel. It is a fact that many people overlook or underestimate.

I hope that this book will be a useful tool for all coaches and players interested in learning the keys to winning defense. Good Luck!

Introduction

The Milwaukee Bucks built a tradition of excellence by playing hard, aggressive defensive basketball combined with solid, unselfish teamwork over a long period of time. At the start of the 1991-92 season they had compiled the second best won-lost percentage among all NBA teams for the 25 years of their existence. They had only three head coaches in all that time — Larry Costello, Don Nelson and myself.

The Bucks averaged 50-plus wins per season in the decade of the 1980s, despite playing in the Central Division. Although the Central was rather weak the first half of the '80s, it became the toughest of all divisions in the history of the game after the emergence of the Detroit Pistons and the Chicago Bulls in the middle years of the decade. The Central set an all-time record for the most victories among five teams in 1988-89 and set another one in 1989-90 by becoming the first division to have six teams play .500 or better for an entire season. The division produced five NBA champions and one runner-up in the six years from 1988 through 1993.

The key to the success of the Central Division was the general commitment to defense. It started with Don Nelson in Milwaukee in the early '80s and accelerated with Chuck Daly's Pistons and both Doug Collins' and Phil Jackson's Bulls. The division that also boasted outstanding coaches like Lenny Wilkens, Mike Fratello and others had no pushovers.

DEVELOP A PHILOSOPHY

Whether it's in the NBA or on the playground, one thing is necessary to win consistently: a commitment to playing strong, aggressive defense, both as a team and as individuals. This commitment is possible only after developing a *defensive mindset*, which means that each player makes a commitment to challenge every open shot and drive, and tries to force the opponent to make an extra play in order to score.

Our philosophy starts with the belief that a good defensive team must eliminate easy baskets as much as possible. To do that they must do the following five things every game:

- Have a great transition defense. Control the fast break.
- Prevent scores created by dribble and cutter penetration. Control the individual breakdowns.
- Attack the rebound and loose ball. Control the second shot baskets.
- Rotate to cover/prevent open men. Control the open shots.
- Force the opponent to make an extra pass or play.

An essential component of the *defensive mindset* is to control the immediate threat, and to do this requires knowledge of how to defend all the basic two- and three-man offensive exercises. Other essentials:

- Talk on defense. There has never been a great "silent" defense.
- Help on defense. Be willing to give yourself up for teammates.
- Defend against all penetrations. A good player is always in position to defend his man, the ball, and the foul lane.
- Have the courage to be physical, to put bodies on people, to make the first hit on blockouts and to challenge cutters.

After a team or individual is committed to playing the most consistent defensive game possible, a basic game plan for setting a halfcourt defense follows. The defensive game plan set forth in this book is confined to halfcourt man-to-man defense, but this in no way precludes the possibility of multiple defenses. The increased pressure today's fine three-point shooters put on zones has given rise to more man-to-man defense at all levels, and this happens to be a defense which can be adjusted to give different looks to the offensive opponent. This gives well-coached teams three or four defenses for the price of one. While a team's defense is largely in the coach's hands, it's good for each player to have an understanding of the various options available to him in trying to stop his defensive assignment.

This book shows upper level players and coaches how to perform advanced techniques of individual and team defense. It is not a book for beginners; neither will a player or coach want to try to do all of the techniques mentioned in one year. The concepts discussed are those that should develop over a period of time. Players and coaches should select those things that are meaningful to them and incorporate them into their own situations.

Part One

Developing Individually Within a Team Concept

Commit to Defense

It's not overwhelmingly difficult for a committed group of players with only average individual basketball skills to put together a very good team defense. Many good defensive teams are far better than the sum of their parts. Certainly each player must decide that he is going to improve as an individual defender as the season progresses to help accomplish this, but he must also make a commitment to the team that he is going to do his part within the system to help his teammates.

The old slogan was, "I'll get my man, you get yours!" But today's successful defense is anchored by people who say to one another, "I'll get my man and yours too, if you need my help!"

It's impossible for a player to accomplish many of the things he must do as an individual in the team defense, unless he knows he has the backup support of his teammates.

To instill our philosophy, we drill our team defense to be able to accomplish the following items — which we call *The Defensive Seven* — on a consistent basis:

1. **Have a great transition from offense to defense.** Don't give up fast breaks with quick, easy, offensive shots. Make the opponent score five-on-five against a set defense most of the time, not two-on-one or three-on-two.

2. **Push the ball to a sideline in order to establish a good weakside defense as early as possible.** A good weakside helps fortify the entry side, puts them in positions to attack penetration, and makes better defenders out of the players on the strong side.

3. **Keep the ball from reversing easily from side to side.** To allow the ball to swing easily creates defensive problems for the weakside people, preventing them from giving adequate help angles.

4. **Concentrate on stopping penetration via the dribble and pass.** Setting the defense early helps accommodate this.

5. **Prevent a consistent low post attack.** Do early work to prevent good positioning inside; challenge cutters and post up people. If the ball does get to a good position inside, it is vital to have a system of attack in terms of helping, trapping and rotating to reduce the damage.

6. **Rotate to assist a teammate** who has gotten into trouble by getting beat on a drive, cut, post-up or by losing his man.

7

7. **Rebound and pick up loose balls.**

Performing The *Defensive Seven* combines with *The Defensive Mindset* to create a solid defense. The payoff for the players who commit is that no individual defender has to be quite as good a one-on-one defender if everyone is helping each other.

In the end, each player must do his best to know and to develop the individual skills and to understand the team concept. When the players on a team commit themselves to one another to be a cohesive defensive unit, they get the feeling like that of an army going to war together. They feel they are a part of something that each can be proud of. They have spirit and camaraderie. And they have a team that plays consistently well.

TEAM DEFENSE IDENTIFICATION SYSTEM OPTIONS

In all of our team defenses, we prefer that ball contact be initiated in the backcourt — even when halfcourt zone pressing — but we number the different team defenses in our arsenal according to where the rest of the team defense comes into play on the attack. We have used number systems, color systems, hand signals and combinations of these to label our defenses. A coach must decide what works best for him in communicating with his players from the sideline.

Number System

40 SERIES — the first number (4) indicates pressure defenses attacking full court from underneath the opponent's basket to the top of our own free throw circle. The second digit in the number, such as the "1" in 41 indicates our regular man-to-man defense that starts by putting on some fullcourt pressure with the man defending the player inbounding the ball. The number "42" signals the run and jump style at fullcourt; "43" calls for the 1-2-2 zone press; "44" is the call for the 2-2-1 and "45" can be for yet another press such as a 2-1-2, or whatever other defense is desired, if another one is deemed necessary. No digit larger than 5 would be used in any of the defensive numbers to facilitate signalling with one hand.

30 SERIES — the first number (3) indicates three-quarter court pressure defenses initiating the attack basically in the area between our own free throw circle and the midcourt circle. The "31" call specifies that our regular halfcourt man-to-man will start by putting on some three-quarter-court pressure with the man defending the player inbounding the ball. The number "32" signals the run and

jump style, with pressure beginning at the three-quarter-court level; "33" calls for the 1-2-2 at three-quarter-court and the "34" indicates a 2-2-1 zone press to begin in the 30 area of the court.

The important thing is to try to have the signals be consistent and to make some kind of sense in order to ease the learning task for the players.

20 SERIES — the first digit (2) indicates pressure defenses attacking at the halfcourt line, including (or not including, as the coach prefers) the basic halfcourt scoring area defenses. The numbering should be generally consistent with the 30 and 40 area signals but the pressure will start in the back court near the halfcourt stripe.

10 SERIES (an optional series) — the first digit (1) can indicate the prime scoring area defenses or be used for out of bounds defenses in the front court. Numbers used would be 10, 11, 12 and so on. We have used 14 to indicate all men automatically switch *except* the 5-man and 15 for *all* men to switch automatically on picks and crosses.

1 SERIES (also optional) — indicates scoring area defenses or special defenses. Numbers used would be 1, 2, 3 and so on.

Hand Signaling System

The use of numbers to designate various defenses permits hand signals to be used by the coach to communicate with the players on the court. Sometimes, however, it is difficult for players to see clearly exactly how many fingers the coaching is holding up during the course of play, and confusion results. Defenses called from a timeout are obviously not a problem.

A coach will often use special hand signals instead of numbers or colors, or he may use them in addition to the numbers or colors. That is, the 44 defense might mean that the team is going to run a 2-2-1 zone press at fullcourt, and the hand signal for that defense would be two fists over the head. Examples of various hand signals are as follows:

- One fist straight up — a 1-2-1-1 at fullcourt.
- Two fists straight up — a 2-2-1 at fullcourt.
- An open hand up — fullcourt man-to-man, five-on-five.
- Two open hands up — run and jump fullcourt.
- One fist out to the side — a 1-2-1-1 at the 30 area.
- Two fists extended out — the 2-2-1 zone at the 30 area.
- One open hand out to the side — man-to-man at the three-quarter- court with all five men up on defense.

These are only examples, of course. Coaches can devise their own system, with their own definitions for each hand signal.

Other signals that can be used are the thumb(s) up or out, the fist(s) down, the hand on the chest, a fist in front of the face or at chest level or on top of the head, and so on. A team is free to use its imagination on this, but the signals should be ones that are easily identifiable.

Don't worry so much about the opponent stealing the calls; worry more about all five of your own players catching them.

USING COLORS AS DEFENSIVE LABELS

We have used colors such as "blue," "red," "yellow" and so on to indicate points of pressure or different overplays. Some coaches hold up color cards to communicate to players the desired defense, a method that eases the biggest problem with verbal signals — no one can hear the calls in a loud, tightly-packed arena.

Again, certain numbers or hand signals can be used in conjunction with the color system. It's all a matter of preference, and the main point to remember is that the identification system used is for the purpose of communication, especially during play. Any system should make sense for ease of learning.

We will not deal with fullcourt attacking defenses in this book, except that it's impossible to avoid discussion of our "1" defensive concept in the backcourt, as in our 41, 31 and 21 defenses. These are the numbers we use to indicate our normal man-to-man defense, which begins at some point in the backcourt.

It may seem strange that a 41, 31 or 21 call would be used to indicate our scoring area defense, but this is because of the need to keep emphasizing that *defense starts when we shoot the ball*. Once that becomes ingrained in players' minds, it's obvious that a halfcourt defense must begin in the backcourt, except for those times when the ball is already established in the frontcourt (such as an inbounds play).

THE 41-31-21 DEFENSES AND OUR HALFCOURT DEFENSIVE SYSTEM

By beginning our halfcourt defense in the backcourt, we not only make the offense use up some of their shot-clock time in the backcourt, but we contain any rapid advance of the ball more effectively. Naturally, this gives the rest of our defense more time to hustle back to get into their halfcourt defensive set. It also enables our defense to try to make the ball cross the halfcourt line on the dribble near the sideline.

It is a great help to our team defense if the ball is dribbled rather than passed upcourt. And, by getting the ball to cross the halfcourt line in an outside lane, we get a big head start on our weakside defense. Our 41, 31 or 21 defense is what sets all this up for the rest of our halfcourt concepts.

Our signal for the 41 defense is simply to hold up *one finger* for ease of communication. *One finger out to the side* calls for 31 and *one finger down* indicates 21. With that one finger we can communicate whether our defense is to be 41, 31 or 21. We also have referred to these positions as hard (41), medium (31) and soft (21).

THE 41 DEFENSE AFTER SCORES AND FULLCOURT OUT-OF-BOUNDS SITUATIONS

The point guard will *point one finger up* to signal the 41 defense, with the defender on the inbounds passer up in a hard position, a concept formulated largely by Bucks' assistant Frank Hamblen. Whoever is defending the man making the inbound pass gets into one of two positions, as shown in D-1 and D-2.

- He can get right up on the man out of bounds (as X5 does in D-1) and try to take away his vision, preventing him from making an easy inbound pass — particularly a long one to the halfcourt line.
- He can turn to get into the area between the ball out of bounds and the opponent's ballhandler to discourage a quick inbound pass to him. Ideally, he prevents any pass at all, or at least for two or three seconds (D-2).

While X5 does his job, the other players quickly get into good containing positions on defense and prepare to influence the offense to bring the ball up the court slowly. They must put a premium on preventing any middle penetration or easy downcourt passes. The man who is defending the opponent inbounding the ball recovers back to his man after the ball is passed inbounds. His objective is to slow the inbound pass and to discourage their best ballhandler from advancing the ball, but he must keep his own man in front of him as well.

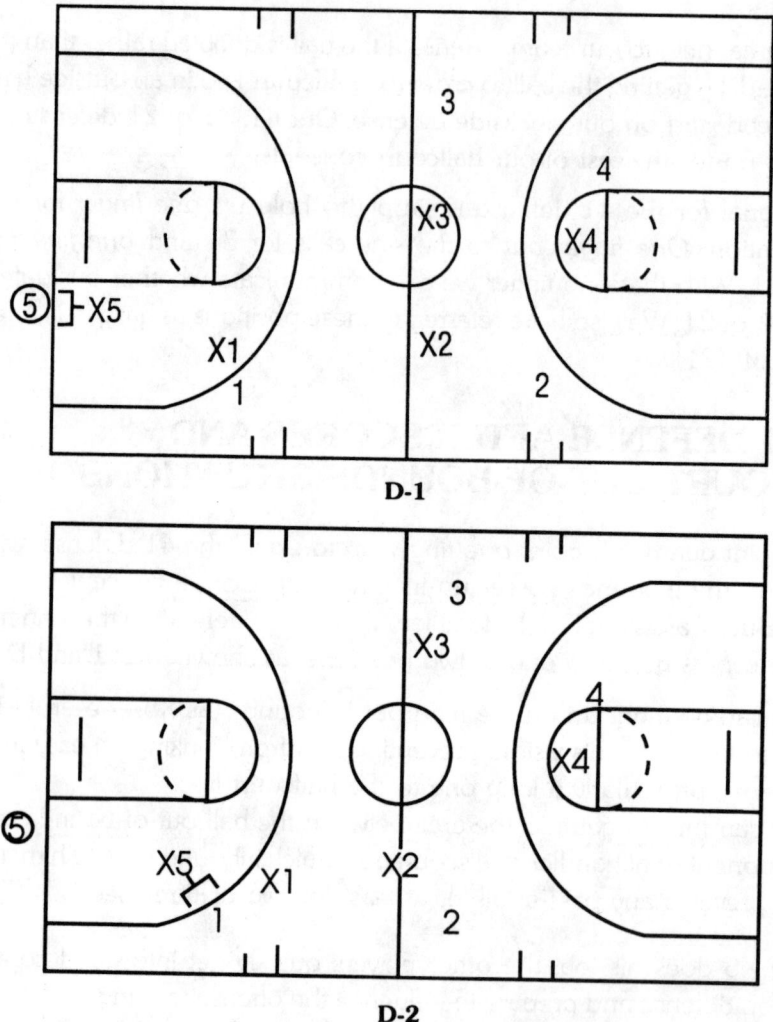

D-1

D-2

THE "31" DEFENSE AFTER SCORES AND ON INBOUND PLAYS

The point guard points *one finger out* to the side to call for the 31 defense. The defender on the man inbounding the ball gets to the area between the foul line and the top of the circle and moves a couple of steps toward the point guard as X5 does in D-3. This puts the defender on the inbound passer in a "medium" position relative to his man as opposed to the "hard" position in the 41 defense. He will stay in the area bothering the ballhandler and discouraging middle penetration until his own man comes inbounds and gets within a step or two of him. He then releases to defend his man, but tries to stay in a good triangle position with his man and the ball. His aim is to contain against a pass or drive to the middle as long as he can and still defend 5 (D-4). The rest of the players do as before. They get into positions to help slow the advance and protect against middle penetration or quick downcourt passing.

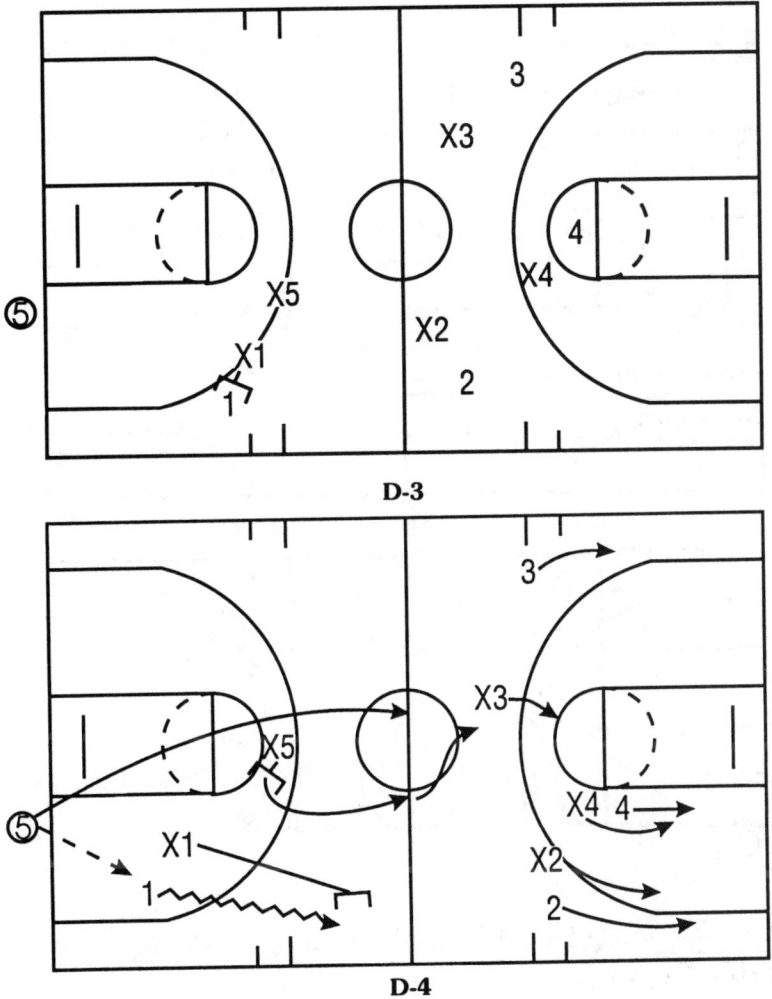

D-3

D-4

THE 21 DEFENSE AFTER SCORES AND OUT-OF-BOUNDS

The point guard will point *one finger down* to call for the 21 defense. The man defending the player inbounding the ball quickly gets to a position in the backcourt between the top of the free throw circle and the midcourt circle. This is a "soft" position and is used to jam the middle against the quickest of point guards.

He stays in this area to prevent middle penetration until his man approaches to within a step or two of the level of him as in D-5. This is very effective when playing against teams with a jet- quick guard and a quick-attack philosophy. Players with extreme quickness are sometimes too quick for a bigger player to be able to bother them at all in a 41 or 31. They out-maneuver the bigger players too quickly. Again, the objective in the 41-31-21 positioning is to keep the offense away from middle penetration and this softer position helps the slower player.

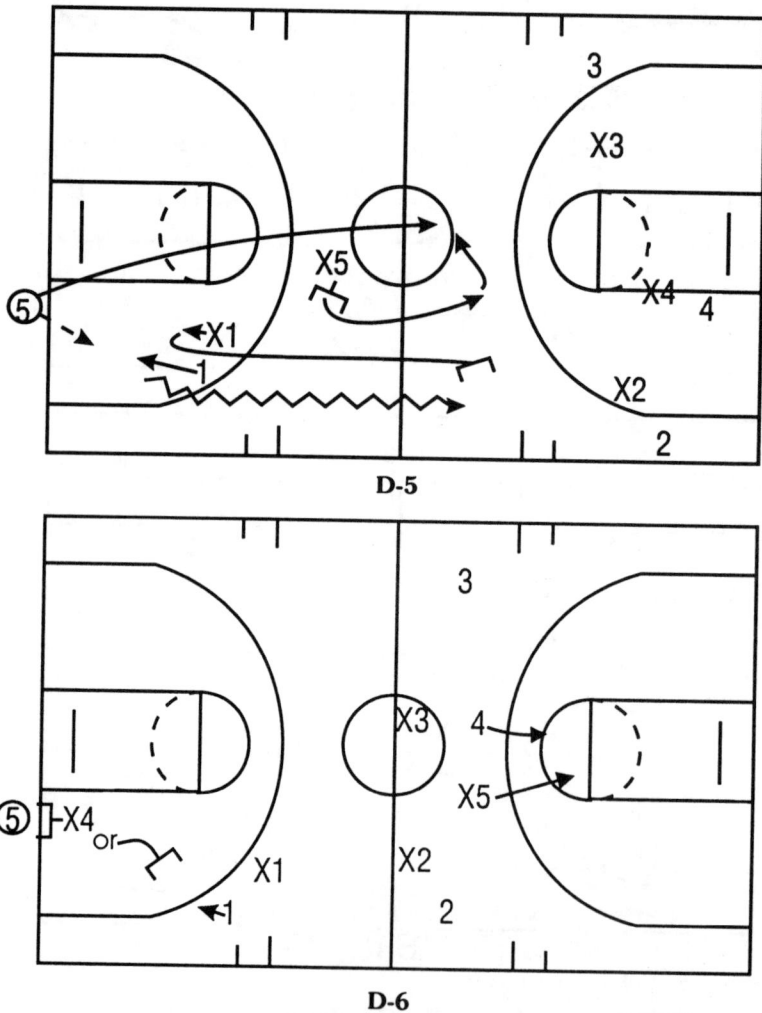

D-5

D-6

The rest of the team should react as in the 41 and 31 defenses.

POSSIBLE ADJUSTMENT IN THE 41-31-21 DEFENSES TO CHANGE THE POINT DEFENDER

Occasionally, a player might feel uncomfortable performing the role of point defender in 41-31-21 (the man defending the player throwing the ball inbounds). When that occurs, it is acceptable to have another player assume the role and allow the actual defender on the man out of bounds to switch assignments and go back down the floor on defense. This usually involves X4 (or possibly X3) becoming the "designated point defender." Regardless of who throws the ball in among the bigger players, the designated man would start the defense in whatever 41-31-21 position had been called. The players can adjust to getting back to their own man after the ball is in the frontcourt in most cases. D-6 shows X4 defending 5, while X5 goes downcourt and takes 4.

THE 41 DEFENSE AFTER MISSED SHOTS

The point guard cannot call this action, but it's really not necessary for anyone to call it. Players must be drilled to have an automatic and consistent response to missed shots. The player nearest the rebounder attacks the rebounder immediately to delay his outlet pass or dribble, as shown in D-7. Basically, all the other defenders get into proper containing defensive positions as quickly as possible to slow the advance. We will discuss this later and in detail under "The 2-2-1 Offensive Rebound Play," page 53.

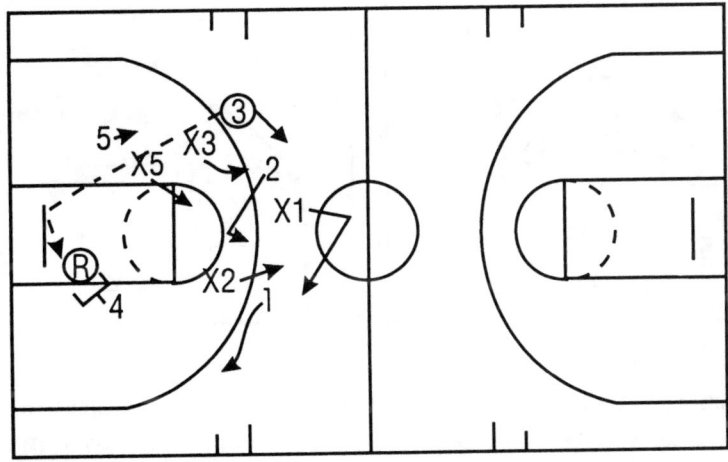

D-7

ESTABLISH A BASIC OVERPLAY IN THE HALFCOURT DEFENSE

We use the terms *fan* and *funnel* to indicate the direction of the overplay on the ball that is desired after the ball is in the frontcourt. Our basic overplay is the *fan* method — the overplay that influences the ball away from the middle. We're always in that mode unless we explicitly say that we are going to *funnel* the entire offense (or just one player) as part of our game plan, or as an adjustment in a huddle. We want the ball to be taken to the outside toward the sidelines and baseline as opposed to being passed or driven toward the middle.

Many coaches have long held to the theory that it's better to overplay and turn the ball toward the middle, "where the help is." The problem with that is that today's players are too skillful to allow them into the middle of the defense. From there, they can not only score and/or draw fouls, they have many angles for outlet passes to open shooters or inside to big men left open by defenders who have had to attack the ball penetration (D-8).

On the other hand, penetration toward the baseline does not enable good angles for passing the ball to open spot-up shooters (D-9). Any penetration that is too quick is a problem in any direction, but it is worse on the baseline. The worst defense is the one that influences the ball to the baseline and then does not have an alert team defense set to react to a too-quick penetration, because a layup will result.

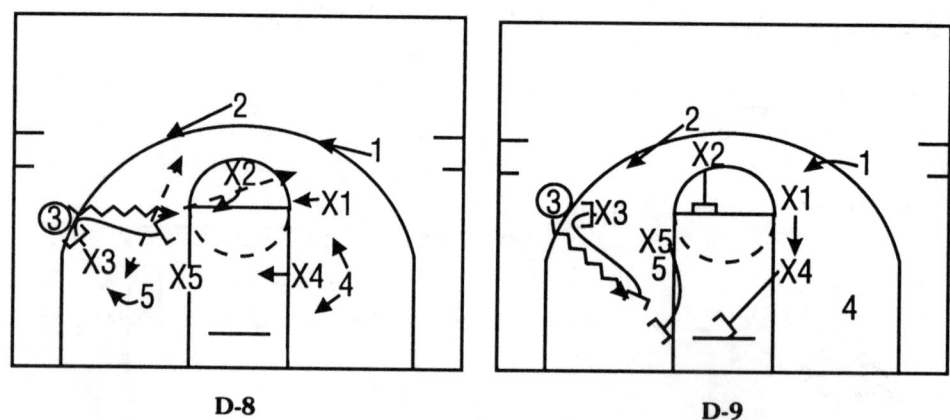

D-8   D-9

Occasionally we reverse our overplay from fanning to the outside to funneling toward the inside, but we do so only for good reason and knowing that we must do a great job of reacting to the middle penetration that funneling encourages. For example, we might funnel an offense that has a high post center, because the low post area is more exposed and more vulnerable to the baseline drive than a low post offense is (D-10).

We also will change our individual overplay to funnel the ball handler into our defense on most pick-and-roll plays. Some clearout situations also cause us to prefer to overplay the ball by funneling it toward the middle.

Unless it is specifically changed, though, it is understood that our defense begins in the *fan* overplay.

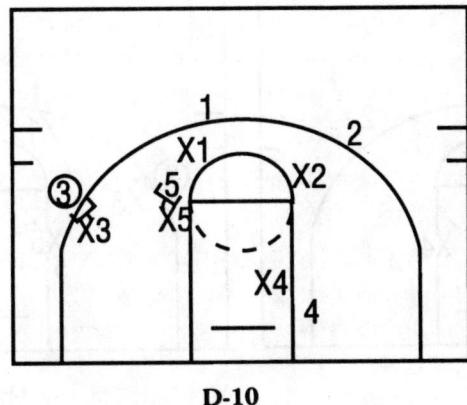

D-10

ESTABLISH A DEFENSIVE PERIMETER

As we've indicated, the simple signal "1" is the call to initiate the defense fullcourt even though the main defensive attack will be in the frontcourt. It is important for the team defense to establish a *line of demarcation* inside of which they are going to make it extremely difficult for the opponent to make a penetrating pass or drive. The colors in our communication system in the halfcourt defense relate to the selection of this *defensive perimeter*. The numbers 41- 31-21 simply stand as reminders that we will start our defense at a given point in the backcourt.

The color selected determines what our defensive perimeter is to be in the scoring area, as follows:

Blue indicates that our defensive perimeter will be at 19 feet in a containing, jam-up-the-middle defense. That is, we will make *every* effort to prevent anyone from receiving a pass or penetrating into the area from 19 feet on in toward the goal. We will allow the ball to be caught on the wing past the 19 foot mark but we will try to keep the ball from being reversed too easily in our normal fan overplay. We must overplay the wing and corner toward the inside when the ball is at either of those locations to help prevent the penetration into the middle.

The man defending the offensive player in the *swing spot* at the top of the circle has a key role in this defensive effort. He must extend his defense a step or so further than the stated defensive perimeter when the ball is on the wing to help prevent the easy reversal pass. He will not be called upon to give support to penetration if the wing defender does his job as he overplays to fan the ball to the baseline (D-11).

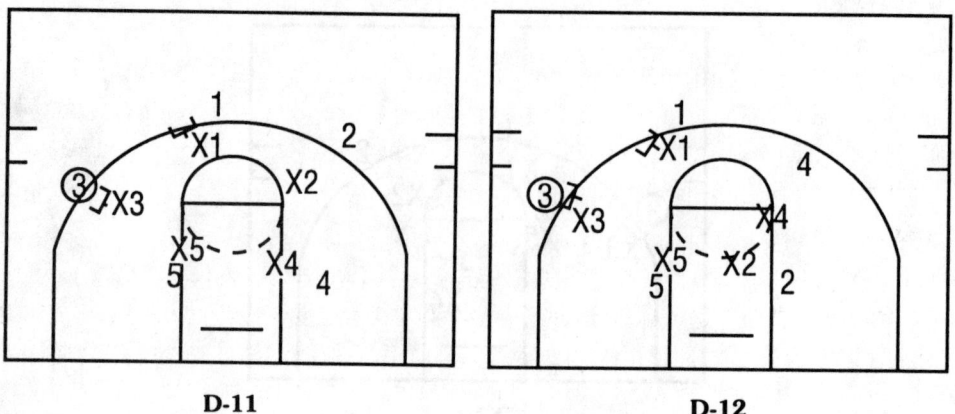

D-11   **D-12**

Yellow indicates that our perimeter will be 21 feet. We will allow the entry pass no closer than 21 feet from the goal, if we are performing it well. Again, after the pass is committed to a side in our fan overplay, we must extend the defender at the swing spot on top of the circle to a step or so further than the defensive perimeter to discourage the reverse pass, as X1 does in D-12.

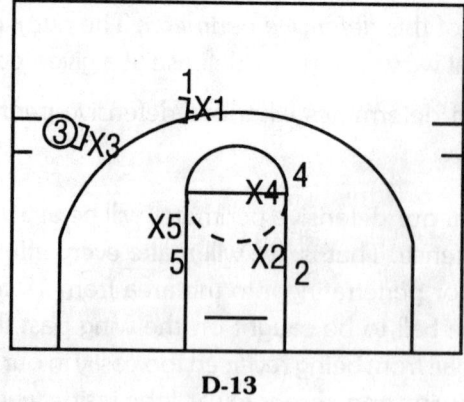

D-13

Green indicates that our perimeter will be 23 feet. Again, the defender at the top must extend himself into the pass lane from the wing to the swing spot at the top to deny the easy reversal (D-13).

In our defensive system then, a defensive call of "41 Blue" indicates that the man defending the inbounder should initiate the defense fullcourt and the team will establish a man-to-man defensive perimeter in the front court at 19 feet. A call of "21 Green," as another example, would mean to drop the man on the inbounds thrower to the halfcourt line. The defensive perimeter would be at 23 feet.

TRAPPING WITH MAN-TO-MAN IN THE FRONT COURT

We have come to prefer the number 22 to call for our extended man-to-man trapping in the front court in preference to using a color. It starts at the halfcourt line (the 20 area), and the second "2" reminds players that the 22 defense means to two-time (trap) the ball.

Number 22 indicates that we want to extend our defense to trap in the front court. Furthermore, to locate where we want to set the traps, we call "22 up" with the number held straight up to indicate we want to *trap the ball high* on either side of the halfcourt line as indicated by the X's in D-14. We originally said that we would wait for the ball to cross the halfcourt line to trap it, but because many teams get right up to the halfcourt line and stop, we give the players the option to trap right then, if they choose to do it (D-15). Coaches may also choose to trap this way right at the mid-court circle (from a general 2-3 formation, though it's still man-to-man) as a change-of-pace trap. This requires athletic people. It can be called "22 middle."

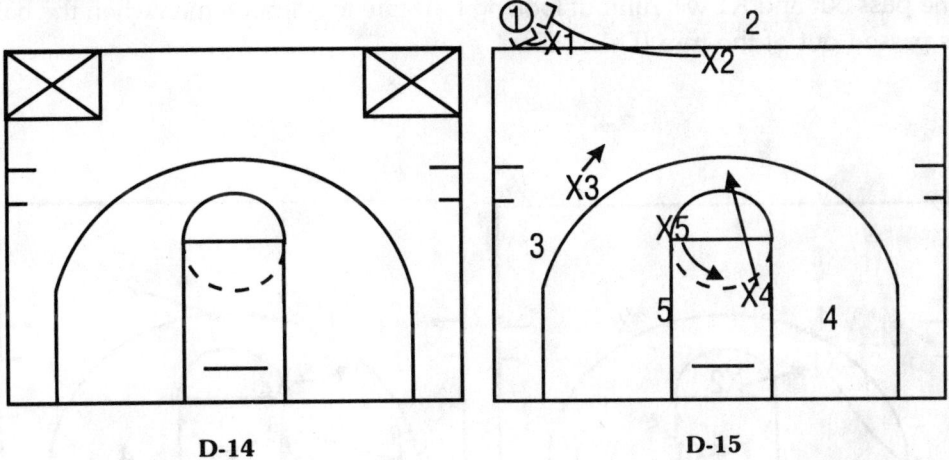

D-14   D-15

A call of "22 side or out" with two fingers held out to the side indicates we want to set a trap in the wing area between the foul line extended and the 28-foot hash mark. It can be with the two front men trapping (usually), as in D-16, or it could be that the forward comes up to trap with a front man, as in D-17. If X3 comes up to trap, X5 needs to be mobile or it's a risky trap. Player X3 would rotate off the trap as the ball is passed out and look to trap again or rotate to an open man.

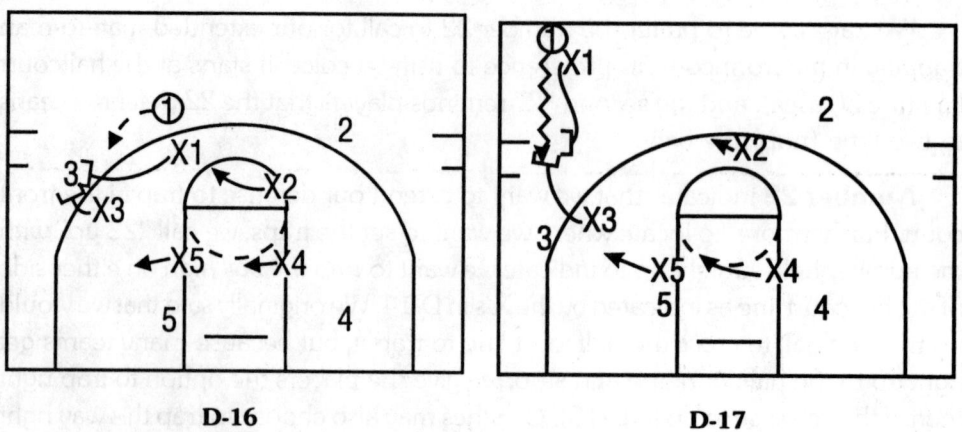

D-16   **D-17**

A call of "22 down" indicates that we want to trap the corner. The call, of course, would be with two fingers pointing down. Player X2 will zone up to play the pass out and X1 will run out looking to rotate to an open man when the ball is passed out of the trap (D-18, 19).

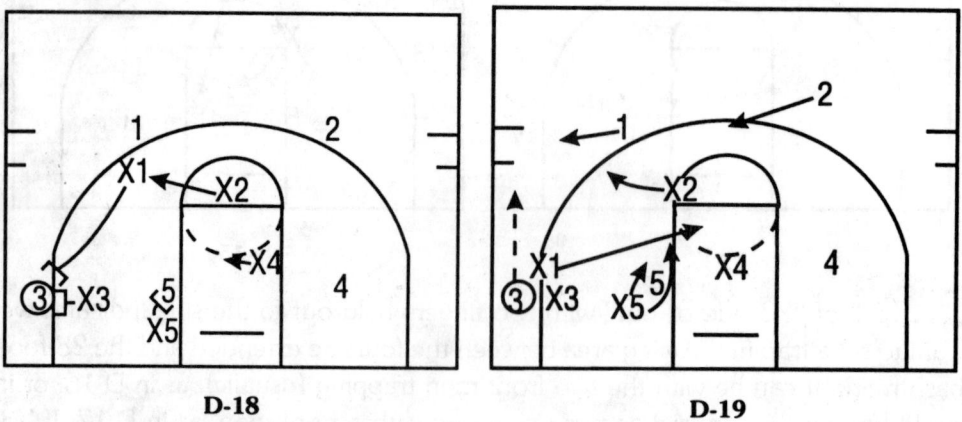

D-18   **D-19**

An optional trap is the elbow trap, called with the words "22 up," made with the elbow bent instead of extending the arm straight up (D-20). If the pass goes down to the low post, X1 would continue down to trap, as in D-21. If the pass goes across outside, X1 will follow to find an open man.

Note: Players X2 and X3 must zone up on 1, 2 and 3 when X1 traps. If the pass goes across to one of those players, X1 will follow and pick up an open man (D-22). Talking and pointing are musts. A quick review of diagrams 15-22 will reveal that the weakside players must get into the two weakside "zone spots" (above and below the foul line) whenever there is a trap of any kind in an outside lane.

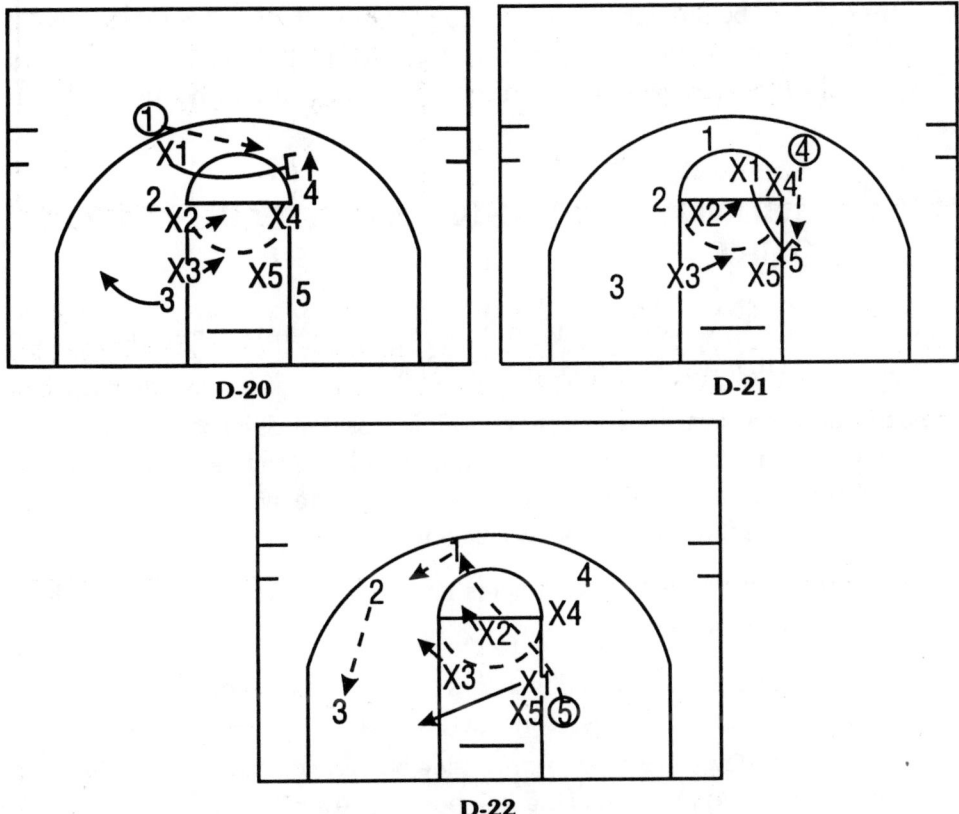

D-20   D-21

D-22

SPECIFIC FRONTCOURT OUT-OF-BOUNDS DEFENSES

It is best to have a separate set of signals for out-of-bounds defenses. They can be numbers or a combination of numbers with hand signals.

Because of the frequency of the out-of-bounds situations on the side during the process of a normal basketball game, it's a good idea to have several defensive tactics available. In the NBA it is absolutely essential. Not only do out-of-bounds plays from the sideline occur frequently, but NBA rules prevent the offense from passing the ball into the backcourt from the side-out situation. This makes it inviting to set up stunting defenses, because you have five defenders against four offensive players. The passer who is out-of-bounds cannot dribble or travel and has only five seconds to pass it in. It is one of the most difficult situations in offensive basketball.

Although non-NBA teams are allowed to pass the ball into the backcourt, it is still a good idea to have some special defenses available for these situations. Teams often have good set inbound plays from the sideline, and some trick defenses can help hinder their flow. More importantly, the game-deciding timeouts often are followed by the ball being put into play from the front court sideline. It is not wise to allow an opponent to run their desired plan of attack. If you are to get beat, make the opponent do it with something other than what was called in the huddle.

OUT-OF-BOUNDS DEFENSIVE STRATEGIES IN THE FRONTCOURT

There are many options available in selecting defensive strategies against side-outs. Some that we have used are as follows:

Number 10. This signals our basic, no-frills position defense. The defender on the man inbounding the ball plays up on him and tries to hinder his vision. He puts hand pressure on the ball as best as he can. Whatever defensive perimeter we are using at the time is what we will stay in.

We caution our players of the dangers involved in defending side-out plays; however, such as the following:

- We do not want to allow a direct pass to the low post from out of bounds, as in D-23. Thus, X5 must front the low post.
- We do not allow a pass to the strongside baseline corner, because the next pass can go too easily into the low post (D-24).
- We do not want to let the ball reverse easily. This final point is very critical, because if our defense prevents the pass to the low post or corner, the next-most dangerous option is the quick swing of the ball (D-25).

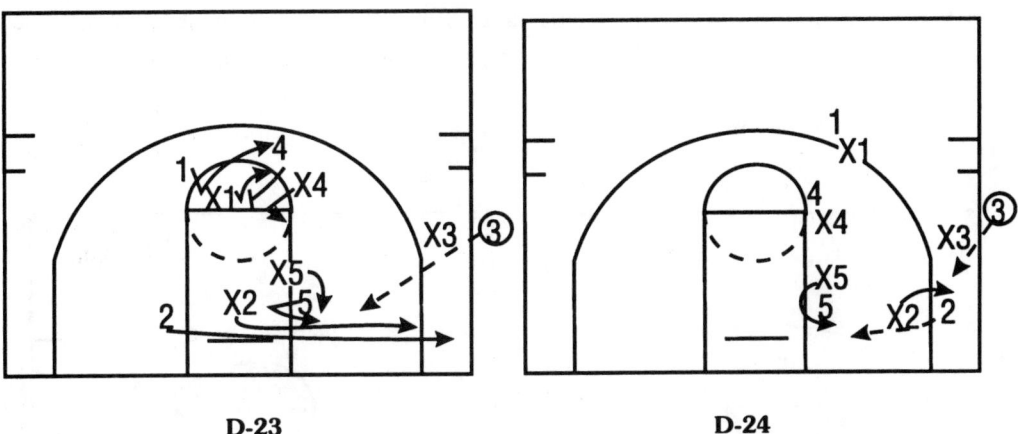

D-23   **D-24**

If we can keep the ball from reversing easily, we can do a much better job of defending their play, just as is the case against any offensive maneuver.

We want to switch on all readily switchable cuts and picks, such as when the switch exchanges equal-sized defenders or a big man inside and a little man outside. If we do any stunting out of the 10 defense, it would be to pre-switch any screening action we know will be coming up. As in D-26, we may pre-switch (invert) X1 and X5 when we know that 5 is going to set a downscreen on 1 to initiate the play. If the opponent learns to pull 1 to the corner and post up 5, we will not pre-switch since the post up would hurt X1 (D-27).

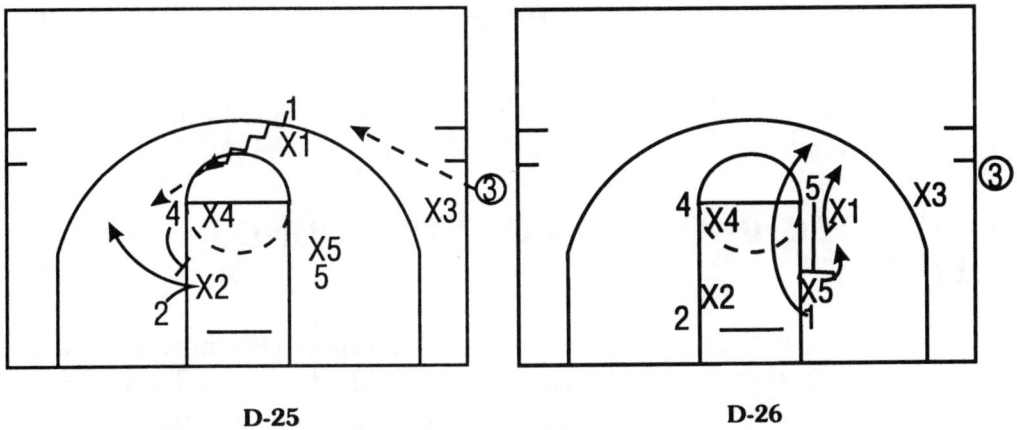

D-25   **D-26**

Number 11. This signals the defender on the ball to pressure the ballhandler out-of-bounds for only a count, or maybe two, and then to turn and deny the ball to the first man who breaks open. The other four defenders try to deny their men from receiving a pass. The objective here is to get a five-second violation.

The tactics can be varied to have the man on the passer let his man go entirely free and concentrate on denying the first open receiver, or maybe to deny their best scorer or main ballhandler from receiving the ball, particularly when only a few seconds remain on the clock. Again, the point is to make the opponent try to beat you with something other than the play they called in the huddle (D-28).

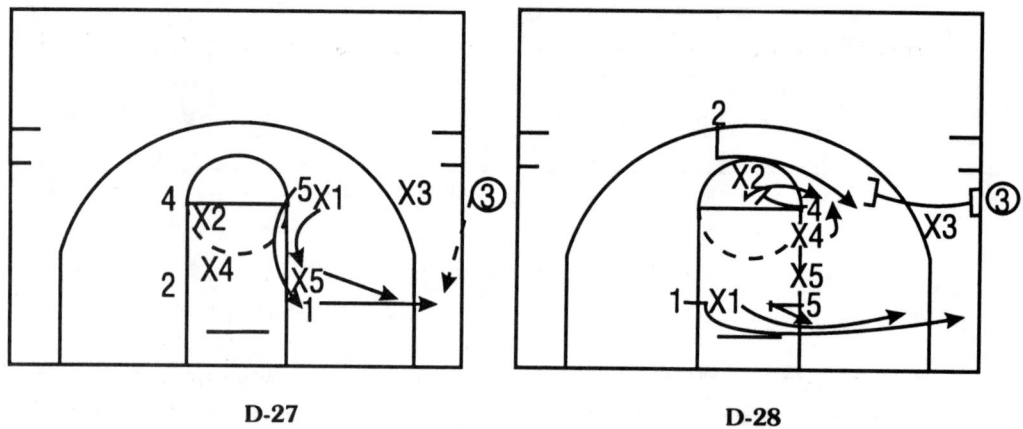

D-27   D-28

Number 13. This is a defense to be used when a quick shot or a three-point shot is expected. Depending on the time left for the offense to shoot the ball, the defense can make some adjustments, such as the following:

- Switch and deny on every screen or cross.
- Start with the big men on the inside and the smaller players on the perimeter, then perform automatic switches to help maintain the situation of big in-little out.

Note: The defense has problems if no switching is done in this situation, because the offense is likely to get a shooter open with good picks.

OTHER TECHNIQUES IN OUT-OF-BOUNDS DEFENSES

The defensive coach can call for a trap to be set on the first or second pass inbounds, or the coach can use the same "22 up," "22 side" or "22 down" to call for a trap when the ball goes to the wing or corner after it comes inbounds. Much of the same strategy that is effective against side out-of-bounds action is effective against end-outs as well.

End of Game Controversy

On side-out and end-out plays at the end of a close game, it is difficult to determine how the defense should play. We have followed the general strategies below:

- If we have not already been charged with a delay-of-game warning, we employ a strategy we brought into the NBA in 1980. We instruct our defender on the ball to get one after the ball is handed to the inbound passer. The defender waits one count to allow the opponent to give away the play it intends to run, then steps up inside the three-foot restraining area *without actually touching the ball or the inbounder* to get the delay-of-game warning. The offensive team's play will have been given away. If the offensive team has no more timeouts, it will have to run the same play unless it has been drilled to have a counter play in this situation.
- We definitely put pressure on the inbound passer if the clock is showing five seconds or less. Pressure on the passer with a long- armed, bigger player is both safe and sound strategy with only a few seconds remaining. With more time (certainly with 10 or more), the strategy does not demand ball pressure. Of course if your strategy does not prevent a score, the newspapers will say you did it wrong. Still, one can defend a strategy that denies the ball to a key player by pulling a defender off the ball.
- Whether or not to foul a player before he can shoot a three-point shot that will tie the game in a short-seconds situation is another tricky decision. At levels where the intentional non-flagrant foul is not a technical, this is a major point. Our NBA strategy has been to make them shoot the ball when we are ahead three points and there are more than five seconds left on the clock. The reasoning is that the shooting percentage will not be too high when we know that the shot is coming and that with time on the clock, we can still score again. Furthermore, they could score two free throws and still have time to steal the inbounds pass and score a basket to beat us. At levels where the three-point shooter is awarded three free throws after a foul, the intentional foul is not good strategy.

Again, our strategy has been that we foul when the ball is inbounded with five seconds or less or after the opponent has worked the clock down to that point.

I must admit, however, that twice in NBA games this strategy backfired on us. We fouled, the opponent made the first free throw and missed the second. You guessed it! They rebounded the ball and scored and we went into overtime. The good news is that we won both games anyway. But the point is that there is no sure way to win every time.

SUMMARY ON DEFENSIVE PLAY CALLS

Teams must decide exactly how they want to apply the above strategies during practice before the first game is ever played. The worst time to decide these things is in a huddle with thousands of fans around and the cameras on. If a team and coach can get together on a strategy ahead of time, it will add confidence and save the inevitable second-guessing in the ranks when the decision is made during a game. Nothing guarantees winning 100 percent of the time, but if a team can agree upon a strategy ahead of time it will have a better chance of surviving as a unit through the ups and downs of a season.

We have discussed play-calling and numbering systems a great deal in this section. A system of communication can be set up in any number of ways, but it should be something you like and can take pride in and, more importantly, will be easily understood by everyone.

RISK CALLS

It is sometimes advisable to include a "risk" call as part of the numbering or communication system. That is, a team might want to press fullcourt and be very aggressive and risk-taking to pick up steals or to raise the tempo of the game. Or, a team might press to slow down the opponent or break its rhythm. Steals would be considered an added bonus in the latter instance.

At times, the defense will want to run a trap from the man-to-man at the halfcourt level and the same proposition will be true. That is, it may be that the defense is best served by going all-out in a desperate attempt to catch up or to upset the opponent mentally; or the situation may dictate that it is best to be conservative and containing.

It is not a question of intensity, because the good teams play whatever defense they play with a high level of intensity. When a defense plays in a containing, conservative manner, such as when it is defending a 19-foot perimeter instead of a 25-foot perimeter, it does not mean that the players should not play it with a high level of intensity. A good player is intense in performing his assignments in every form of defense.

Adjusting the defense involves calculating the risks. A player who plays good position defense and contains his assignment within the designated perimeter of defense should not be considered a lazy player. Neither should a player who is supposed to be in a conservative containment be rewarded for being a "hustler" when he flies out of the team defense, rolls under the scorers' table and comes up with a hand full of air, forcing his teammates to scramble to cover for him and expose the middle of the defense that was intended to be packed in tightly.

We have used a "thumb up" signal to indicate that we want to increase our risk-taking and a "thumb down" signal to indicate that we want a very conservative approach to whatever our defensive call is. When a defensive call is followed by a "thumb up," if a player has a question on a risk, the answer is "yes." The answer is "no" when the call is "thumb down." Using no specific risk call after a defensive call means that the players are on their own to use good judgement on the level of risk they take.

CLOCK-ENDING DEFENSIVE ADJUSTMENTS

When there are only 10 seconds left on the shot clock, it's wise to call out a signal such as "clock," or use a color. Both the offense and the defense should always be aware of how much time is left. An intelligent offense will make adjustments for the final 10 seconds of the shot clock to get off a good shot rather than a heave from 25 feet.

Defensively, some adjustments can be made to make it more difficult for the offensive team to get the kind of shot it wants. Some of those tactics include the following:

1. Switch on every pick to prevent an easy catch-and-shoot action. The offense does not have enough time to capitalize on a mismatch.

2. Trap the pick-and-roll action automatically as early and as aggressively as possible. Make quick rotations to steal. It's difficult for the offense to make the two good passes necessary to beat the trap.

3. Trap the low post, preferably from the top of the defense, and rotate quickly for the steal. Again, force the offense to have to make two passes to get the ball into position to score in a short-seconds situation.

4. Apply the "star player" trap rule. Trap a really good offensive player who has the ball on the wing, corner or low post with the nearest man and force him to give up the ball. If the "star player" is out front be a little more cautious, but still look for an opportunity to trap if possible. If they are going to score, make them do it with less than their best player. At every level teams have players who are clearly better offensive players than their teammates. Make these people give up the ball when you can, and particularly so when there is little time for their teammates to make adjustments. When trapping the ball out of the hands of a great player, be sure that the defender who stays on that player (whether you rule it to be the original defender or the trapper) stays in position to deny a return pass right back to him. All the work would have been done for nothing if he gets it right back.

DEFENDING AGAINST THE "RUNOUT" PLAYER

Quite often an opponent will forego blocking out an outside shooter in order to run out to his own basket in hopes of receiving a quick long pass as soon as his team retrieves the ball. This is especially true when the defender has found himself out of position and has had to take a desperate run at the shooter.

The automatic rule for the defense is that the *shooter* must go with the "runout man," whether he is his own defensive assignment or not. He cannot go in for the rebound. He must become the first safety man on defense. He is the only one who will be able to defend this tactic on a consistent basis.

"FOUL FOR PROFIT" INSTEAD OF WASTING FOULS

Fouling is not against the rules, as such. Fouling is included as part of the rules. Like any rule, whether it is a tax law, civil law, or basketball law, the smarter individuals will find ways to make the rules work for them to their most advantageous way. Smart basketball coaches and players will always know the rules. If you do not, read them this week.

The point is that each player is given a certain number of fouls to use per game. They can be wasted on non-profit items such as reaching/grabbing in the backcourt instead of containing; grabbing or reaching around behind a driver in the front court instead of moving one's feet; fouling a jump shooter after he has already released the ball; softly touching a layup or postup shooter to give him a good opportunity to score a three-point play, charging in a out-of-control drive, etc.

A player who "fouls for profit" is one who uses his first two or three fouls in the first three quarters of a game to prevent easy scores. He does not allow an easy layup or a put-back on an offensive rebound. He fouls with enough force to guarantee that the "easy basket" is not made. While it is important for the players who play the most minutes for a team to be able to stay in the game, using one of two smart fouls will not be a problem. Then, late in the game, even the best players may have to take a foul for profit (possibly even their last one) if it keeps the opponent from making the critical, certain score.

A well-prepared team will know who are the poor foul shooters on the opposing team. When a player is known to struggle with the foul shot, the smart defender will foul when he sees that this type player is going to make a sure two points, provided the defender still has some fouls in his "bank" to use for profit.

Not only will points be saved by putting the opponent on the foul line, the psychological edge is still held by the defense in that they did not "give up an easy basket." It must be a point of pride to prevent the easy scores. Good preparation, position, and execution are the best ways to do that. But when those fail, a good tough foul will still get the job done. Remember that the opponent is looking for all the easy goals he can get and he gains confidence each time he gets one. Nothing helps a struggling shooter more than to get a couple of layups. Now the pressure is reduced for his next shot and his confidence is elevated, thus making him a bigger threat on his next attempt. It is a double-edged sword and the defense must make every attempt to maintain the upper hand. It all goes hand in hand with having the courage to be a physical team player.

FREE THROW DEFENSE

When the opponent is shooting a free throw, it is a crime to allow one of the offensive rebounders to get the missed attempt. The rules guarantee the defense the best positions and so the defense must concentrate to be sure to recover every rebound. You have fouled for profit, hopefully, so do not let them off the hook by being able to get the ball back to try it all over again. Your profit becomes a wasted foul when that happens.

It is not enough to block out the rebounders along the lane and the shooter. In the NBA, an alert player standing above the foul circle behind the shooter will sometimes crash the boards for the offensive rebound. Michael Jordan has made some spectacular baskets this way. The defense should line up with an opponent on free throws. In the situation where the offensive player is in a position to crash the board, it is best to face front the player in order to block out his path to the goal as X2 does to 2 in diagram 29.

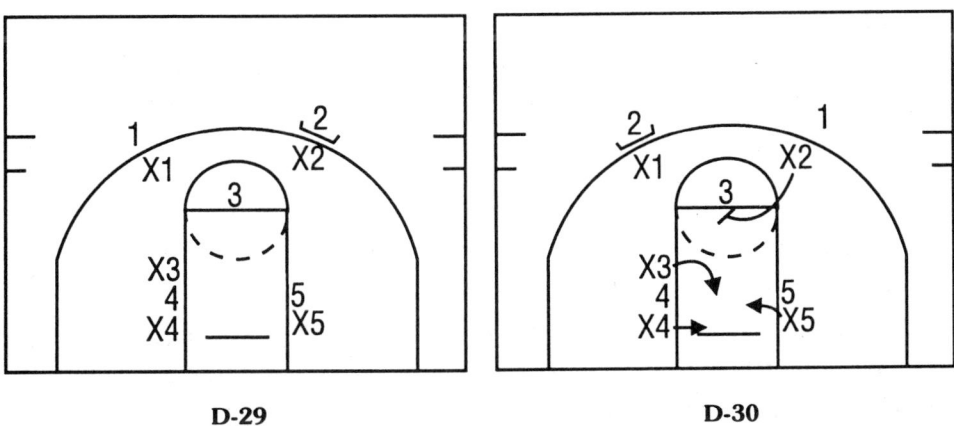

D-29   D-30

A different way to get an advantage on the free throw rebound in the NBA is to allow three rebounders to go to the basket (D-30). But to do that, X2 is called upon to block out the shooter. It is best not to do that if 2 is a logical board crasher, however. If that is the case, X1 can check the shooter, X2 can face front 2 and the three big men go to the board. This ploy is best done from a timeout in a situation where the free throw rebound is an obvious necessity. But it can be used more often; it becomes a matter of teaching it and giving it a signal /name.

GENERAL TRANSITION DEFENSE TECHNIQUES FOR HALFCOURT DEFENSE

Note: For a more specific transition attack that is a recent innovation refer to the "2-2-1 Offensive Rebound Plan" later in this chapter.

As mentioned, it's best to make defensive contact in the backcourt in all defenses when that is possible. Unless a fullcourt zone press is in order, our defense will be 41 Hard, Medium or Soft after scores or when the ball is thrown inbounds in the backcourt.

The defender on the ball can perform a tactic often called "playing the ball," or "putting your nose on the ball" to force the ballhandler to zig-zag in his path as he advances the ball up the court. However, it's important that the defender not turn the ballhandler into the middle of the court near the halfcourt line. Unless the defender knows that he has a trap coming at that moment, he will be turning the ballhandler right into a position very favorable to the offense (D-31).

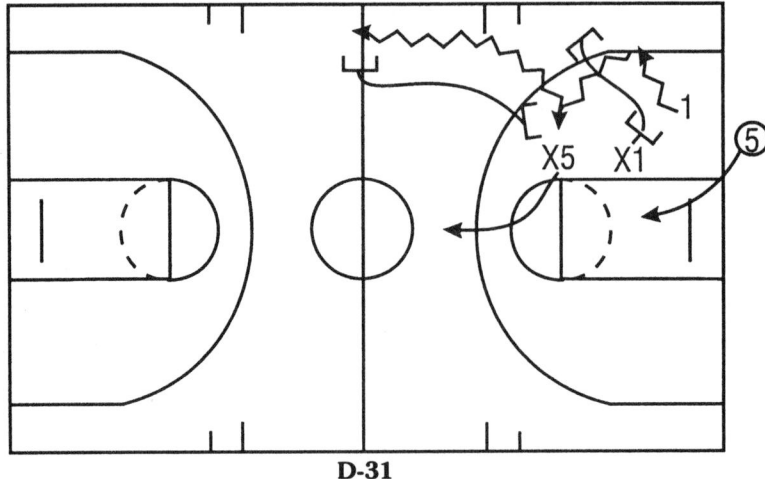

D-31

Therefore, it's best to do any turning that can be done early in the backcourt, and it is not paramount to do it at all. Be sure that the defense is in a position to angle and contain the ballhandler in such a way as to influence the ball to be dribbled across the halfcourt line in an outside lane as X1 does in D-32. He does not want to reach in and get beat in the backcourt — an all too-common defensive error at every level of play. The key word remains "contains."

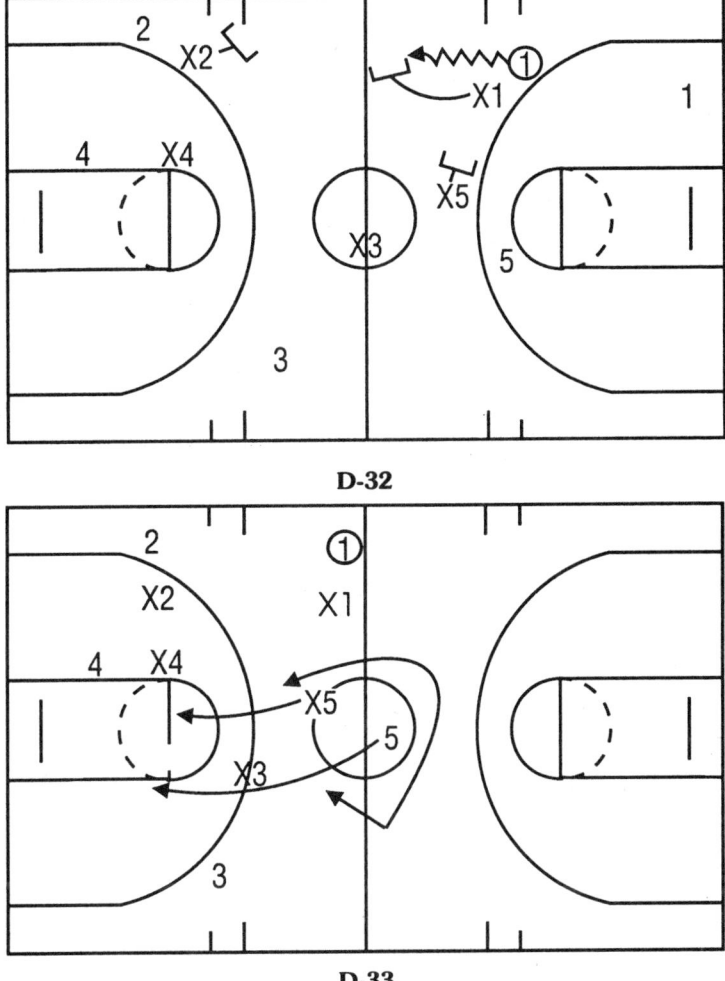

D-32

D-33

By accomplishing this, the defender on the ballhandler allows the weakside defense to begin its move toward the middle to give better help. And it allows the strongside people to concentrate on getting into position to deny passes to the wing and post areas that would be inside the team's defensive perimeter. Basically, it allows the defense to establish its defensive perimeter more quickly and safely as the ball enters the front court (D-32).

UTILIZE TRIANGLES TO CONTAIN THE ADVANCE OF THE BALL

Players other than the man defending the ballhandler must slow the advance of the ball, of course. And it's not enough for the rest of the team merely to run back quickly on defense, though that is the second best strategy. The best strategy is for the teammates to make a quick transition with purpose. That helps the ballhandler prevent the two things that will speed up the opponent's attack: getting the ball to the middle or making a quick pass up the sideline.

To help keep the ball from the middle, the defender nearest the ballhandler toward the middle of the court must form a triangle (as equilateral as possible) between himself, the ballhandler and his own man. In this position as in D-34, X5 is able to discourage any penetration with a dribble or pass by Player 1 and still account for his own man.

To help keep the ball from being passed directly up the sideline, the player nearest the strong side sideline must form a second triangle. This triangle is between himself, the ballhandler and his own man. It is a flat triangle in which he will be in a position closer to his own man than he is to the ball as X2 is in D-35. In this angle, X2 is able to discourage an upcourt pass to Player 2 and is still in position to help X1 if Player 1 tries to penetrate past him.

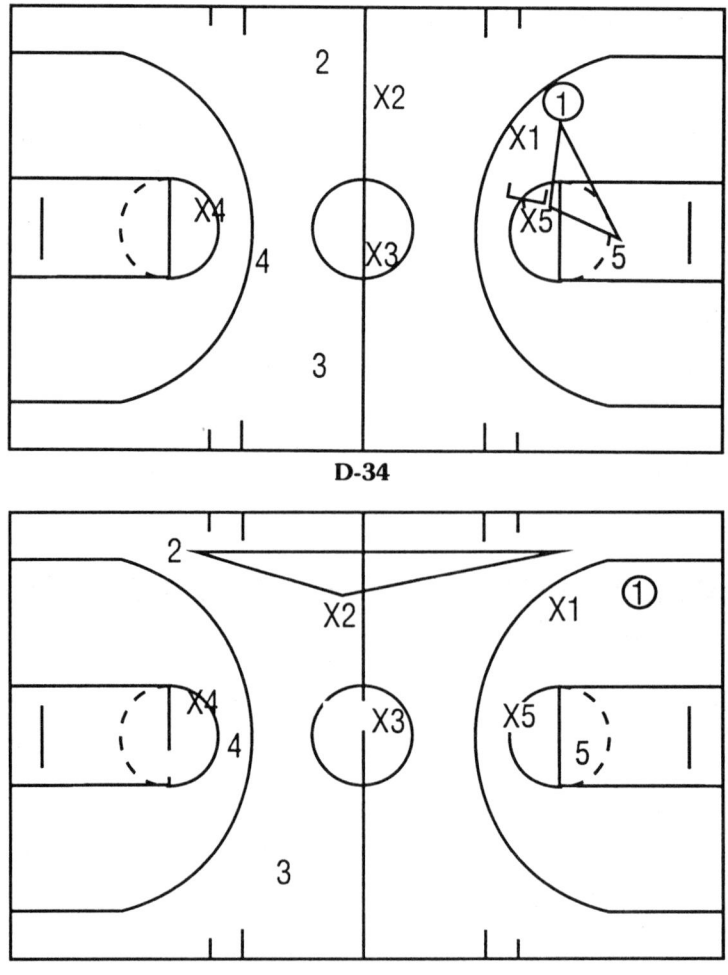

D-34

D-35

This leaves two more defenders to account for (X2 and X4 in the diagram) and those two men are very critical in helping stop an easy long pass and, more importantly, in preventing a middle attack. These players not in the positions where they are involved in setting the crosscourt triangle or the downcourt triangle must get back quickly and open up to the middle to discourage any pass or dribble penetration there.

Note: Transition defensive alignment after scores generally lends itself to a 2-2-1 formation, even when the defense is man to man. This is an important concept in getting the two triangles set and performing the basic transition jobs. Those tasks are to:

- Slow the outlet pass.
- Protect the goal.
- Pressure, but contain the advance of the ball.
- Prevent the sideline pass up the court.
- Prevent middle penetration.

INFLUENCE THE BALL TOWARD THE SIDELINE

Thus, D-35 shows all five defenders effectively playing the 41 defense. Each is doing his part to help slow the advance of the offense and to help make sure the ball is advanced up an outside lane with the dribble. It is easy to see that this puts the defenders in great attack positions in the front court.

Players X2 and X3 can communicate to get to the side of the floor their men occupy or can switch men with each other. The main point is that they must know the jobs of hindering the quick downcourt sideline pass and discouraging middle penetration. Diagrams 36-42 show X2 and X3 on opposite sides of the floor from the previous diagrams.

TEAM ADJUSTMENTS AS THE BALL CROSSES THE HALFCOURT LINE

With the ball in the front court, the defender on the ballhandler contains the ball with pressure (but he does not want to get beat with the dribble) and to influence the ball toward the sideline. X5 moves on into the post to defend 5 and 2 moves over to the front. Player X2 gets in a triangle position relative to the ball and his man, but he flattens the angle to put himself closer to his own man in D-36. X1 should not need help in the middle, because he will not allow 1 to penetrate the middle. This allows X2 to move up to deny 2 an easy swing pass from 1, since we do not want the ball reversed now that we have our weakside defense set.

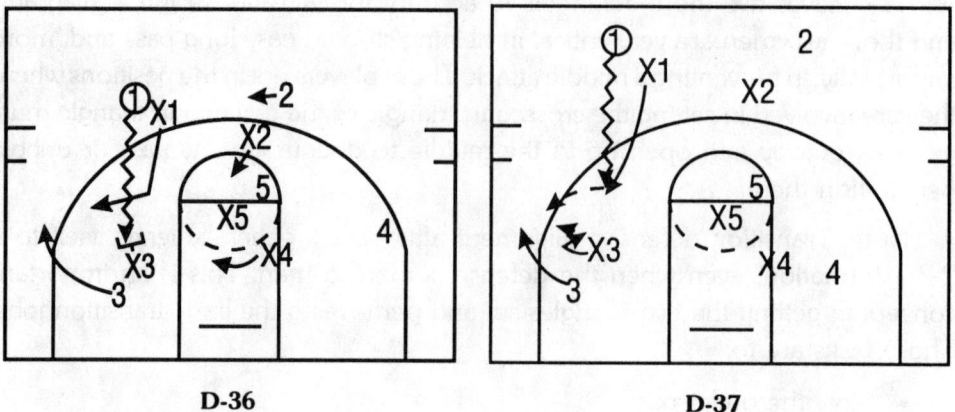

D-36   D-37

ALLOWING THE WING PASS OUTSIDE THE DEFENSIVE PERIMETER

D-36 shows X2 in the flatter triangle and X4 in a good helpside angle, defending his man, the ball and the lane. X5 is in a low post defensive position, denying a direct pass from the front. Also in the diagram, note that X3 is denying 3 a catch inside the agreed upon defensive perimeter — 19, 21, or 23 feet. But X3 has a second responsibility and that is to help X1, if he should get beat quickly by 1. X1 is giving 1 an advantage to the outside in our normal fan defense, so he must be able to receive help in that direction. So in D-37, X3 drops to an inside angle as 1 tries to beat X1. His hope is to flex in toward the inside angle to discourage 1 and influence him simply to stop or pass the ball out to 3. X1 would recover to 1 and X3 would recover back to his own man in that case. But if X3 had to commit all the way to 1 to stop him, he would.

If X1 were beaten badly and forced this move by X3, X1 would then have to rotate on over to 3, if 1 kicked the ball out to him after penetrating (D-38).

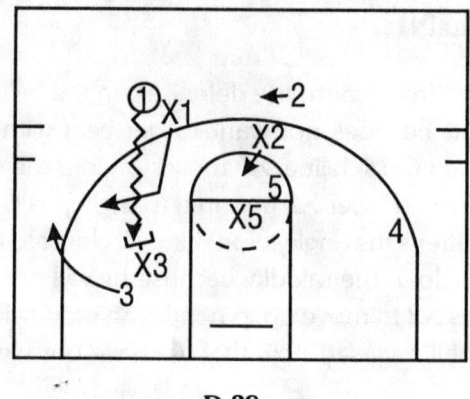

D-38

FORCE A HIGH ANGLE CATCH ON THE WING WHEN POSSIBLE

When thinking about allowing the wing to catch the ball outside the defensive perimeter, we want the wing defender to try to force his assignment to catch the ball at an angle higher than the free throw line extended. There are three reasons for this:

1. By denying to a higher angle, the wing defender puts himself in a tighter angle to help X1 in case of penetration by 1 in transition. Notice the smaller amount of space that 1 has to work with in D-39 as compared to D-40 where X3 allows 3 to get open below the foul line.

2. If 3 catches at the higher angle, he has a longer distance to go to get to the basket on a baseline drive. The longer path gives the low post and weakside defense more time and space to be able to move to help attack penetration.

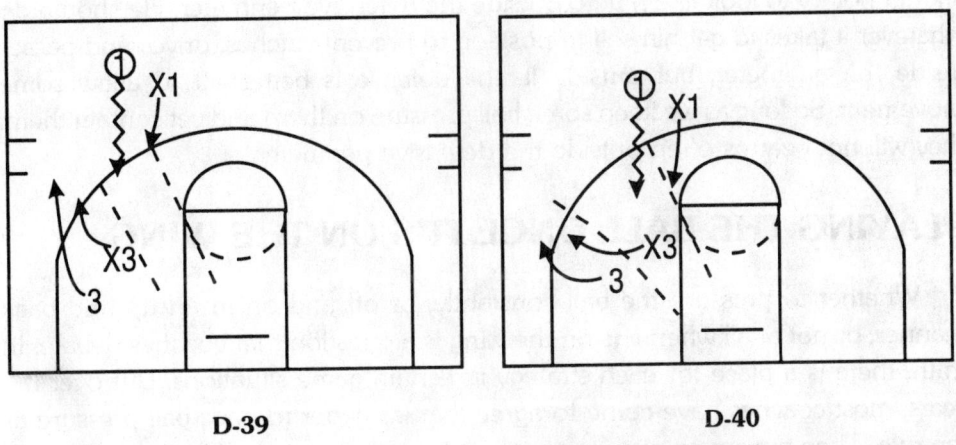

D-39   **D-40**

3. If 3 catches higher on the wing, it's easier for X5 to get a defensive angle on 5 in the low post. The angle to pass inside is far more difficult in D-41 than it is in D-42.

When the ball gets below the imaginary straight line between the wing and the goal, the post defender needs to worry about getting to the baseline side to defend the post, unless the posted man is down so far toward the baseline that it's unnecessary.

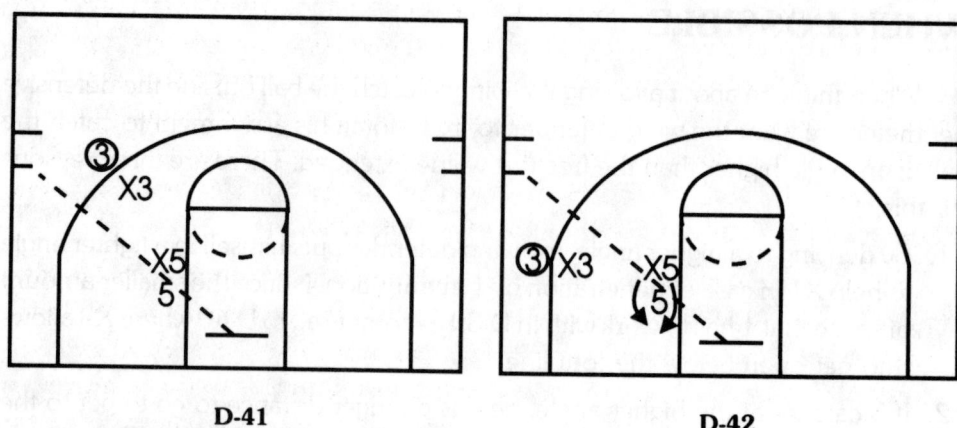

D-41   D-42

It is not a mistake to allow a man to catch the ball on the wing. In fact, it's *easier* to set the team defense if the ball is on the wing or in the corner, so a defender should not try to look like a hero outside the defensive perimeter. He should do whatever it takes to get himself in position to prevent catches, drives and passes inside the perimeter, but outside it, the defense is better off to allow some movement. So long as we keep some ball pressure on them and yet contain them, they will not beat us often outside the defensive perimeter.

PLAYING THE BALL ONCE IT'S ON THE WING

Whether to pressure the ball constantly, or off and on in an up and back manner, or not at all when it is on the wing is a question that coaches debate. In truth, there is a place for each strategy in certain game situations. But over the years, most coaches have come to agree that it's better to have ball pressure as the rule. Then a team or player can adjust from that occasionally if the situation calls for a different approach. Basically, more good things happen for the defense when ball pressure is exerted.

While ball pressure will work best for most players, there are occasions in the NBA when another adjustment makes more sense. For example, teams that play Hakeem Olajuwon will often dare the wing player to shoot the long shot as opposed to passing to Hakeem. After denying the man out to the three-point line, the wing defender may drop right back in Hakeem's lap. This discourages a pass inside and helps squeeze Olajuwon off of the offensive board, where he is very effective. The down side is that Hakeem's team works hard on its three-point shooting for this reason and can sometimes cause problems for this coverage. It's important to know which players are shooting the three well at game time and to know when to adjust to another coverage.

Another case in point is Michael Jordan. He puts the team that wants to pressure the ball hard on the wing in a different dilemma. While some players are strong enough and quick enough to get up and play tightly on Jordan for a while, no one has yet been able to do so consistently over an extended period of time. Ultimately, Jordan will break down the overly-aggressive pressure defender and penetrate past him. Jordan is the best ever when he's in a penetration situation. He can get to the goal, pull up for the short jumper, or dish it off to a teammate left open by the defender trying to stop the penetration.

Still, defensive philosophy and general game plans are established to cover game situations at a 90% level of success. Exceptions can always be made for specific games and/or players, if the team is grounded in well conceived and well understood principles. Therefore, good ball pressure makes sense as a general practice because most players aren't good enough offensively to try to penetrate when there's a defensive player in their face. The great majority of players will play better when they are in a "comfort zone." If a defender plays up close and tough inside that comfort perimeter, all but the outstanding players will function less effectively as penetrators, passers and shooters.

There is always a question as to how much of an overplay a defender can afford to play in keeping the ballhandler from penetrating middle, while still keeping him from beating the defender too quickly to the baseline before help can arrive. Diagram 43 shows the position the defender can take if he is quicker than the ballhandler, especially if the defensive teammate in the post can communicate that he is in good position by yelling "low post." Or , if the corner is occupied by an opponent, the defender can get up into this higher more aggressive position. In these cases, he knows help is ready.

However in diagram 44, we see the position of a defender who knows that he is defending a player who is quicker than he is and is not sure that help can arrive. He still has a fan overplay with his body position and should be able to angle the ballhandler's middle penetration up high toward the area above the foul line if he drives middle and also angle him to the sideline if he drives to the baseline.

The key to the foot position is to use the inside foot (the one opposite the baseline, nearest the halfcourt line) as a gauge. The more advantage the defender thinks he has, the higher toward the halfcourt line he can play. If the defender thinks he is at a disadvantage, he has to drop his foot position more toward the baseline.

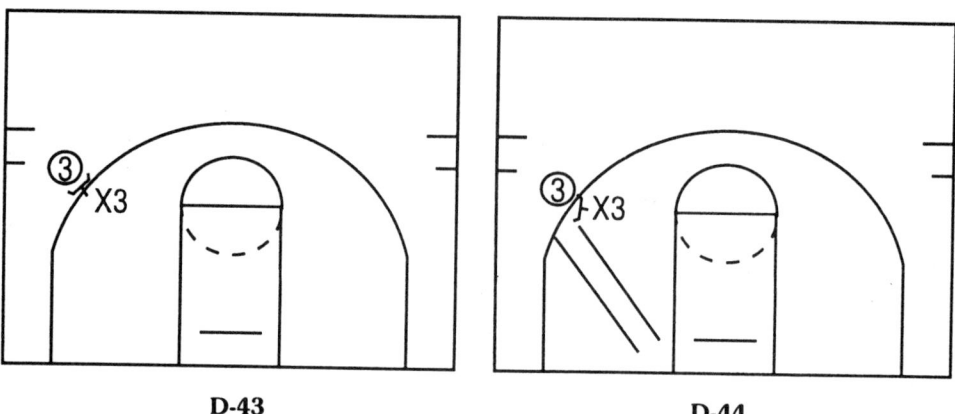

D-43   D-44

Another way to play the foot position is to have the defender try to get into position where his foot position straddles the non-pivot foot of the ballhandler. Some players find this difficult to do, while others handle it well. Whatever helps the individual to accomplish his goal is acceptable. When a player fails to do that, the coach needs to step in and help him adjust his position. Remember that the objectives are to pressure the ball and still contain the ballhandler so that he does not beat the defender to the middle at all and does not beat him to the baseline too quickly.

Ideally, the penetration will be able to be angled by the defender along the lines in diagram 44 so that it is not necessary for a teammate to leave his own man to help attack the penetration. X5 can flex in toward the action, see that his teammate has taken strong individual responsibility and be able to get back to his own man quite easily without giving up an easy draw and kick pass for a shot.

Once it has been proven that an opponent thrives on pressure defense, there's always time to soften the coverage and try other defensive strategies such as playing looser or trapping. Any number of possible adjustments can be made.

DO EARLY DEFENSE WORK IN THE LOW POST

While there are numerous techniques for playing individual low post defense, the most important is the initial contact made as the two opponents in the post fight for turf. D-45 shows how X5 can bump 5 away from the premium spot in the low post by making early contact, making the "first hit" that is necessary in establishing good physical inside defense. Because X5 "did his work early," the offense is forced out from the block area, allowing X5 to be able to play a flatter angle on 5, maybe even behind him. This lower angle on body position will give X5 the rebounding position edge when a shot goes up.

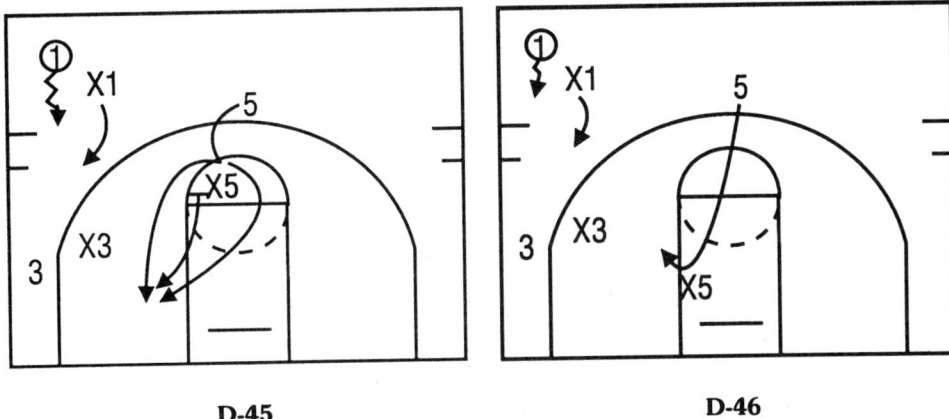

D-45   D-46

In D-46, X5 fails to rise up to meet 5 and establish early position, so 5 gets his prime spot. The closer to the goal the offense is allowed to set up, the higher the defensive angle must be by X5 — and the more important ball pressure on the passer becomes, because an easy pass to a good low post player who is in prime position puts the defense in a bad way.

If the defense allows the offensive low post player to set up right on the foul lane line or even in the paint, the individual defender must try to establish a front, or near-front position on the posted man. All but the big shot-blockers should opt for fronting when the posted man has a foot in the paint. Again, when a player has to get up in front, he must yell out "front" to alert all his teammates so that each can adjust to this new position (D-47). The ball pressure must increase and the weak side must drop to be ready for the lob pass.

The defender nearest the middle from the ball-handler must deny his man the ball in order to stop the lock-and-seal action on the reversal of the ball (D-48).

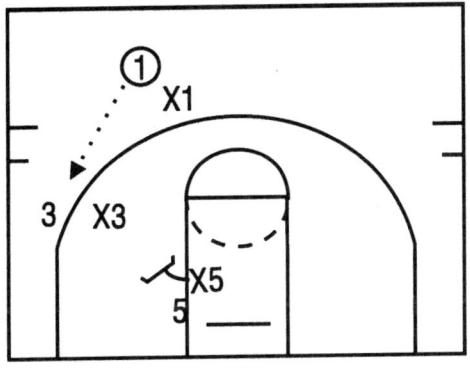

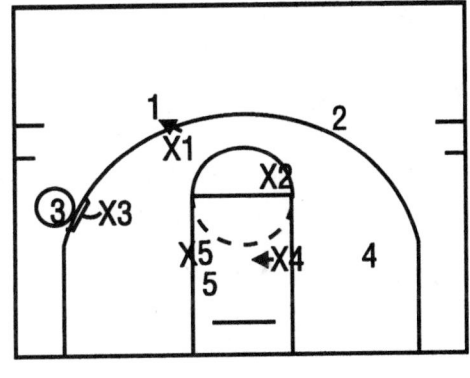

D-47   D-48

Diagrams 49 and 50 show how the distance the offensive low post player is from the goal determines the general body position of his defender. The closer the man is allowed to set up, the higher the defensive angle must become (meaning that the defender has to get to an angle that is more of a denial angle). Again, the higher the angle necessary, the more at risk the defender becomes. Therefore, the case for doing one's work early in the low post is an easy one to make. Scouting reports and a knowledge of the abilities of one's own players will affect the game plan strategy that a team decides upon. But this general analysis will apply in most cases. Since every player may have to defend in the low post at one time or another, it's important that each player be drilled on this aspect of defense.

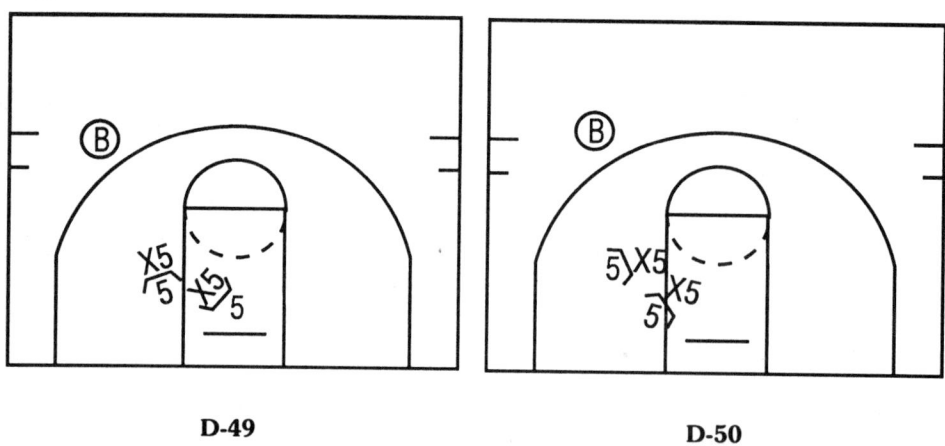

D-49   D-50

DEFENDING THE STRONGSIDE CORNER WHEN THE BALL IS ON THE WING

In general it's good for the defense when the ball is thrown into the corner area, so denial is not generally applied there. The exceptions might be if the opponent is having success feeding the low post from the corner, or if they execute a corner play action particularly well. For example, the Chicago Bulls can sometimes get their corner series going quite well out of the Triple Post Offense. When that happens, a denial of the corner pass is an easy way out of that situation.

For the most part, however, it's easier to defend the ball in the corner because the sideline and the baseline become defensive allies. D-51 shows how everyone responds to the ball thrown into the corner. X2 plays the strong fan defensive position to encourage 2 to dribble baseline.

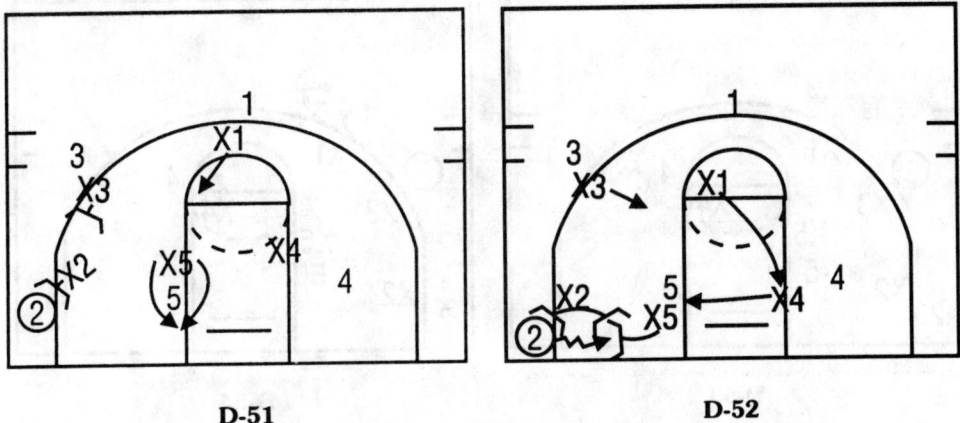

D-51   **D-52**

X5 has moved over the top of 5 (or under him if 5 was out from the lane far enough that X5 had a shorter defensive angle) and is ready to attack 2 if he tries to penetrate baseline. X3 is in a denial position for the pass back to the wing because the defense wants to keep the ball from swinging. The defender on top, X1, drops to zone the free throw line area, anticipating a steal of any lob pass thrown out of the corner. Player 2 has very few angles by which he can hurt the defense, but a pass up to the wing will allow 5 to pin down X5 and 3 or 1 could feed the ball to him in a threatening spot.

Weakside player X4 is in a crucial position. He is the farthest away from the ball and he drops even more into a help position. If 2 drives the baseline as he does in D-52, X5 must attack him with X2. When that occurs, X4 has to be ready to jam right in to cover the basket area and prevent a short pass to 5 from 2. In that case X1 would drop on deeper in a V-back to cover the weakside baseline area vacated by X4. X3 would loosen and zone the pass out of the trap.

DEFENDING THE TOP WHEN THE BALL IS ON THE WING IN THE FAN MODE

The defender at the top of the defense is as critical as the low post defender when the ball is on the wing. He is defending the "swing spot" of the offense. A good defense will not allow the ball to be reversed easily, since reversal breaks down the weakside defense and puts a lot of pressure on the inside defenders to change their body positions to prevent an inside pass. Any number of bad things can happen to the defense when the ball is reversed easily and frequently.

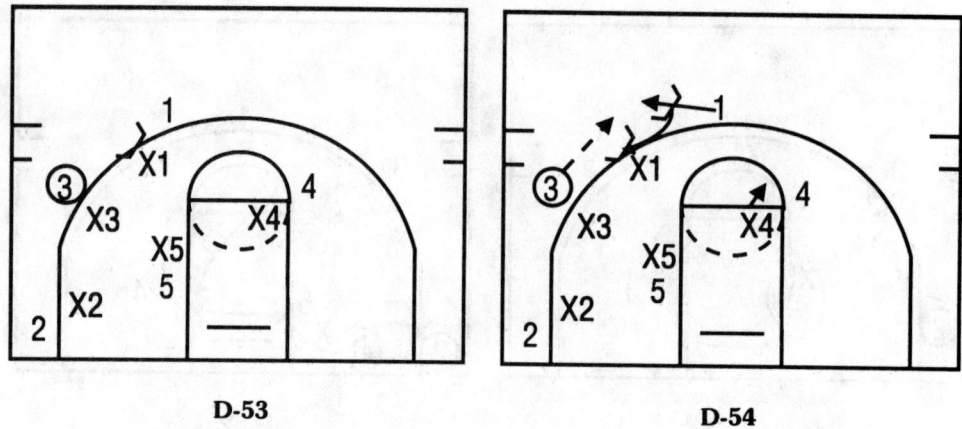

D-53   D-54

With the ball on the wing and the defense in a fan overplay, X1 must discourage the swing of the ball out to as far as 25-30 feet (D-53). Both the weakside and the low post defense should be set. Easy reversal of the ball will destroy this. If the ball is swung as high as 25-30 feet, both the weak side and the low post can adjust, since the passes become longer. When 1 gets the ball, X1 will still overplay the ball back toward the original side to try to delay the reversal (D-54).

DEFENDING ON TOP WITH THE BALL IN THE CORNER

The defender at the top must react if the pass comes out of the corner up to the wing, since he is the key man in helping make the fan overplay work. He drops to the foul line when the ball goes to the corner as in D-51. If the ball goes to 3 on the wing, he must deny the reversal pass wherever the defensive perimeter has been established. As usual, he will add three to five feet to the defensive perimeter to help prevent the ball from swinging from the first side to the weak side as in D-55. By challenging the pass out to 28-30 feet, he buys time and space for X5 to regain low post position on the low post.

DEFENDING ON TOP WITH THE BALL ON THE WING/FUNNEL MODE

If the defense shifts to the funnel mode as X3 does in D-56, the defender at the top has an entirely different responsibility. Since the ball is being overplayed to be turned into the middle of the defense, X1 must drop off his man altogether as he assumes the role of the primary helper to attack wing penetration. He is not at all responsible to prevent a reverse pass to his man outside of the stated defensive perimeter.

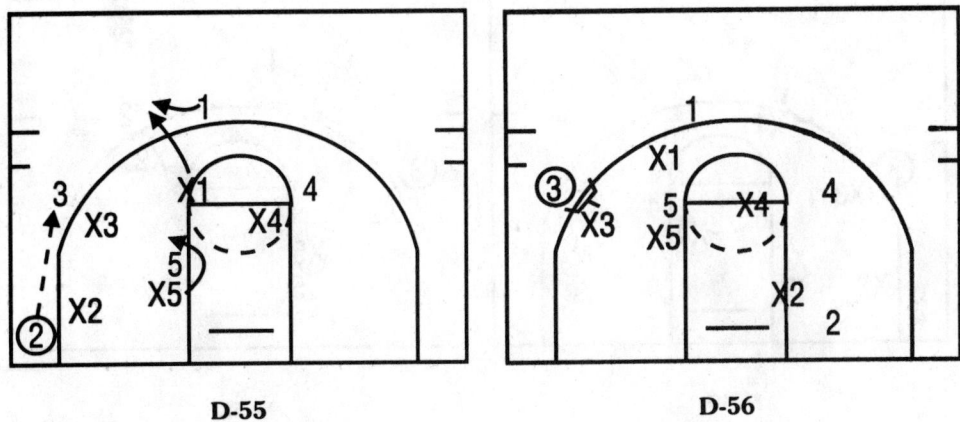

D-55   D-56

WEAKSIDE DEFENSIVE POSITION WITH THE BALL ON THE OPPOSITE WING

The weakside defense is freed to be effective when the ball is on the opposite wing in the fan overplay. There may be one or two defenders opposite the ball depending on whether or not the offense has filled the strongside corner. In D-57, X4 is alone on the weakside and in D-58 he has X2 with him. Either way, he must be alert for lob passes to 5 (when X5 fronts) as well as to his own man. However, his prime role is to remember his triple responsibility of defending "the ball, his man and the lane." By doing this he will be able to do the tough jobs he is being counted on to do:

1. **Prevent his own man from receiving the ball inside on a cut to the basket**.

2. **Be ready to attack penetration.** While his biggest worry on penetration is to get to the basket area on the baseline drive, he also must be ready to help even on middle penetration should X3 make a big mistake and get beat by 3 to the middle.

3. **Be ready to rebound.** The weakside defense must always be thinking "rebound", since most misses carom off to the weak side.

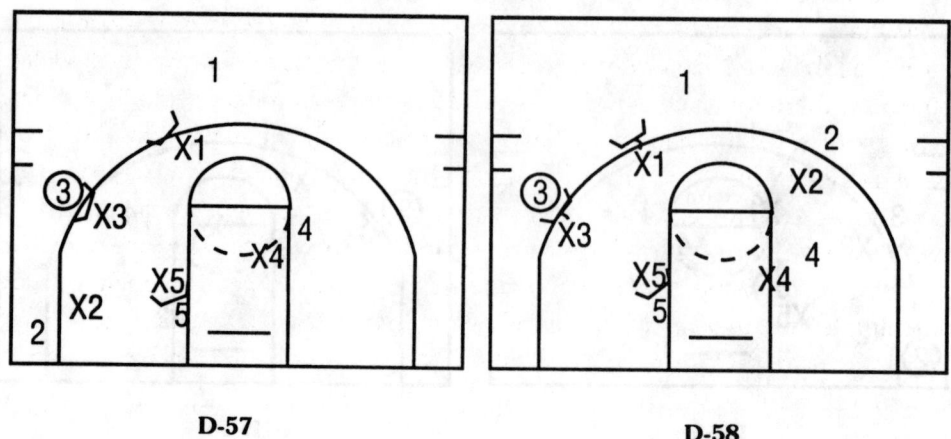

D-57   D-58

A GOOD DEFENSIVE SYSTEM HAS A WELL-UNDERSTOOD SWITCHING CONCEPT

The best defensive teams in the NBA maximize the use of switching in the man-to-man defense. They use it often and effectively, while most college coaches use well-defined switching concepts significantly less than their NBA counterparts. There are two reasons for this. First, there isn't nearly the equality or depth of talent on teams at levels lower than the NBA. Thus, the need to switch to prevent open shots is not quite as vital; furthermore, the lack of equality and depth also applies to the calibre of defender that would be called upon to switch to a superior offensive player. The other reason is that when faced with the need to do more switching, many high school and college coaches have opted to go into a zone defense, instead of adjusting the man-to-man coverage. I know I certainly did in my ten years in the college ranks. That was before I became immersed in the endless possibilities of man-to-man defense one is forced to learn to survive as a coach or player in the NBA.

With the emergence of the three-point shot and the increasing ability of players everywhere, switching is becoming more common at all levels of basketball. An advantage that the NBA and even international teams have with regard to switching is that the time clock is only 24 and 30 seconds in length respectively. This gives less time for the offense to exploit mismatches that may have resulted from switching. The 45-second clock (now, with the 35- second clock this is less true) allows more time for exploiting mismatches, but there are two saving factors for switching: one, most teams don't do a good job of isolating the mismatch to capitalize on it anyway, and, two, the defense can always trap the mismatch. Good switching techniques allow a team to have the advantage of playing man-to-man combined with the ability to cover the shooter/cutter freed up by successful screening action.

FOUR BASIC GUIDELINES FOR SWITCHING:

1. **Switch with teammates of equal or near-equal size on screens and crosses.**

2. **Switch to keep big players inside and small players outside on screens.** Do this on changes and crosses away from the ball when possible, and on matching up in transition defense, as well as in recovering on rotations. Any communication that can allow a switch to accommodate the big in-little out concept is usually worthwhile.

3. **Switch within fifteen feet of the goal** when one of the players involved has the ball or is about to get it as X5 does for X2 in D-59.

4. **Use the "emergency switch rule."** That is, switch whenever a situation arises in which a switch will challenge an open shot, regardless of the mismatch as X2 does for X5 in D-60. While X5 should get through on this action, sometimes he may fall down, get lost or just forget his job.

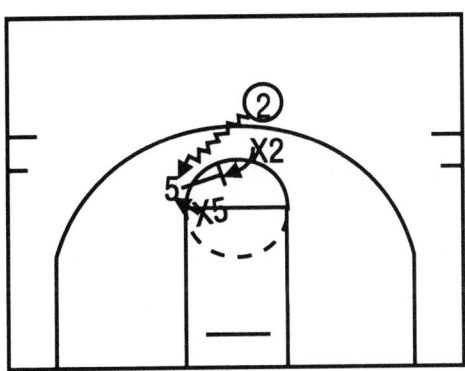

D-59

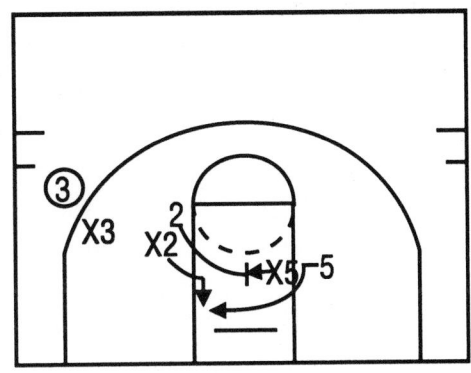

D-60

The reason for switching follows the basic principles of challenging every shot possible, forcing an extra pass, and of taking away an opponent's preferred options to force them to do something other than they want to do. Overriding every other reason for switching is our firm belief that mismatches won't beat us, but open shots will. Easy open shots will beat the defense at every level.

OTHER ELEMENTS TO SUCCESSFUL SWITCHING

Communication. Even though we have rules for switching and a game plan to dictate in which particular situations we'll switch against a given team, no switches are considered automatic. Players must physically come together when possible and call out verbal signals such as "switch", "let me through", "stay", "get through", "I've got high", "you take low", etc. In addition to the verbals, it's necessary to use the hands to point and pull or push each other through switches and stays when necessary.

Switch and deny should be considered as one big word — "switchandeny" — because both actions go together when done properly. That is, when there is a switch, something must be denied to each offensive player involved in the switching. If neither one has the ball, the defenders switch aggressively to stay in a position to deny each one the next pass. If one of the players has the ball, the defense works to deny the pass to the one who does not have the ball and to deny an easy shot or route to the basket to the one who has it. This helps prevent the laziness in defense that can occur when a lot of switching is used. Accepting this point can help players better understand that switching is not an easy way out of performing hardnosed, aggressive defense.

The picker's defender should play up close to the picker. Although there can be a few situations in which the coach determines that the defender on a picker should play loose off of his man, it is best to get into the habit of being on the body of the picker. If a defender is up on his man as he sets a pick, it's easy to take a step back to loosen up to give a teammate help or let him through; but it's more difficult to move up to help in time when a defender is too far away from the picker at the outset.

Switching that occurs in areas close to the goal (roughly 15 feet or closer) will definitely be of the aggressive "switchandeny" nature. The defender on the picker must be close to the picker's body to be able to get to his new man on the switch before he can shoot easily (if he has the ball), or before he can have an easy opening to catch, if he does not have it.

D-61 **D-62**

In D-61 X5 cannot switch or even make a convincing fake-switch ("hedge" or "show"), because he is too far off 5 as 5 picks for 1. However, in D-62 X5 is up in a position whereby he can switch to 1 and can push 5 up away from the goal with his inside hand as he does. In playing physically like this, he can slow 5's roll to the basket and break the rhythm of the ballhandler. He may even be able to draw the offensive foul from 1.

Areas where most of the switching will be done. The backcourt is an ideal location for switches and pre-switches. (The latter is a switch done ahead of time by two players inverting their assignments because they know there is a high likelihood they will be switching anyway. This way they do not have to try to get back to their own men in the frontcourt.) There is plenty of time to get rid of mismatches that occur 80 feet from the basket and a lot of time can be wasted by the offense in the backcourt as the offense struggles to bring the ball up against a good, aggressive switching defense.

The fifteen foot rectangular area in front of the basket is another common area for switching, as D-63 demonstrates. If the ball is involved, we apply the switch as part of our normal switching rules, as mentioned earlier. But even if it's not, a man allowed to be open within fifteen feet of the basket can cause a lot of damage to the defense; therefore, most proponents of the switching defense will say that a switch to deny into even the worst of mismatches is superior to allowing a free catch inside. Remember that the mismatch can always be trapped, but the easy open catch usually leads to a quick shot before anyone can be of much help.

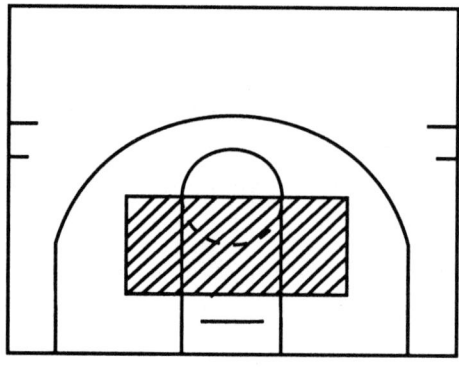

D-63

REBOUNDING IS A CRUCIAL ASPECT OF DEFENSE

The best defense is to be on offense. The opponent cannot score when our team has the ball, unless we're called for a technical foul. Therefore the team that goes after every rebound and loose ball is a better defensive team because they do the best denial defense of all — they get the ball more.

There is a lot of talk about denying the opponent the ball. The irony of it is that when we use that term, the opponent already has possession of the ball. True denial is when our team puts its bodies on people and gets the ball when a shot is coming off the glass or is rolling on the floor.

There is a common misconception that rebounding is "big man's work." That is partly true — it is certainly "man's" work in the hardest, toughest sense of that word. (Of course, many women are very good at this "man's" work!) Besides being NBA All-Stars, Michael Jordan, Magic Johnson, Alvin Robertson, and Oscar Robertson have at least one other thing in common: they are all guards who have lead their teams in rebounding.

Many players have made places for themselves on teams by being rebound specialists when their overall game was not strong enough. Good teams often have this kind of role player on their team. The annals of the NBA are filled with stories of limited players who had long, fulfilling careers by dedicating themselves to identifying with defense and the rebound. While lesser known than a lot of players, men like Paul Silas, Kurt Rambis, Larry Smith, Charles Oakley, Wes Unseld, Michael Cage, and many others had long and productive careers on good teams as rebounders and defensive specialists. Moses Malone was a three-time MVP on the strength of his primary talent — rebounding. Malone turned a lot of his offensive rebounds into points.

TEN STEPS TO BECOMING A BETTER INDIVIDUAL REBOUNDER

1. **To be an effective rebounder a player must make it a top priority.** A player has to want to be a defender and a rebounder. They go hand in hand and the same dogged determination is required to become successful at each. Success in both begins in the mind, not in the size of the body.

2. **Make the first contact when a shot goes up in the air.** In fact, Moses Malone began getting position when he thought a player was going to shoot. Think "body — ball" immediately. Hit a body and only then should a player look for and move toward the ball. The best method of blocking out is to step toward the nearest opponent and reverse pivot into him with a low, wide base. The object is to tie up the opponent's lower legs with the tail end. Spread the upper arms out wide with the elbows bent and the hands pointing upward.

3. **Keep the hands up for better rebounding.** Do not leave the hands down and do not reach back to hold the opponent as so many players do. Not only is it a foul, but a player will not get as many rebounds if the hands aren't held high. In position with a reasonably wide, low base with the arms spread and the hands up, a rebounder can feel his opponent move. He can move a step or two with him to keep him sealed behind him as he pursues the ball.

4. **Determine to go after every ball.** If a player goes after twenty balls, he may get four or five. If he goes after four or five, he won't get any. Good rebounders go after more balls than average players do. They aggressively pursue a ball after blocking out, not being content to get only the ones that come their direction. While some great, quick- jumping players have become outstanding rebounders without utilizing blockouts, it is still better to use the technique. The automatic blockout, even if it's just a touch and go, that precedes an aggressive pursuit of the ball is sound basketball at every level.

5. **Make space for yourself to rebound when the shot goes up.** The forward step into your man followed by a reverse pivot will help give more space between your body position and the goal. It's easy to rebound a ball in front of the body, but very difficult to jump backwards to get one. A player must establish his position early so that he does not get pushed in underneath the basket into a position where there are virtually no rebounds.

6. **Be relentless.** Good rebounders do not give up on a ball because they get blocked out or seem to be out of position. They work to get themselves into the action by spinning around people or by going to the baseline under the blockout and knifing back up into the lane to battle for the ball. They jump the second and third time for the ball.

7. **Get to the logical rebound angles.** Go to the weak side for rebounds when possible. Seal off rebounders who have deep inside position. Push them deeper and lock them up so they cannot get out. Then chase down any long rebounds.

8. **Guards should consider rebounding a challenge,** especially the defensive rebound. On both ends of the court there are now more long rebounds than in previous years because of the proliferation of three-point shots. Long shots that are missed equal long rebounds. Guards who are alert and tough will claim a lot of these balls.

9. **Plan for offensive rebounding by taking decent shots.** Shots that come within the framework of the offense should give the offense more of an opportunity to rebound because the shots are expected and a well- constructed offensive attack will take into consideration the positioning of rebounders.

10. **Study your teammates' shooting habits and learn those of your opponents.** This way, you'll know whose shot rebounds softly and whose come off the board hard. This will help in the anticipation of rebound angles and in the execution of the above ten steps.

THE WEAKSIDE SEAL-OFF

We have already alluded to the point which is common knowledge among basketball people, that most missed shots rebound in the direction opposite the spot where the shot was released. An underestimated tactic called "sealing off the weakside rebound" can be very helpful in increasing the chances for rebounding weakside misses.

In D-64 player 2 shoots from the right wing. X2 touches 2 and gets to the middle (foul line area) for the long rebound. X1 executes the seal-off by putting his right hip on player 4. X4 already has blocked off 4, but 4 would have as a good a chance of getting the rebound because he has in effect also sealed off X4 from getting any long rebound. However, X1 has come down and put his inside leg (right leg) between 4's legs and locks 4's tail end up with his right hip. X1 is facing the baseline in this position and has vision of the ball in flight. If the ball rebounds short, X1 can help tie up 4's legs so he cannot jump as well. If the ball rebounds long, X1 will be able to seal 4 off and run down all of the long ones (D-65).

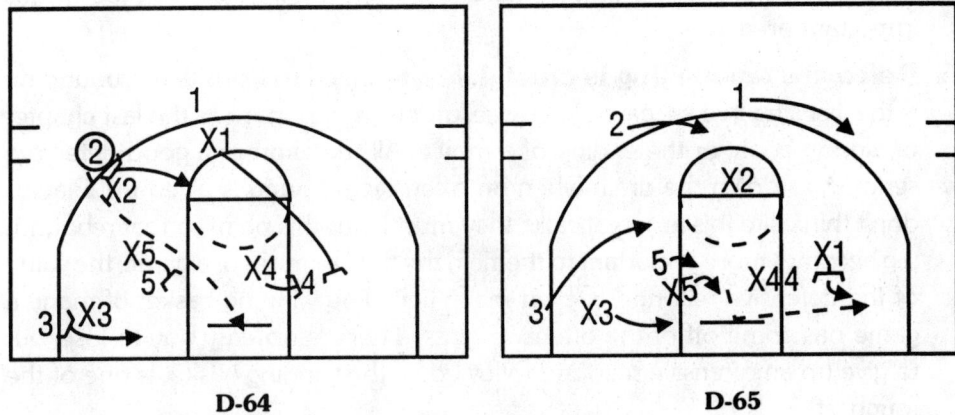

D-64　　　　　　　　　　　　D-65

REBOUNDING COMPLETES DEFENSE

On defense every player needs to consider himself a rebounder. Both defense and rebounding begin with a state of mind. As mentioned earlier, some outstanding guards on excellent teams have led their teams in rebounding in the NBA. Defensive rebounding is a much easier task than is offensive rebounding. There cannot be an actual plan when it comes to defensive rebounding, because the offense generally dictates where the defensive players will be. Nonetheless, it is important to drill several factors to increase defensive rebounding effectiveness. Basically, each individual should work on the following aspects:

1. **Players inside of 15 feet should block out** by executing the step toward the nearest opponent and reverse pivoting to block out.

2. **Outside defensive players should make at least a touch on their men** and then move to rebound the ball or be back on defense.

3. **Defensive players should try to prevent the opponent from getting around the blockout and regaining inside position.** If a choice must be made, it is generally thought to be better to turn players into the middle and away from the baseline when it comes to rebounding. It can be argued to do it the other way, but if an offensive player is allowed to get to the baseline side, it's easy for him to slide right up and under the blockout and get the ball. A ball rebounded on the baseline side of the basket is usually an easier two points than one rebounded in the middle of the pack.

4. **Moving toward the weakside and executing the weakside seal-off will also enhance defensive rebounding.**

5. **It's important to find ways to reward players for their defensive rebounding.** A coach must make it a high priority and he must pass out not only accolades but also playing time to players who do a good job in this important area.

6. **Defensive rebounding is crucial.** Players need to learn that rebounding is the last step in a successful defense, and is as important as the last chapter of a good book, or the ending of a movie. All the effort of a good defensive series goes down the drain when an offensive rebound is given up. Players don't think like this automatically; they must learn this point so that rebounding becomes more important to them. In the final minutes of a game, the value of the defensive rebound is even magnified. The winning basket of many a game has come off of the offensive glass. There is no *easy* way to lose, but to give up an offensive rebound followed by the winning basket is one of the toughest.

A PLAN FOR OFFENSIVE REBOUNDING

Just as such items as the set offense/defense, transition offense/defense, press offense/defense, etc., require a plan in order to be effective, so does offensive rebounding. It's just as naive to assume that players will naturally get enough offensive rebounds without a well-conceived plan as it is to assume they will run an effective, well-spaced offense on their own.

When a coach decides to put a play into the offense, he has to decide several things: who will shoot and where he'll shoot it from; who sets the pick; where the main rebounders will be when the shot goes up; and how switching will affect the play. Two of the most important considerations are providing defensive balance and a team rebounding plan. These two aspects are interrelated.

The best strategy for a successful set play will involve a good shooter being freed up for a shot he likes from a spot where he feels comfortable. The rebounders will be in position to retrieve a missed shot and the backcourt will be ready to defend against a fast break if the rebound goes to the opponent. Plays that have these components are not only sound, but tend to take pressure off the shooter. Plays lacking one or more of these elements will often cause a fast break, thus putting more pressure on the shooter to hit the shot.

Our teams have done well over the years in the area of offensive rebounding, having set team and league records in this category. Part of this has been because of individual effort and part of it is due to having a plan for offensive rebounding. Our plays have followed the basics mentioned above. However, it's important to remember that more unplanned shots are taken in a typical game than are taken as a result of set plays. This is where a broader plan for offensive rebounding becomes important.

Teams that use primarily a motion offense (any variation of the passing game) and teams that complete broken plays with motion will often end up getting a shot with poor rebounding coverage and/or defensive balance; thus a way to help correct these flaws becomes necessary. This requires players to understand the game and to react to a plan of coverage for rebounding and defensive balance. The smaller men have a set of responsibilities, while the big men have their own assignments.

THE 2-2-1 OFFENSIVE REBOUND PLAN

This rebound concept involves getting our players into a loose 2-2-1 formation as soon as one of our players shoots the ball. This plan is an elaboration of the general transition defense plan discussed earlier. The guards start this off by filling the "back" or "first safety" spot in the 2-2-1 as X1 does in D-66. A coach may decide to have the guard furthest from the goal when the shot is taken call out "safety" or "I'm back"; or he may designate a specific guard for that role (except when he is driving or posting up). However it is done, the safety role must be filled immediately when the offense shoots.

Continuing in D-66, Players 4 and 5 were inside and are able to get to the "front" or "inside" positions in the 2-2-1. Player 3 shot the ball and immediately does what we prefer all outside shooters do — he gets quickly to a "middle" position in the 2-2-1 to look for the long rebound. Player 2 gets the remaining "middle" spot. If player 2 had been the guard to take the "back" or "safety" position initially, player 1 would have filled in at the middle. These positions give the offense an opportunity to get the short rebound as well as the long one, while putting the team in good defensive positions to execute specific transition defensive jobs, if they are unable to recover an offensive rebound or if the shot goes in as in D-67.

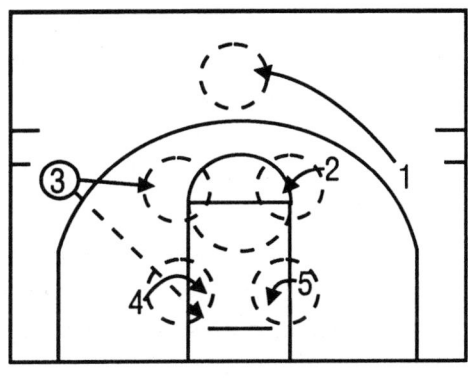

D-66

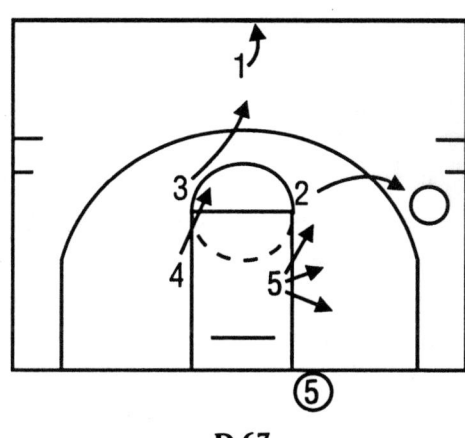

D-67

While there are an infinite number of configurations the offense could be in when the shot goes up, the duties of the players are pretty well covered with a rule for the 1 and 2 players, another rule for the 3, 4 and 5 players and allowing for an exception when a guard posts or drives all the way to the goal.

General Rules for the 1 and 2 Men

The first one able to get back must call out "back" or "safety" and rotate back as 1 did in D-66. He is called the *safety* man. A team may well prefer that either the point guard or the off-guard be designated as the safety (exception: if 1 or 2 is driving to the basket or is posted up, he cannot get to the safety spot. The other guard must rotate quickly to become the safety).

The guard who is not the safety must call out "middle" and he gets to one of the middle spots in the 2-2-1 at the nearest free throw elbow (exception: again, if he is driving or posted up, he may not be able to get to the middle right away. But unless he is in position to pressure the rebounder, he will still try to get back to cover the outlet pass or at least catch up with the flow of the ball as quickly as possible).

The smaller player in the middle of the 2-2-1 will become the *outlet defender* when the opponent rebounds the ball and will move to converge toward the outlet receiver in an effort to slow down the outlet pass. He will not be able to steal or deny the pass often, but he wants to get in a position to be able to contain the advance.

General Rules for the 3, 4 and 5

Two of these three men should already be inside or else should converge toward the goal to fill the two "front" or "inside" spots. The remaining one will get to the other "middle" spot and look to crash the board only if he thinks he will come up with the offensive rebound. If the shot goes in , we are in excellent position to go right into a 41, 31, or 21. But the tough transition job occurs on the rebound.

The transition jobs for the 3, 4 and 5 men will be as follows: the player nearest the rebounder (usually one of the players in the "front" or "under" spots) must pressure the rebounder's outside shoulder to slow down the outlet pass. He is called the *jammer* and should concentrate on putting hand pressure on the ball, the same concept as discussed in our 41 transition defense after our scores. Having a label for each duty helps in the teaching of the roles.

The other front (inside) man must immediately run back to defend the basket at the other end of the court. He is called the *sprinter* and his role is crucial. The coach will spend more time reminding him of his job than any other. His best action is to sprint back to the opposite foul line and wait to read the transition. He defends against the long pass and he gets in a position to do post defense early by bumping the opposing post man away from his desired spot. He is also in position to play his man as a trailer, if he decides to trail instead of post.

The bigger middle man (quite often the 3 man, but it could be 4 or 5), must run back immediately just like the sprinter does. He is called the *release man* and his job is to release the *first* safety man from having to defend the basket against the long pass. Assuming the release man is the 3 man as in D-66 and 67, 3 runs back and releases 1 to be able to move over to form the sideline triangle to defend the sideline pass (D-68, 69).

The release man temporarily has the responsibility of defending the basket until the sprinter passes him by. The sprinter sets the release man free to help defend the middle against penetrating passes or dribbles. The defense is ideally still in general 2-2-1 positions. By communicating, X1 and X3 in the middle spots may change positioning with each other to get nearer their own assignments when that is convenient.

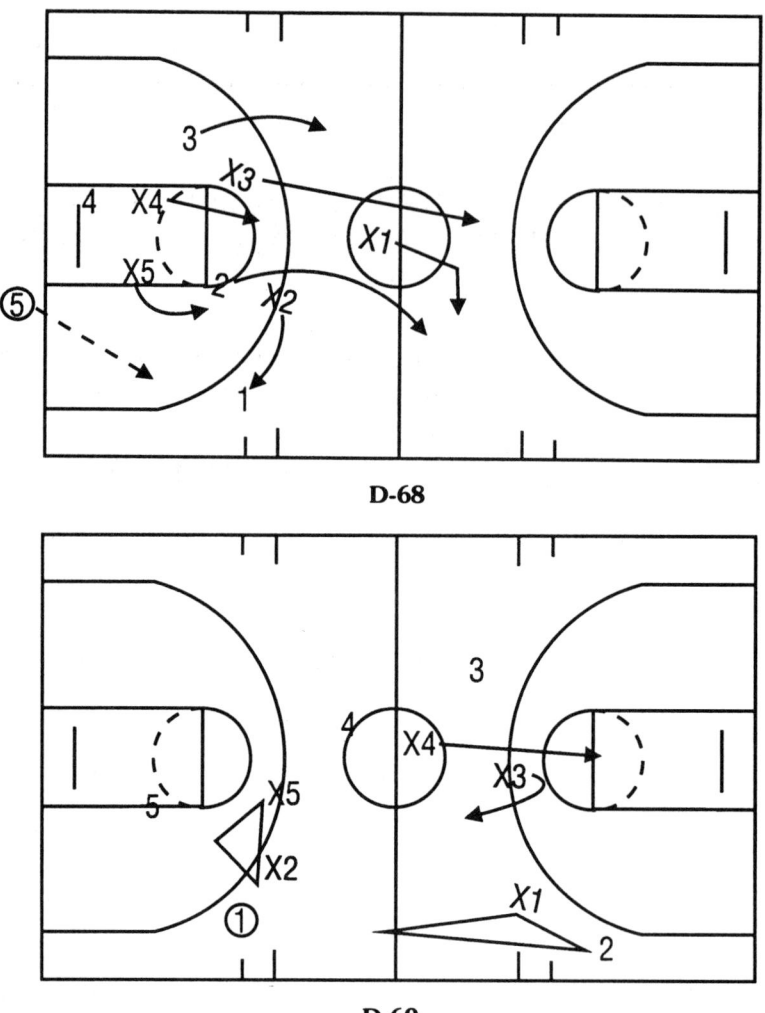

D-68

D-69

Diagrams 68 and 69 show the players now being designated with X's since they are obviously on defense. Safety X1 is defending the sideline after release man X3 passed him by and X3 moves up to defend the middle as sprinter X4 passes X3. The X5 jammer will stay with the middle triangle as long as the inbounder or rebounder is in front of him and then will go on down court with him, leaving the release man to cover the middle triangle. The outlet man, X2 contains 1's advance up the floor. He doesn't try to steal the ball from 1; he's more interested in containing him in an effort to make him dribble the ball up the court near the sideline. X1, the first safety, is now the sideline triangle defender. Note that there may be an exception when one of the guards is already inside due to driving or posting. Even then two of the three bigger players may go ahead and get to the board. In this case the formation would be a 3-1-1 instead of the 2-2-1. It is just as well if the 2-2-1 is still formed, however. In this case, the smaller of the two middle men would converge toward the outlet pass and try to contain the advance until the guard caught inside can come to release him.

EXAMPLES OF UTILIZING THE TRANSITION DEFENSE PLAN WHEN THE OFFENSE FAILS TO SCORE

Setting the 41 defense after an unsuccessful offensive attempt. Naturally, successful transition from offense to defense is easier when the opponent has to take the ball out of bounds after scores. However, the inevitable missed shots and turnovers occur all too frequently. Great teams and players at all levels will be good at defensive transition especially in these latter situations. Since the offense's first objective should be to *score* easy baskets, the first objective of the defense must be to *prevent* easy scores.

Since the NBA uses a 24-second shot clock, there is even more of an advantage to delaying the advance of the ball whenever possible. If the offense can be forced to use up eight or ten seconds to get into their set offense at the half-court and if the defense is good at the clock-ending defense in the last eight or ten seconds, it leaves only a few prime seconds for the offense to work their magic.

Since other levels of play allow more time per possession, this strategy is not quite as vital as with the 24-second limit, but it is still effective and a better plan than simply trying to stop an opponent without having a good concept of the relationship the clock plays in the game of basketball.

It takes three things to play a game properly — a ball, a goal and a clock. Every practice and strategy should take each into consideration all the time.

In the end the 41 defense can stand on its own merits as a defensive concept. It not only uses up the opponent's time on the shot clock, but it breaks their rhythm and quickly puts the defense in the preferred mindset of being on the attack.

Just how closely the transition defense after missed shots can come to matching the 41 defensive concept already described, depends on how effectively the outlet pass is delayed and equally as much on how well every defender reacts to executing his transition duties. Having a label for each duty helps in teaching of the rules.

PRESSURE ON THE REBOUNDER/SLOW THE ADVANCE

In pressuring the outlet pass, the defender (jammer) will try to follow the path of the ball with his hands. This is called putting hand pressure on the passer or "tracing the ball", or "mirroring the ball" by some coaches. Whatever one calls it, it is best for the defender to try to harass the outlet pass, specifically in hopes of getting a deflection as opposed to stealing it or just having the hands up in the air without purpose.

As the outlet man receives the pass, the jammer will drop to form the front triangle to help discourage middle penetration by 2. In diagram 70, X4 jams the rebounder. The defender farthest from the ball, X1, assumed the safety position as the ball was shot. He must be passed up quickly by the release man, X3, so that he can be freed from his safety responsibility and move up to the middle on the ball side to be ready to discourage a quick sideline pass.

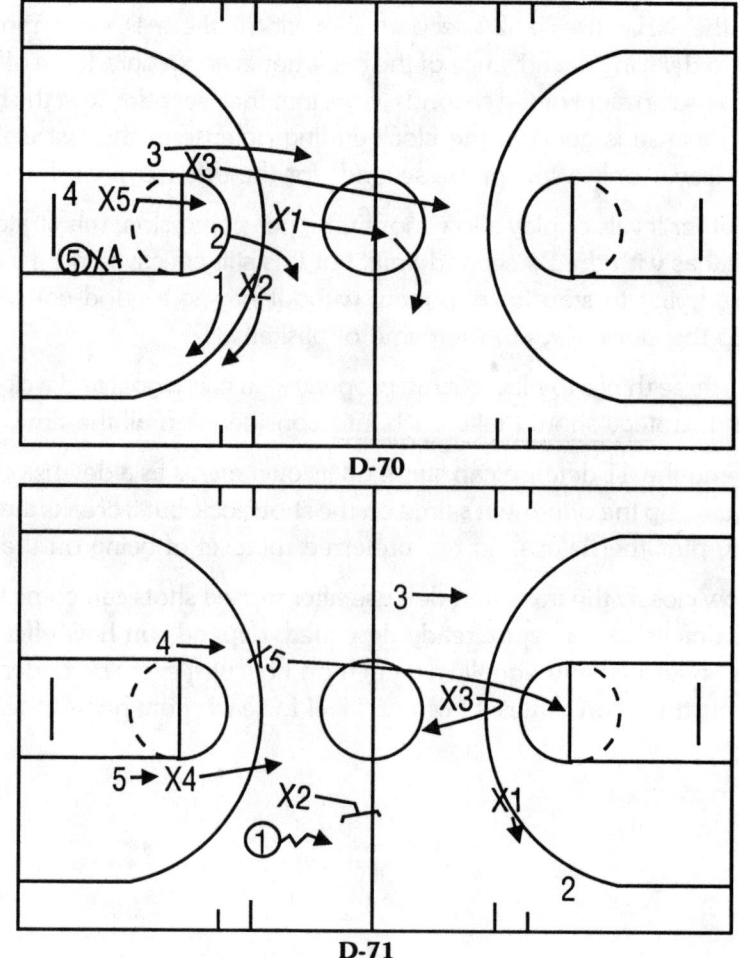

D-70

D-71

In D-71 X3 runs past X1 so that X1 no longer has to protect the basket. (To stop the transition it is acceptable to have X1 on 2 and X2 on 1, even if the matchup is not ideal. The purpose is to contain, not stop. If it becomes easy for X2 and X1 to recover to their own men later, they will, but it's usually not necessary. If X2 is a really bad defender, he can be told to try to be the safety each time in order to let X1 try to get to the outlet man.)

Again, while mismatches are no big deal, X1 and X3 can communcate to switch jobs with each other if players 2 and 3 are on opposite sides of the floor from those in diagram 71. The two middle players must do the jobs of controlling the middle penetration and the downcourt pass.

ADJUSTING AFTER PRESSURING THE REBOUNDER.

Continuing in diagram 71, once the responsibilities of pressuring the rebounder and getting a safety man back are fulfilled, the rest of the players are thinking about doing their jobs to contain a rapid advance of the ball. In the diagram X1 intimidates 1 from throwing the sideline pass by setting up the downcourt triangle, while X5 is the sprinter and goes hard down the middle to release X3 from the safety. X4 gets to the middle triangle after the rebounder releases the outlet pass to help X2 keep the ball out of the middle for as long as the rebounder stays in front of X4.

A common error is that players try to make a stop in the backcourt by reaching, grabbing and over-committing for steals. While now and then a big play occurs, more often a lot of damage is done by the high risk play in the backcourt in transition defense. If the risk is taken within the system of an organized press, that is a far different matter. Transition defense requires a containing approach.

Another frequent mistake is that a big player will pace himself getting back on defense, if his own man is further from the goal than he is. It must be made clear that his job is not just to beat his own man down the court — it is to sprint back to release the smaller players and to defend the goal against all comers.

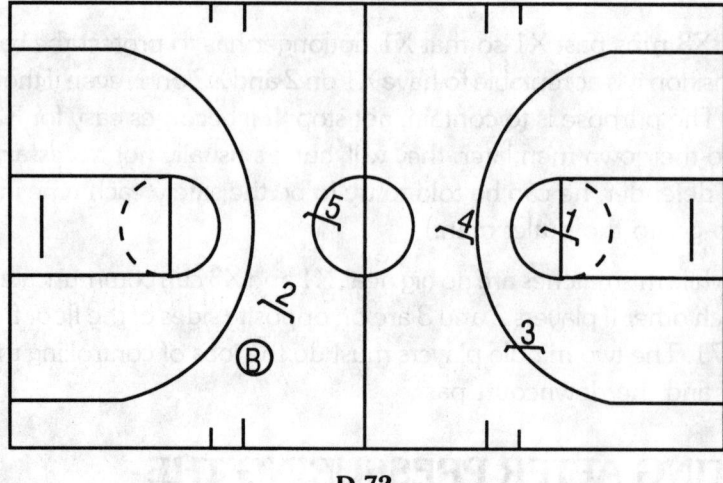

D-72

D-72 shows the angles that good transition defense strives to take away and their order of priority:

1. Defend the basket.
2. Contain the ball.
3. Threaten the up-court sideline pass.
4. Jam diagonal middle penetration.
5. Discourage lateral reversal or penetration.

The error most players make is that they think their job is to get back and find their own man and that's all that is required. What is demanded in the advanced thinking is to get the job of containing done by the players who are in the best position to do the most effective job. If players end up with other than their own men, it is no big deal. They can match back up later, or not at all. Getting each transition task done is far more important than getting proper matchups.

Therefore, the man nearest the rebounder will pressure him, whether it is his man or not. The bigger man left inside races back, even if his own man broke his leg on the previous play. The smaller man nearest the potential outlet receiver tries to contain him. The first safety man is released to fan out to prevent an easy pass into the sideline area and that release man protects the middle. This describes the duties to be done and it is a team job that must involve everyone.

It is more important to have a good defensive transition system than it is to have one for the offense. Yet, most teams have very little defensive transition organization beyond telling the players to hustle back. Coaches should worry about the tasks that are necessary to be completed to stop the easy baskets. A transition system that is well understood will help reduce the easy scores. Then a team needs a good halfcourt defensive concept in order to win.

Thus, pressuring the rebound and outlet can assist the team defense in getting set up like they do when the opponent takes the ball out of bounds after our scores. That is the whole objective.

TEN STEPS TO SUCCESSFUL TRANSITION DEFENSE

1. **Get to 2-2-1 (or 3-1-1) spots and begin to play defense.** Rebounding the ball back on the offensive board is the best defense of all, because they cannot score if you have the ball.

2. **Pressure the ball with the jammer.** Pressure the rebounder if they rebound the shot and give pressure to the outlet pass in 41-31-21 if the shot is scored.

3. **Cover the safety spot to protect the goal from the long pass.** Depending on your team, it can be X1 or X2 that is designated as the safety and the other as the outlet man, or it can be a read as to which one reacts first to getting to the safety spot. In any case, in the halfcourt offense either X1 or X2 should fill the safety role, freeing X3, X4 and X5 to get to the basket or middle.

4. **Cover the outlet man with the outlet defender.** The outlet man will be the guard who is not the safety in the ideal situation. From the middle position in the 2-2-1 the smaller man will either be on the side of the rebound or should cross over to the other side to release the bigger middle man from the outlet responsibility. (Should one guard be stuck under on the drive or postup, he can still often get to the outlet man in time to contain him. Only if he is jamming the rebounder will he be unable to fulfill one of the roles of safety or outlet man.) Diagram 73 X2 calls "outlet" and frees X3 up to get back as the release man. X1 has already called out safety and X4 is the sprinter, while X5 jams the rebounder.

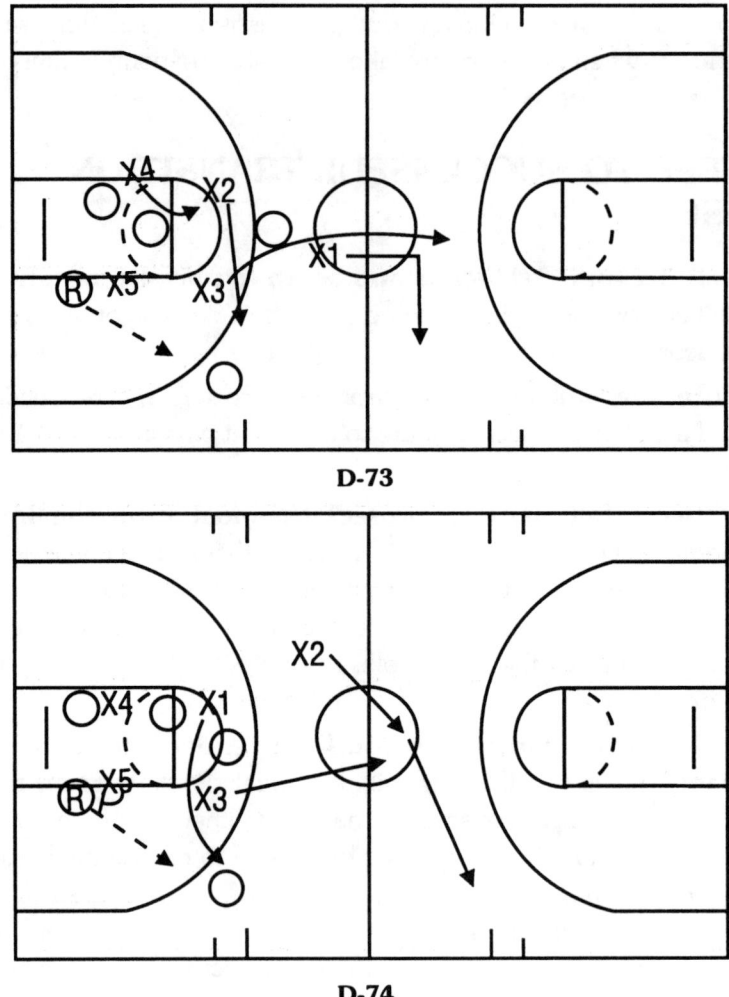

D-73

D-74

5. **Release the first safety man with the release man** (the other middle man) so the first safety can move to the sideline triangle.

6. **Run the sprinter out** (the biggest man not jamming the rebounder). Normally this will be X4 if X5 is jamming the ball and vice versa. But it could be X3. It would never be X1 or X2 because they have basically two jobs to do — safety and outlet.

7. **Discourage the sideline pass.** The first safety man should move over to the sideline area and form the sideline triangle as soon as the release man gets back and yells "release", or at least points for the safety man to move over to the sideline. In diagram 74 X3 releases X2 to the sideline triangle, though he could cover it himself by communicating with X2.

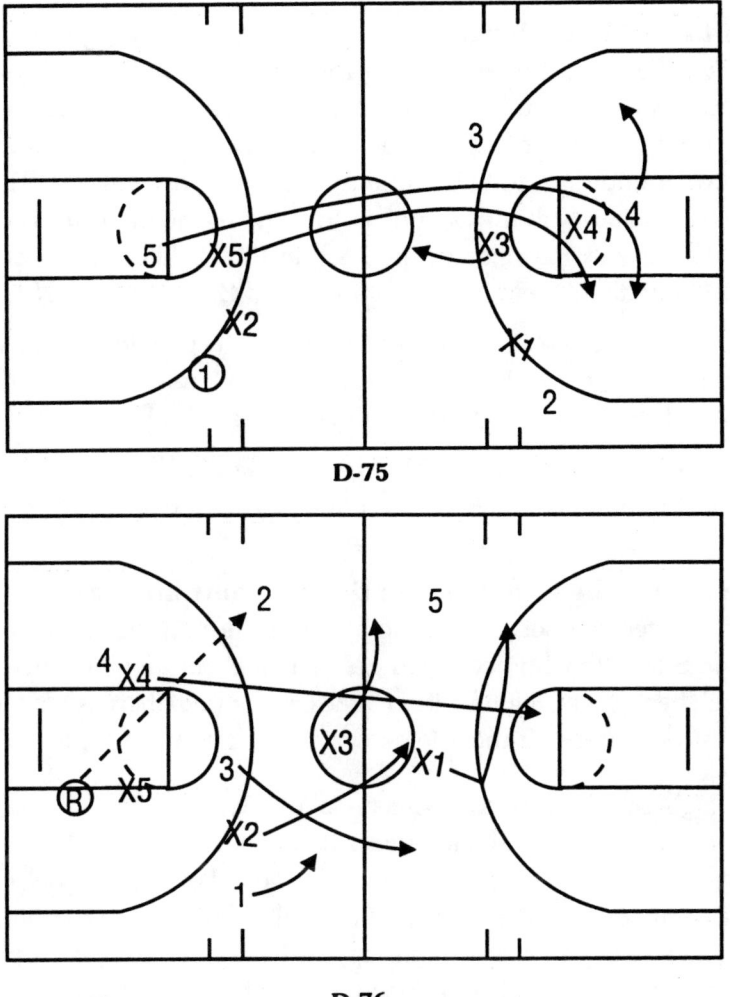

D-75

D-76

8. **Fill the middle of the court.** The release man will be the middle defender at the halfcourt level. He will help stop any middle passes or penetration at the midcourt level. For example as in D-74, if X5 is the jammer, X4 is the sprinter and X1 is the outlet defender while X2 is the first safety. X3 is the release man and he is free to defend the middle once the sprinter passes him.

If X4 is the jammer, X5 would be the sprinter and X3 would ideally be the release man. If X3 were the jammer, X5 would be the sprinter and X4 would be the release man. The point is that the three big men will normally fulfill the roles of jammer, sprinter and release man and the guards will do the jobs of first safety and outlet defenders. The first safety man gets released to cover the sideline triangle. The sprinter will become the final safety man. By communicating, players can exchange roles with one another, however.

9. **Form the middle triangle.** As the ball is thrown to the outlet man, the jammer drops back immediately to form the first middle triangle with the outlet defender to help keep the ball from penetrating middle. He stays up in the front of the 2-2-1 formation as long as his man is in front of him. Since we are not in a zone but in a man to man in the 41-31-21 transition defenses, he stays with the man he is covering as the man cuts on down the court. This leaves the release man, X3, in the middle area to continue to keep the middle triangle intact in an adusted 2-2-1 front (D-75).

If the ball is reversed in the backcourt, that is a plus for the defense. The opportunity for a quick, easy score is denied normally and that is the purpose of the transition phase of the defense.

If the rebound is outletted crosscourt as in D-76, X3 can contain the ball and serve in the outlet role and X2 will take X3's job in the middle. Or, they can communicate to change positions.

10. **Make the ball be dribbled over the halfcourt line near the sideline.** Now the defense is set, even if the matchups are not perfect. Do not worry about it. Stay with whomever you get matched with until a convenient time to switch back. Once the transition attack is stopped, there is time for players to adjust defensively. If there is no switch back, that is OK, too.

Some high school and college teams may want to use this same 2-2-1 transition defense system, and after a time they may want to signal that the team will stay in a 2-2-1 zone. This can be done on a verbal or visual signal. Or it might be that the team will stay man to man if the ball is brought up the defensive left side, but it will be a zone if it is brought up on the defensive right. Or perhaps it's a man to man unless the ball is reversed; then it becomes a zone.

Another adjustment that a high school or college team can make out of the 2-2-1 system is to have a call that allows the defense to trap with the jammer on the rebound and go right into a 2-2-1 zone press off of the missed field goal.

Utilizing the 2-2-1 system offers a lot of exciting possibilities and it gives organization to a vital phase of defensive basketball that is largely overlooked or at best, undertaught. Coaches may want to use all, part or none of this in their system, but understanding the concepts can help each coach and player organize a better transition defense.

DEFENSIVE TRANSITION AFTER A TURNOVER: ERASE THE MISTAKE

Should a turnover occur that puts the ball out of bounds on the end or side for a throw-in in the backcourt, the defense can set up a 41-31-21 defense. They should call out and set up one of these immediately. There are two reasons for this:

First, it gets the defense doing exactly what they are supposed to be doing — playing defense instead of complaining to officials.

Second, we have used the concept of "erasing our mistake" by putting on an aggressive risk-taking defensive approach immediately after committing a turnover. The point is that we can negate our turnover, if we can cause the opponent to commit their own turnover or take a bad shot. It not only works out pretty well in theory, it gets the defense thinking properly right away after an error.

REMINDER NOTES ON REBOUNDING

Defensive End

1. Get a body, get the ball.
2. Make the first hit.
3. Everyone is a rebounder on defense.
4. The best denial defense is getting the ball.
5. Pursue as many balls as you can.
6. Attack the weakside rebound area. Most misses go to that side.
7. Seal off the weakside rebound area. Prevent their weakside man from getting the easy rebound.
8. Get the long rebound. Long shots equal long rebounds.
9. Turn bad shots, open rebounds, long rebounds and corner shots into fast breaks.
10. Not much bad can happen as long as it's our ball.

Go get it!

Offensive End

1. When a shot goes up, try to fill the 2-2-1 spots.
2. The weakside middle man can go to the board if he gets a good opportunity to rebound the ball.

3. We want to be able to execute the 41 defense after our missed shots out of the 2-2-1 so as to contain their transition.

4. When a player shoots an outside shot, he should normally move to the middle to read for the long rebound, unless he knows he is going to get the ball right back by going after it.

5. Whoever shoots from the corner should immediately move toward the middle as his feet hit the ground. He must not stand and watch to see how it all comes out. Missed corner shots cause fast breaks. One reason is that the shooter takes himself out of the transition defense by standing and watching his shot.

6. Know the transition defense plan and be ready to execute it from the 2-2-1 set.

7. Communication is important so that everyone knows who is back and who is middle in the rebound formation, and who is doing the transition jobs of jammer, safety, outlet, release and sprinter. Any of the roles can be adjusted or exchanged with communicating through talking and pointing.

STOP THE SECONDARY BREAK ATTACK

Once the initial thrust of the offense is contained, the defense may have a tendency to relax. The job of transition defense is not complete just because the opponent did not get a 3 on 2 or 2 on 1 fast break. Nor is it complete simply because all five defenders have gotten down court ahead of the offense.

Aggressive offensive teams who are looking for the easy basket can be even more effective with a controlled 4- or 5-man secondary break game that attacks the defense in transition before it is totally set. A good secondary break team can gain easy goals in a number of ways:

- Using the turnout technique on the baseline (D-77).
- Using the first trailer to cut through the middle for a pass or as a quick post up player (D-78).

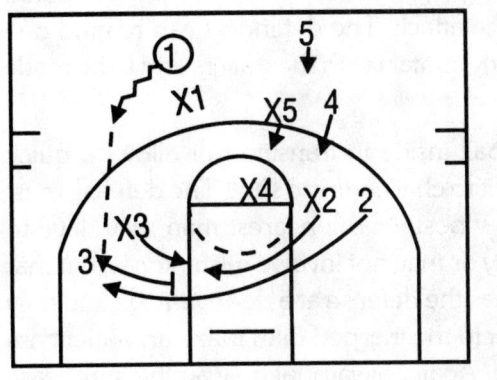

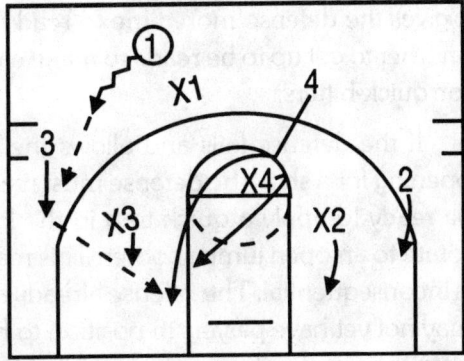

D-77   **D-78**

- Using the second trailer to score a jump shot or to set a pick on the ballhandler for a quick penetrating pick and roll (D-79).
- Using the second trailer to swing the ball quickly to the weakside for a shot — possibly a three-pointer. The threat of the three-pointer cannot be underestimated as a huge transition threat. Our Milwaukee Bucks teams were exceptionally dangerous with Jack Sikma trailing up as the safety trailer for a three-point shot. Dale Ellis was another who could score points in bunches by coming into the transition play late or way out wide on the weakside (D-80).

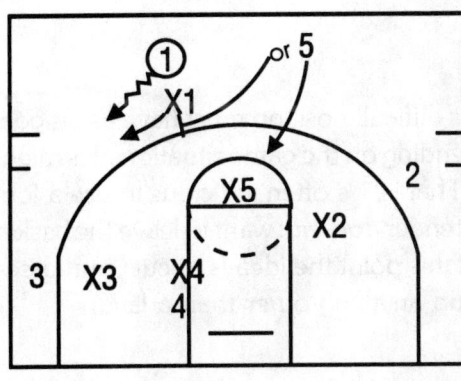

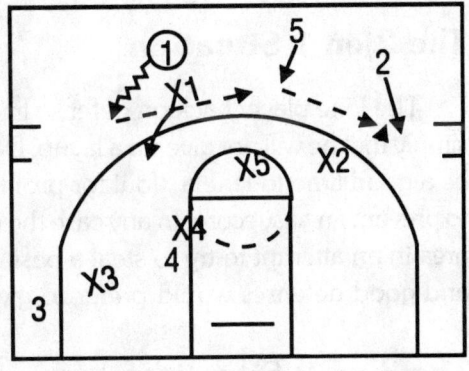

D-79   **D-80**

- Using any number of quick-hitting secondary transition plays designed to get a good shot against a defense that is back, yet not quite prepared to defend.

The advantage of forcing the ball to be dribbled across the halfcourt line is that it gives the defense more time to read the attack. The defenders can remind one another to get up to be ready to make early contact with the trailers and to be ready for quick-hitters.

If the defense fails and allows the ball inside in transition or allows a quick opening for a shot, the defense must react to challenge the shot. The defense must be ready to apply a quick trap in the low post; or the nearest man may have to rotate to an open jump shooter. This may or may not involve mismatches, but that is inconsequential. The offense already has the defense at a disadvantage and they may not yet have players in position to help the trapped man make an outlet pass after the defense has responded to him. Again, always take away the sure, easy play in favor of making the opponent find the next opening and execute the next play.

The easiest play of all is to shoot the open shot.

DEFENDING DISADVANTAGE SITUATIONS

Regardless of how diligent the defense may be, the offense will beat the defense at times and the defenders will find themselves having to scramble to recover to stop an offense that has them outnumbered in transition. This happens most often when the opponent steals a pass or when the offense took an ill-advised shot without good defensive balance.

The 2 on 1 Situation.

The lone player back on defense in this difficult position must have as his goal simply that he will not give up a layup. Depending on the game situation, this might be a good time to take a "foul for profit." That is, it's often judicious to use a foul to prevent an easy score. In any case the defender does not want to leave the basket area in an attempt to try to steal a pass. At this point the idea is to cut your losses and good defenses would prefer to give up anything other than a layup.

The 3 on 2 Situation

Ideally the smaller man of the two will take the top of the tandem 1-1 defensive formation as X1 in D-81. This is a big-in and little-out operation and the job of the top man is to contain the ball as it comes into the free throw circle area. Although most coaches will say that they want the top man to "stop the ball," it's better to use the term "contain." Once the ball is passed, the top man will drop back to help defend the basket. Again, the defense does not want to allow the layup.

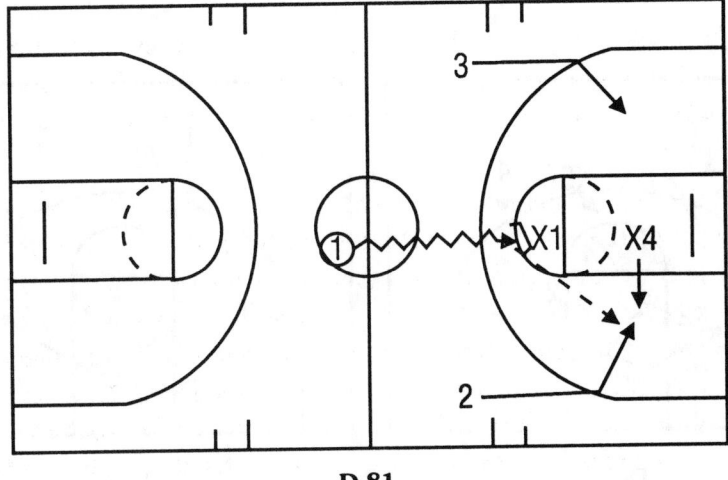

D-81

The back man on the 1-1 tandem will move out to cover the pass. As he does so, he must be under control to prevent an easy fake and drive. It is a huge mistake for either one of the two defenders to get so aggressive that they allow the offense to beat them. The defense is already at a disadvantage and if one more gets beat, it's an even bigger problem. The aim is to contain enough to force either a longer shot or else another pass or two. The time that the defenders force to be consumed will allow that much more time for defensive reinforcements to arrive to help.

"Big in and little out" principles apply in transition. Communication will go a long way toward promoting good defense of any kind, but it is very critical in transition. In the 3 on 2 situation, the big man should call out that he has low and the smaller man should call out that he has the ball. Everyone should try to talk and point as players scramble back on defense with the idea that they will try to get the big men inside and the smaller men to the outside when possible. As stated, however, any man on an opponent is better than no one at all.

On the turnout maneuver by the transition offense as in D-82, the big in-little out concept will prevail. Player 2 sets a screen for 3 as they execute a turnout. With equal-size players involved, the switch is an easy one to make and this one leaves bigger man X3 inside. In D-83, player X4 screens for 2 and so there is no switch because the defense would not want to switch 4 to the outside and leave smaller X2 inside. If 2 were screening for 4, then it would be an easy switch.

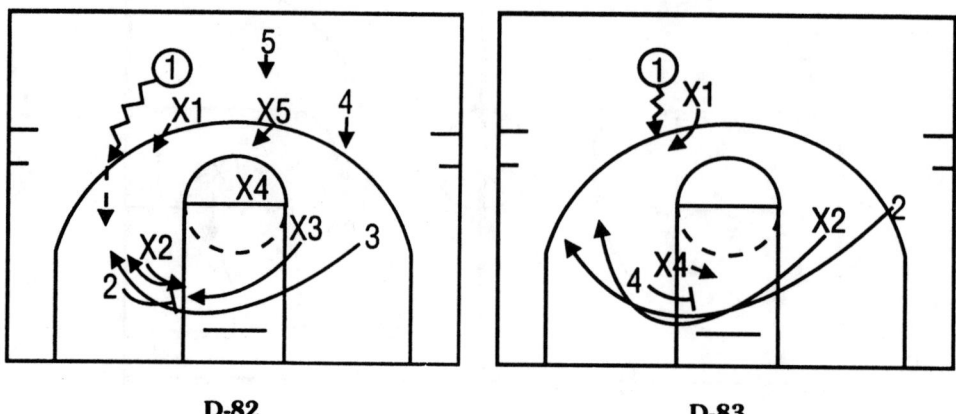

D-82   **D-83**

As we go on with other disadvantage transition situations, it will become clear that the big in-little out concept comes into play many times as the defense tries to get people in the best spots to defend. Defensive backflow is essential for recovery in disadvantage situations.

In D-84 X1 stopped the ball and X2 covered the first pass in a 3 on 2 disadvantage action. X3 is the first man to catch up to the play with defensive backflow. There is no time for X3 and X1 to change right away to big in — little out, so X3 must cover the open man at the top of the circle, player 1.

In the next diagram, D-85, X4 and X5 get to the play with their backflow and through communicating, both of them get inside and X1 gets himself to the outside. X1 and X3 may change men when neither is involved in the action, usually when both are on the weak side.

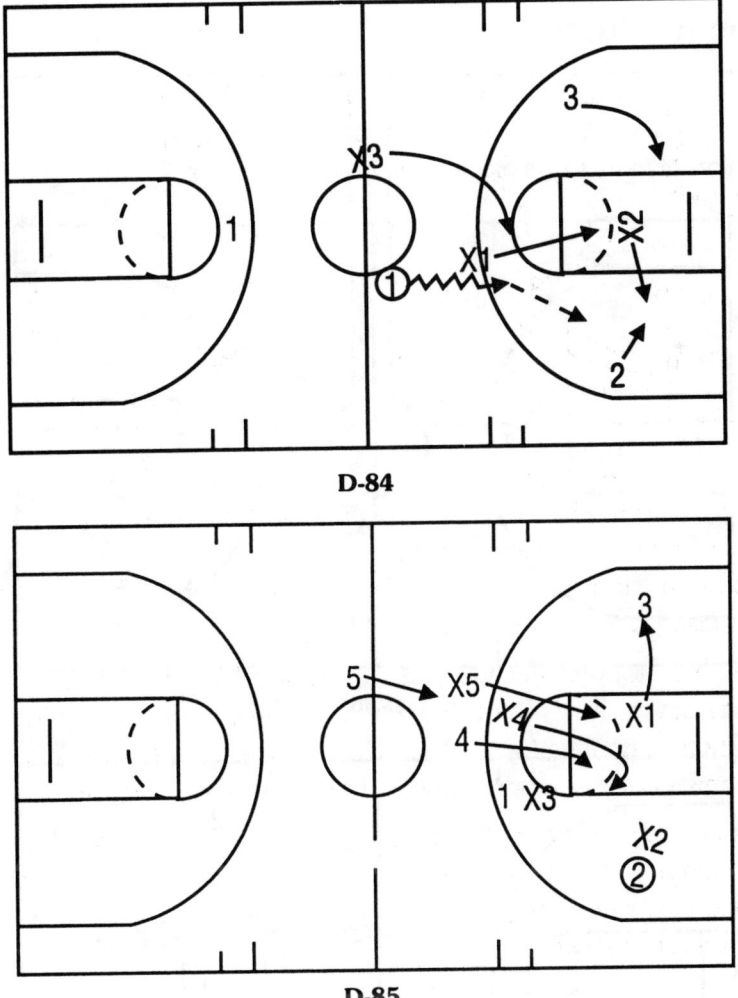

D-84

D-85

The 4 on 3 Situation

In D-86 players X1, X3 and X4 have gotten back and are being attacked by four players — 1, 2, 3 and 4. Defenders X5 and X2 are getting into the play with the backflow. X2 tells X5 to go inside. X5 and X3 can communicate that X5 will take 4 at the low post and X3 moves on out to look for an open man. This gets the big men in and rotates the small men out. They can worry about getting to their specific assignments later.

The 5 on 4 Situation

This will be handled the same as the 4 on 3 in that the defense must protect the goal and rotate to cover the open people. Communicating by talking and pointing in order to try to get bigger men inside will help solidify the transition effort (D-87).

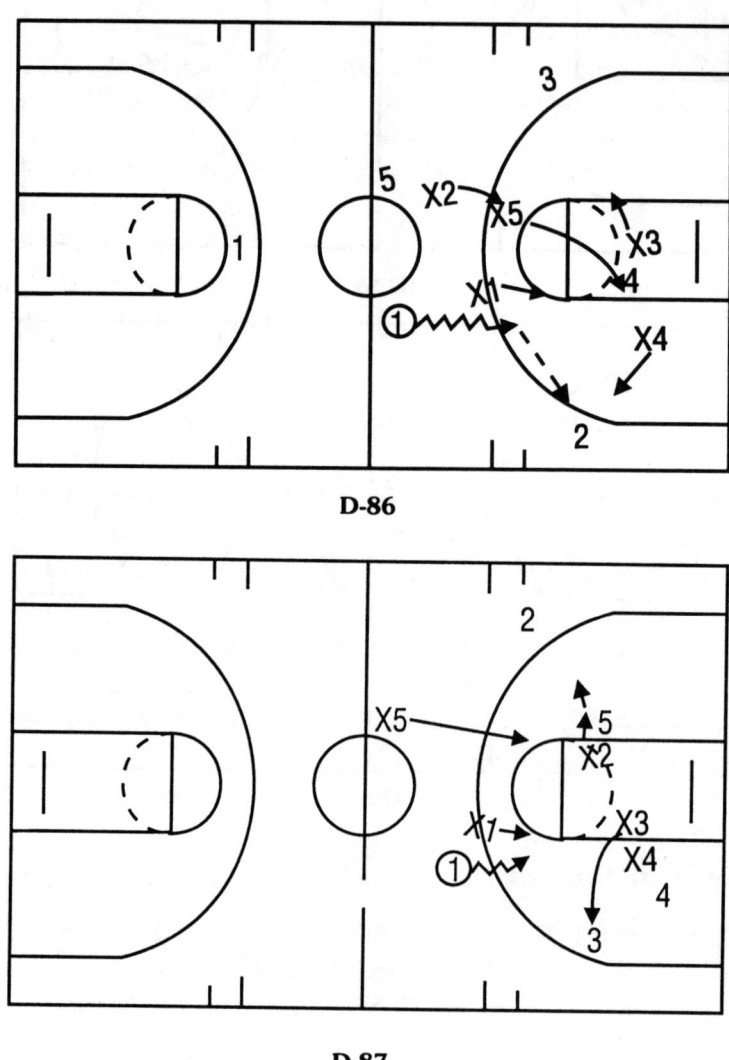

D-86

D-87

POINTERS FOR BETTER INDIVIDUAL DEFENSE AGAINST SET OFFENSES

Post Play

Low post defense. All players need to learn low post defensive techniques. Any player on the team may have to defend in the low post during a game — not just centers and power forwards. Therefore, it is important for each player to learn the basics of low post defense. Regardless of how much technique a player may learn, however, it is still very difficult for a player to defend another equally good player once that player gets the ball in good low position. For that reason everyone must remember to be ready to help a teammate who is defending in the low post by dropping in and being ready to help out when the ball goes inside. As previously mentioned, ball pressure on feeders is one way to help prevent lob passes, as is weakside help.

The best low post defense is of a preventive nature as noted in the discussion of transition defense. By doing one's work early in fighting for position, a defender can break up the opponent's timing and can stake a claim for the preferred real estate. The early bump is very important to remember. The defensive player should "greet" the posting player with body contact as near to the foul line as possible in transition defense. The sooner the defense can make body contact with the offensive player, while the two are jockeying for position, the better. Again, "he who makes the first hit has the advantage" is an ancient basketball truth. By contacting him and diverting the offensive player's path to a wider position away from the goal, or forcing him to cut behind the defender, the defender has made the offensive player do something he did not intend to do and that creates an advantage for the defense.

Basic defensive post positioning. In D-88, X5 has bumped 5 inside the lane and then established a good position to prevent a wing pass. In D-89, X5 made contact and 5 chose to cut over the top. X5 must be strong to force 5 out at an angle toward the corner and then slide under him to establish a position to prevent the pass in from the wing. If X5 lets 5 out-muscle him and go in a direct line to the low post, 5 will have an easy opening. X5 has to be strong enough to hold his own or else his best early contact will be as in the previous diagram where he contacts 5 on the outside and makes him cut inside the lane.

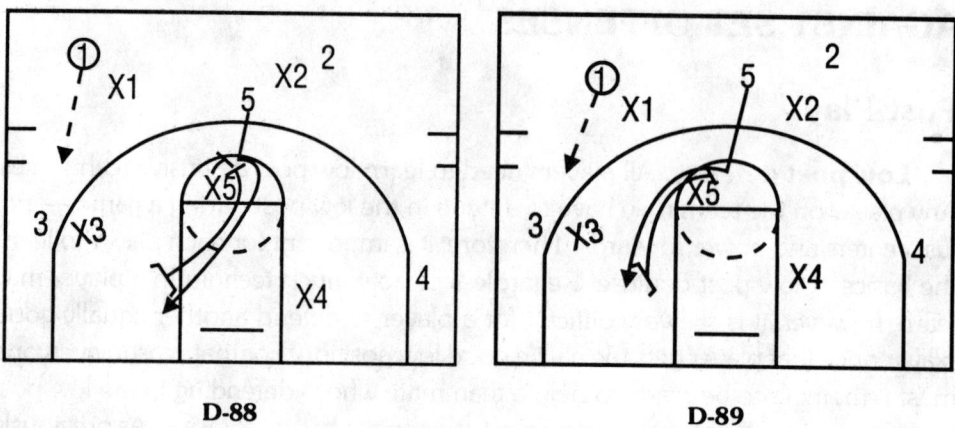

D-88   D-89

Prevent an entry pass from the front angle. A low post defender cannot allow a direct pass to the low post from the top (the high post area, or front angle in general). A pass that comes in from the wing area is easier to defend because the weakside defense will have had a chance to establish itself and can give help to the low post. There is no quick weakside help when a pass enters from the top angle. Therefore X5 must always play the denial angle shown in D-90 when the ball is toward the front.

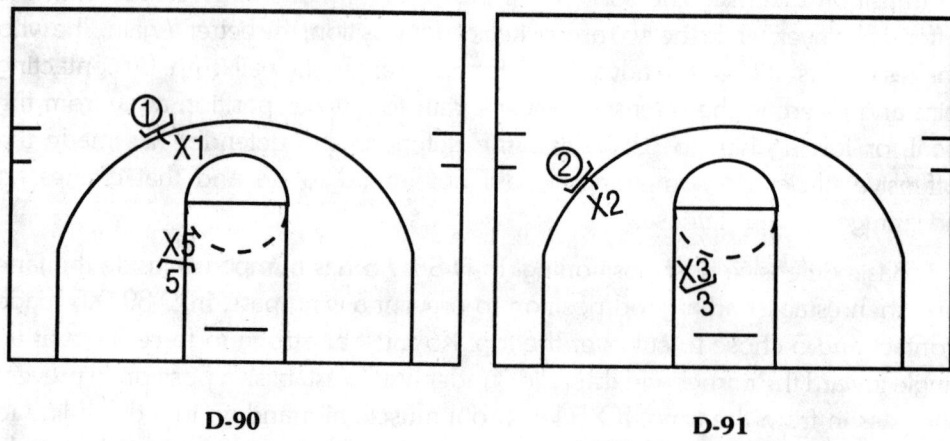

D-90   D-91

Get in front of any player who has a foot in the paint. Unless the defender involved is seven feet tall and the offensive player is a foot shorter, players should automatically do whatever it takes to get a body in front of any player who is this deep into low post position. Technique is not the issue. A player must use his feet, hands and whatever else he has at his disposal to get himself in front. The specific footwork is not as important as getting the job done. However, it is important that the defender use his upper body and his forearm opposite the ball to pressure the upper body of the post player in order to keep the feet and legs in a position whereby they can be moved freely. A defender who has his legs and feet tied up cannot change positions as the ball moves. In addition, the old technique of leveraging a posted player out by driving a knee between the legs of the offensive man is now being called a foul in most leagues (D-91).

DEFENDING AGAINST THE LOB IN THE LOW POST

The post defender must yell "front" when he assumes a fronting position on a man who has established position with a foot or two in the paint. By fronting in the low post, the defender is able to get his best effort at jumping to try to tip a lob pass out away from the basket. In his position facing the passer, he can squat and get a high jump for the tip-out. The weakside defender must be totally alert to come to the lob pass when he hears the post defender yell out "front."

Even with a shot-blocker, it's better to keep the ball outside. There are various considerations in defending the low post when the ball is on the wing. The active, shot-blocking defenders have an advantage in being able to play a little more conservatively in the low post. It is not quite as negative a situation if the ball gets inside in a case like this, if the post defender can take care of business on his own. However, that type of player doesn't come along every year. In reality the player who allows the ball inside easily is making a mistake. He puts himself in a position where he has to play very good defense or commit a foul. By keeping it out, he will put himself in less danger.

Furthermore, the offense gains an advantage in most cases just by getting the ball inside. Not only can a good player score from the inside, but he can make good passes to cutters or spot-up shooters because the defense will normally drop back somewhat to the ball inside and this helps free up the other players.

Study the opponent's inside moves. The defender inside must know the abilities of the man he is guarding and be realistic about his own defensive ability. The better the offensive ability of the inside player, the harder the defender must work to keep the ball away from that area. Fronting when the offensive player sets up deep is one strong method of post defense and is a must if the offensive player gets a foot in the lane area.

The defender must decide if he is going to play in a three- quarter or half-man position, if the posted man is in the area between the paint and that safer area well off of the block. In the three-quarter style the defender will try to get his lead foot in front of the post man's front foot as in D-92.

In three-quarter position his body angle will be such that his tail end is pointing toward the halfcourt circle. If the man is further off the block, half-a-man defensive positioning may be enough to keep the ball away and still give good rebound position as in D-89. The defender's tail end will be pointed toward the corner formed by the meeting of the halfcourt line and the sideline on the weakside of the court. The defender will keep the post man's body centered on his chest with his forearm in contace, of course.

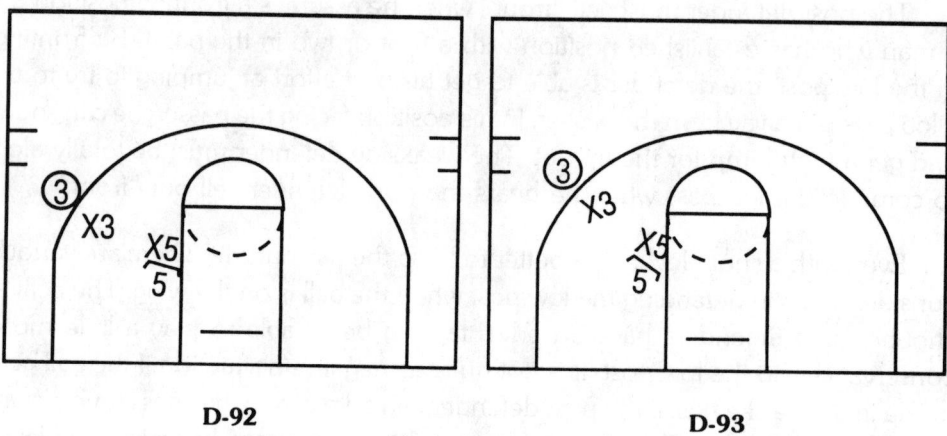

D-92   D-93

BODY AND ARM POSITION

In both the three-quarter and half-a-man defensive positions the defender will keep his outside hand up in the passing lane between the ballhandler on the wing and his man. He must keep his inside forearm on the shoulder or upper body area of the posted man. He will lean into the man and try to control his movement, hoping to muscle him to move on down nearer the baseline to decrease the angle with which the offensive player has to work. If the offensive player can be moved out of the block area, it can be a lot easier to play with a hand and arm out in between him and the passer on the wing. He may be able to get the man far enough off the block to get by with just putting a hand in between his man and the ball. Or he may get him far enough out to be able to play behind him.

Don't let the post man have the advantage of "feeling." Whenever the posted man catches the ball inside, the defender should break contact with his body immediately. The key factor the offensive post man evaluates in deciding which way to make a scoring move is to go opposite the direction from which he feels pressure from the defender. If he feels the defender on the right, he knows he can spin or drop-step left (and vice-versa). But if he cannot feel him at all, he has to locate him first in order to make the smart move. This process takes more time than the drop-step and will often allow enough time for a teammate to give some help, if help is needed.

Get to the baseline side to defend the low wing and corner feed. If the ball and the low post man are in a direct line to the basket and the ball is drag-dribbled or passed to an angle that is below the direct line toward the corner, the defender on the low post man must get to the baseline side of the posted man as in D-94.

He can step out over the top of the player by exercising the "two-step shift move" or he can go behind the man. The farther out of the block the posted man can be forced to play, the more likely the defender can go behind the offensive player. If the posted man is in deep near the foul lane line, the defender will probably have to use the two-step move to get over the top.

The two-step shift move is executed as shown in D-95. The defender quickly gets out in front of the posted player by stepping his back foot out in front of the offensive player and reverse pivoting. As the diagram shows, the defender's body shifts from a position of being on the top side to the baseline side with this simple two-step move.

The teammates out front try to keep the ball from reversing once the post man shifts to the baseline side. Note how X1 and X3 deny their men in D-94 and 95. If the ball does reverse, the defender will have to resume position on the posted man as best he can, but it will be by getting back up from under the man. He will not be able to retrace the two-step method to get back to where he was when the ball was on the wing without getting pinned, if he is playing against a good player.

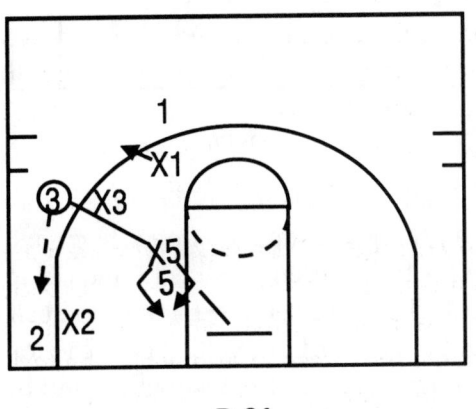

D-94

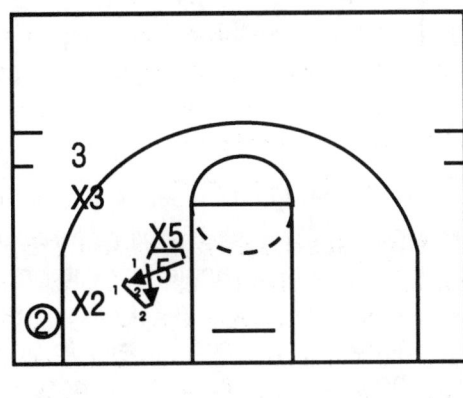

D-95

DEFENDING CUTTERS

Make contact with all cutters to keep the defensive body between the cutter and the ball. Although more physical contact is generally allowed in the NBA compared to other levels, it is important for all players to learn how to use their bodies in order to play a more physical game. One of the most important of these was mentioned in the discussion of blocking out to rebound. Another equally important one is learning how to bump cutters away from their preferred route without actually fouling.

The "bump and release" technique is how the pros play cutters toward the ball. The defender will use what we call the "45 degree technique." As the offensive player cuts to the ball or basket, the defender will contact the cutter with the inside forearm held at about a 45 degree angle. If he has the arm up and out at a 90 degree angle, he will be called for a foul, and he is in a weak position. If he has it down to his side, he will not be able to keep any space between his body and the cutter and can get manhandle easier. He should also think basically of keeping his body at a 45 degree angle above the direct line of the cutter toward the ball or basket.

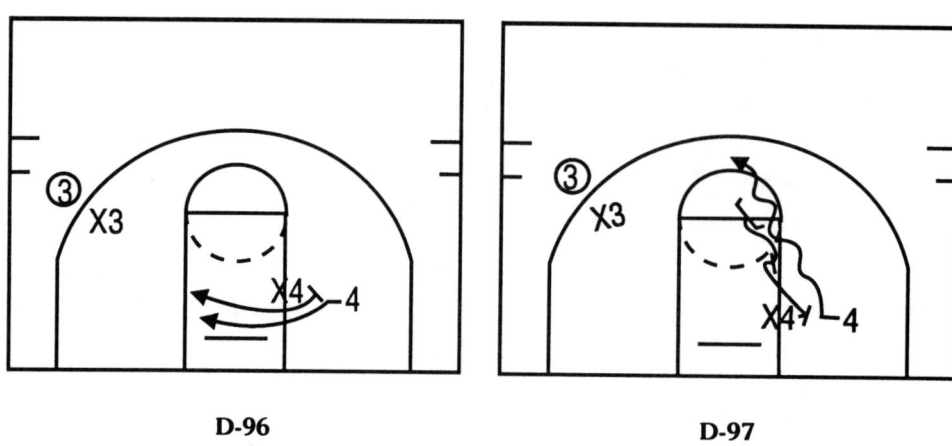

D-96   D-97

In D-96 and D-97 player 4 wants to cut into the lane to receive a pass from the wing. X4 must get his inside forearm (right) angled into 4's upper body and get his body into an angle that will prevent 4 from making a straight line cut to the ball. He will try to force 4 either to cut higher than his direct line to the ball, or to perform a backcut. He tries to prevent the cutter from getting over the top of his body at all costs. The defender must be willing to give every effort and be willing to absorb and administer a little pain in order to maintain a body position between the ball and the cutter.

There is good reason for using the "bump and release." If the defender stays in contact with the cutter's body, he runs two risks. One, the offensive player can use his own body and hands to throw the defender aside and still gain his desired route. Two, referees tend to call a foul on the defender if he appears to be holding the cutter. But a bump followed by a release will serve the dual purpose of breaking up the cutter's route and rhythm and still keep the defender in a good position in front of the cutter's body. If the offensive player keeps coming, another bump and release is in order.

WHEN DO ACTING CLASSES BEGIN?

When is it appropriate to "flop" to ask for a foul in the case where the cutter keeps coming at the defender? Many players flop at the first contact, but those flops are not often called by good referees unless the contact is flagrant. It's best to stay in there, be physical and maintain position. If the contact continues, the defender can consider flopping after the second or third hit. However, it's risky for a defender to fall completely down, because if there's no call, the cutter is wide open. A better tactic is for the defender to do a little acting to emphasize the contact and let out a groan to attract the referee's attention, but stay on his feet.

In the cutter/defender situation, the man who makes the first hit has the advantage. Therefore, the defender must be alert as he is defending off the ball ("ball, man, and lane") so he can step up and make the first contact. If the offensive player bumps the defender first, he can step through the direct line to the ball over the top of or under the defensive man and receive the pass easily.

Defenders on the baseline must always play a half-step to a step higher off of the baseline than the offensive player in order to maintain position to make the initial contact. In D-98 players X2, X3, and X4 are in good high positions (roughly 45 degrees) along the baseline and are ready to initiate contact if either of their men cut to the ball or goal.

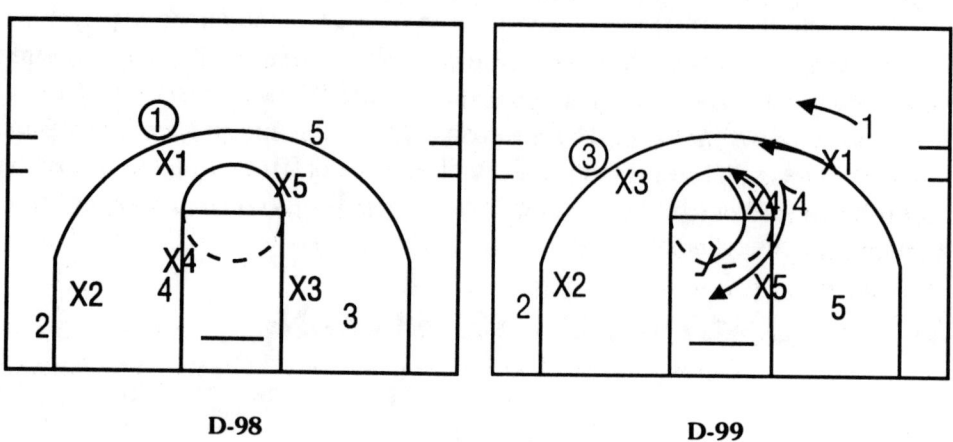

D-98   D-99

GET TO THE BODY OF BACKCUTTERS

Playing a backcutter involves proper technique. If a cutter to the ball allows himself to be pushed on up above the line toward the ball, the defender has an easier time in maintaining body position.

However, if the cutter backcuts to the basket, as 4 does in D-99, X4 must know how to defend against this. He denies the flash cut of 4 by forcing him up toward the elbow. At that point 4 backcuts to the goal. To defend him X4 must open to the ball and reach back to feel the body of 4 as he cuts. He keeps contact and vision of the ball as 4 cuts through the lane. This allows X4 a better chance to jump to deflect a lob pass. If he maintains a strong, wide body position open to the ball, he can prevent 4 from stepping in front of him as well. As 4's angle changes in D-100, X4 can close his stance back up on him. He will continue to try to deny 4 the ball on out to the defensive perimeter.

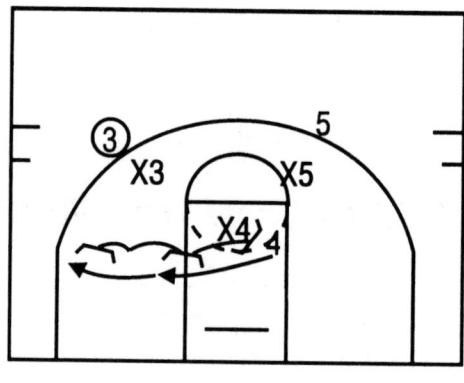

D-100

PLAYING THE PASSER/CUTTER

In playing a man who has just passed the ball, it's important to step back and move slightly in the direction of the pass after the ball is passed. Over-commitment should be avoided, but the defender must put himself at an angle whereby he can defend the passer, if he cuts to the goal looking for a give and go return pass. The reason he cannot over-commit in the direction of the pass is that there are a lot of athletic players who will be able to get a lob pass by cutting away to the basket, if the defender loses position altogether.

D-101 shows that X5 can bump 1 if he cuts straight down toward the baseline, but there is danger of the lob on the weakside, if X1 is too far removed from 1's body.

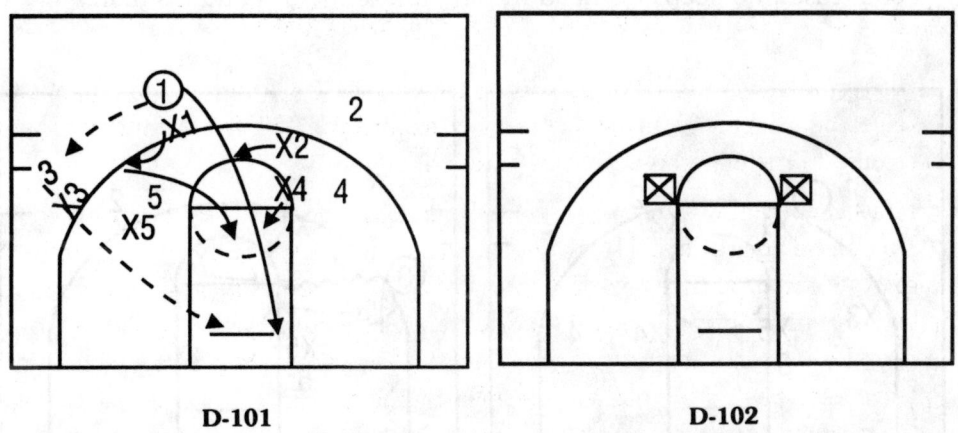

D-101   **D-102**

Deny any pass to the elbow area. It's a mistake to allow a ball to be caught at either elbow spot (D-102). Too many good things can happen for the offense with the ball at either elbow. Most players can score well from there; it is an easy access route to both low post areas and a quicker way to reverse the ball to the weakside than passing the ball to the swing spot at the top of the circle. From the elbow a player can get to the basket in just one bounce. If a player is allowed to catch at the elbow, he must be pressured to prevent an easy pass inside and must be kept from driving middle to the goal.

HOW TO BE "STRONG" ON THE WEAK SIDE

Good weakside defensive techniques are critical to a successful team defense. One of the overriding reasons for using the 41 defense is to be able to get the weakside defense set as quickly as possible. It is vital to ball pressure defense and to attacking all penetration by dribbling, passing and cutting. The weakside players are constantly reminding themselves of their triple responsibility of "ball, man and lane."

In this mindset they put themselves into position to be able to fulfill five responsibilities:

1. **Preventing an easy reversal of the ball.** In D-103 X2 is denying an easy swing at the top in order to allow X4 to be further off into the help area. In the event that X1 makes an error and allows 1 to penetrate the middle, X2 would try to give help to X1, but his main concern is to prevent the easy reverse pass. Note that X2 has an open stance, though a closed stance may be better if X2 is a bit slow or if 2 is an outstanding player. (In an open stance X2 faces the ball, in closed stance he faces in toward his man, and in both cases, he keeps his head moving to see the ball and his man.)

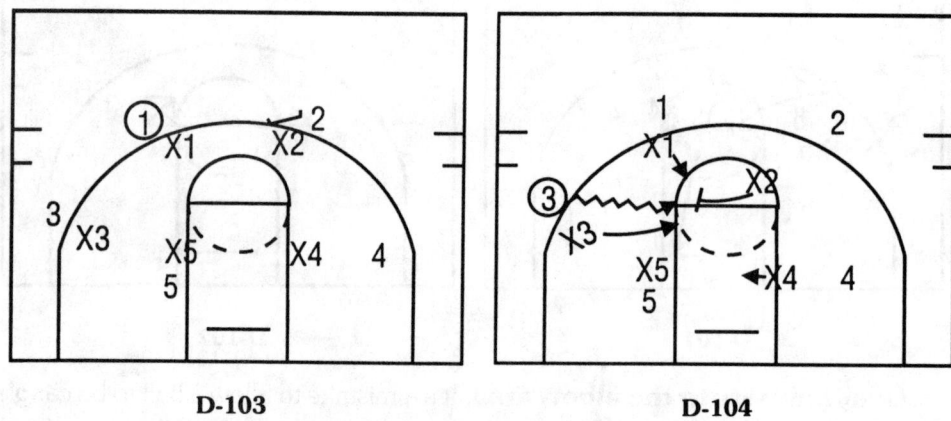

D-103   D-104

2. **Giving secondary help to penetration when defending two passes away from the ball.** In D-104 X2 is two passes removed from the ball and steps in because 3 beat X3 to the middle. X2 will try to get to an angle to force the ballhandler away from a direct line to the goal. His route will be a "banana" route as opposed to a straight line. X1's primary responsibility is to prevent an easy swing of the ball to 1. If X2 fell asleep or was out of position to help X3, X5 would have to challenge 3's penetration so X4 moves to fake 5 and X2 would then rotate down to pick up X4's man (D-105). Drilling to attack from the strongside front, weakside front, and inside is very necessary.

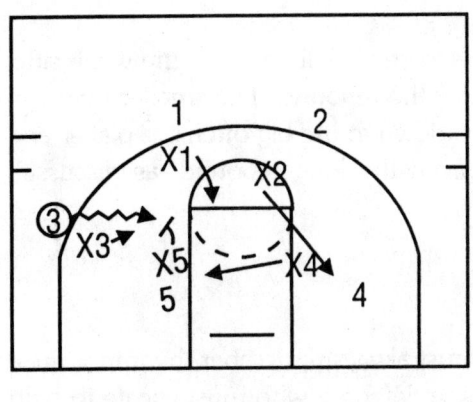

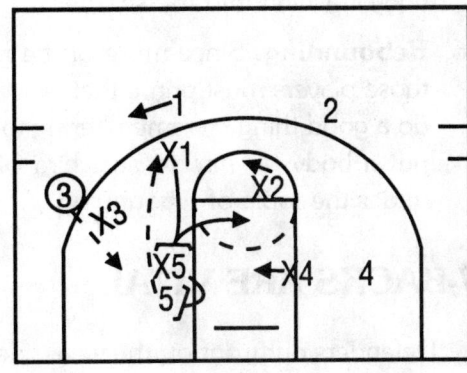

D-105   **D-106**

3. **Rotating to open men in scoring position, whether they are shooters, drivers, or swing passers.** Because X1 trapped the low post in D-106, X2 has to rotate to the open receiver 1 at the elbow area. In D-107 X4 rotates to the baseline penetration of player 3 and X2 rotates to open man 4.

4. **Going for blocked shots when they can get an angle.** If a player is not a shot-blocker, he can at least go for good body position as he attacks a shooter such as X5 does in D-108. The entire weak side must rotate as they see baseline penetration. The baseline player must go to the ball for the trap or blocked shot and the front man must V-back to cover for the baseline man who vacated, as X2 does for X4.

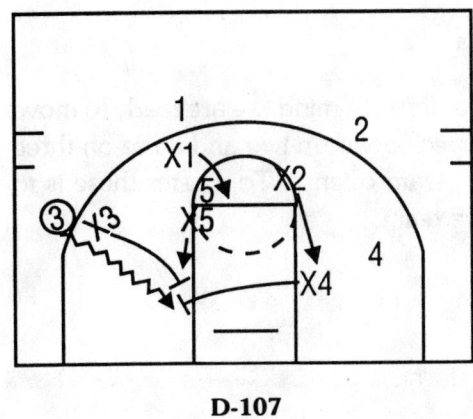

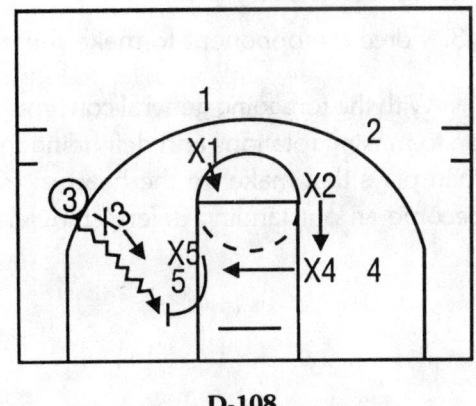

D-107   **D-108**

5. In attempting to block the shot, Hubie Brown correctly advocates a defender doing so with his inside hand (the one nearest the goal). This method will cause fewer fouls by carrying the blocker's body on past the shooter's, and

gives him the same opportunity of getting to the shot with less chance of his body crashing into the shooter's.

6. **Rebounding.** Since more of the missed shots will come to the weak side, those players must prime themselves for the rebound. The smaller men can do a good thing by remembering to go down to the big offensive player and put a body on him to seal him off from the long rebound, as discussed under the topic of rebounding.

V-BACKS ARE VITAL

Defenders out front on the weakside must always remember the importance of the V-backs move to cover for the baseline defender who must vacate to help defend the strong side low post and baseline penetration. The move is called a "V-back" because X2 moves in the shape of the letter "V" as he goes down to the baseline to help and then recovers back up to his own man. It has to be an automatic response to give the kind of help X2 does ;in D-105, 107, and 108. It will not always be a guard in that position when a shot goes up, so everyone must drill it and remember the responsibility.

SUMMARY NOTE ON PART I

Most of the details of the individual responsiblities within the team defense will become more automatic to players when they remember the basic aims of the defense in keeping the opponent from scoring easily:

1. Challenge every open shot.
2. Challenge every penetration.
3. Force the opponent to make the extra play.

With the foregoing general concepts of defense in mind, we are ready to move on to making rotations and defending the specific two-on-two and three-on-three man plays that make up the heart of every team offense. To master these is to become an outstanding defender/defensive team.

Part Two

Rotating in the Half-court Man-to-man to Maintain a Multiple Defense Effect

Introduction

The Milwaukee Bucks were a leader in rotating defenses in the NBA for several years. Don Nelson and his defensive guru, assistant coach John Kililea, set a trend in the late 1970s that was followed by the rest of the league. All NBA teams now use various forms of defensive rotations and opposing offenses have become good at adjusting to the various trapping/rotating defenses. Some coaches feel that the trapping and rotating has been overdone and have now become more selective in using them. Some systems have become very clever in their adjustments because of the skill of many individual players.

There are times when teams seem to do even better when they are trapped than when they are left to play against a good positional man-to-man defense. For example, Larry Bird and Magic Johnson are two such players who passed so well out of traps that they found easy assists when teams doubled them. Other players have developed similar talents in this area.

The problem is that if teams lay back and do nothing but play straight one-on-one defense night after night, they face certain defeat as offenses pick, cut, drive and post them. Being aggressive and creative at least gives the defense some hope.

Rotating on defense is mistakenly thought by some to be limited to just trapping in the low post. While that is one area in which rotating is often used, it's necessary to have an overall concept of rotations in order to use Multiple Defenses. To attack penetration and to defend many 2- and 3-man actions, rotating is a must. A team that is committed to picking up open shooters depends on rotations to cover up for the defender who picks up the open man. Teams who want to trap with the man-to-man at halfcourt and be able to extend with zone presses in various situations can do so most successfully with an organized rotation system.

In order to use traps consistently well and to give help to teammates, all players have to understand the general concept of rotation defense. When they see the whole picture, it becomes easy to make adjustments in the multiple defense system. Most players take pride in being able to attack the opponent with a multitude of looks and adjustments. Smart, tough players enjoy the feeling when they know they have been able to win by keeping an opponent from doing what they wanted to do on offense.

It's that kind of pride and joy in defense that builds a winner. It takes hard work and teamwork and everyone knows it. Champions have been willing to pay that price. And so it must continue to be true that champions at all levels will have enough players on the team that commit to defense as the vehicle they all will ride in, if they are to lead the victory parade.

CALLING THE FIRE DEPARTMENT

"Put out the fire!" The calls and labels involved in our rotation system reflect our attempt to build pride in our multiple defense attack. Each team should find a fun way to characterize its defense, since that helps build pride and camaraderie. One method we used involved characterizing our team as "The Fire Department," going about the business of preventing and putting out fires. It makes it more fun to teach and play defense, if the team can agree on something they can take pride in. To describe our defensive rotation activities we use the following terms analogous to the Fire Department:

- **Fire** — what a player yells as he goes to set a trap. It indicates that our Fire Department has a fire to prevent or put out.
- **Sandman** — the trapper who yells "fire" and goes to trap. He throws sand on the fire.
- **Smoke** — a potential trouble spot where the defense may have to make an adjustment.
- **Chief, Captain, Ladder Man, Hose Man, Three/Four Alarm, etc.,** are all terms that a team can use to reward or identify players who do a good job of defense in terms of stopping a player, of calling out signals, of shot-blocking, of stealing, and so on. Come up with your own terms or games.

My recommendation is that a coach and team try to find a unique identity for its own defense, then fit some of the terms to that identity. For purposes of illustration, we will continue with the Fire Department analogy here.

FIRE DEPARTMENT DEFENSE

A player will call out "fire" to signal to his teammates that he is leaving his own man to attack another. The call can indicate that he has to go put out a raging fire where a teammate is in trouble, or it can mean that he just smells smoke and sees a good opportunity to do some fire prevention.

Scouting reports will help the coach decide when, where and whom to trap.

1. **Examples of when to trap.** Some of the options include:

   - When a specific opponent catches the ball in a prime area such as the low post.
   - When a specific opponent dribbles once or twice in the post or on the wing area.
   - When opponents run isolation plays.

2. **Examples of where to trap.** The defense can look to trap in the:

   - Low post.
   - Baseline or lane area when there is penetration.
   - Wing area against a pick/roll or a 1-on-1.
   - Corners. The "corners" along the baseline and those where the half-line meets the sidelines are nice areas for trapping, due to the help the lines add to the defense (D-1).

3. **Examples of whom may be trapped.** Good candidates for trapping are:

   - Good low post scorers.
   - Good 1-on-1 players.
   - Pick and roll participants.
   - A playmaker in good feeding position.
   - Any weak ballhandler.

4. **There are some automatic trap situations** including when:

   - An offensive player has a defender in a "bad way" (at a disadvantage) and is ready to score.
   - When a smaller player is mismatched in the low post.
   - When a big player is mismatched outside and faced with defending a good smaller 1-on-1 player.
   - When there are 10 seconds or less remaining on the shot clock and the ball is in good position or with a good scorer having the ball.

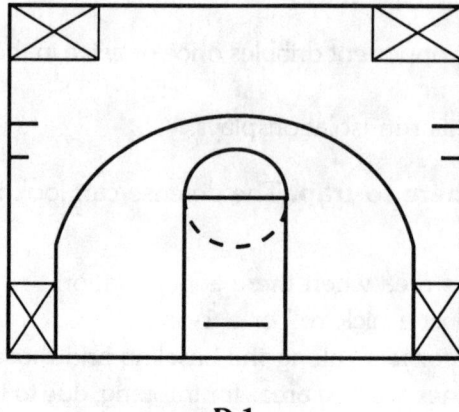

D-1

LOW POST TRAPS

Nearly every good player is skilled enough to put intense heat on the defense if he's able to catch the ball in the low post. We will do certain preventive techniques such as practicing good early defensive body position, giving help from the wing feeder and using different traps. Against some players we will have to use traps a lot and react to cover for the player who has gone to trap by rotating the defense. A teammate must rotate toward the player left open by the man who left to trap, if he is in a threatening position.

THEORY AND TECHNIQUES

There are several reasons for using different trapping techniques:

1. Too much of any one technique begins to be counter- productive because good players learn to adjust.

2. It's not good for the opponent to know, with a high degree of confidence, what defense you're going to run.

3. The ability of players in the low post varies. Some score well, some pass well. Some do both well and others do neither one with a great degree of success. Know which your opponent is and adjust to it.

4. The overall outside shooting ability of the opposing team can make the defense hesitant to leave shooters to go trap very often. A poor shooting crew will allow more inside trapping to be done.

5. The rebounding ability of the opponent is a factor. Trapping alters the defensive matchups and positioning, tending to weaken the rebounding of the defensive team.

6. The general passing ability of the opposing team. Good passing teams can be rough on the extended defenses.

7. The game situation can dictate when it is time to take more chances or to play it safer.

THE FOUR TRAP ANGLES

The numbers in D-2 and D-3 are for quicker teaching and communication purposes. By calling out "Fire!" and a number when teaching or explaining traps in a huddle or practice, it makes it easy to designate who will trap the ball in the low post with just a few words. In a game a player will simply yell "fire!" and everyone will see where the trapper is coming from, making it unnecessary to add the number.

Notice that the "Fire 1" from the wing comes from the ball side in both diagrams and that the "top" is the strongside top and is "Fire 2" in both diagrams. The weakside front is always "Fire 3" and the weakside baseline is "Fire 4." When we talk about "Fire 5" later on, it will refer to trapping from any one of the four spots on a "read" basis.

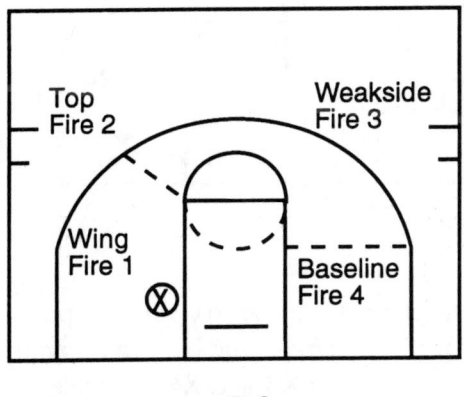

D-2

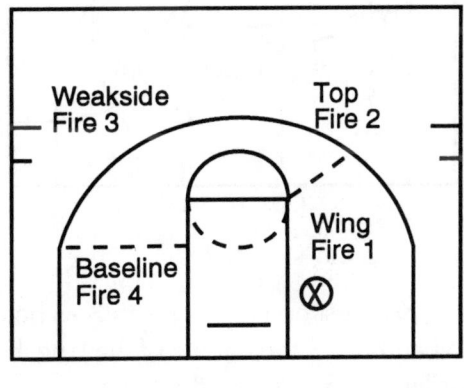

D-3

USING DIFFERENT PLAYERS TO SET THE TRAPS TO PUT OUT THE FIRE

The basic low post traps described as "Fire 1, 2, 3, 4, and 5" are not the only trap methods that are effective, though they do form a solid base and could be considered arsenal enough when setting up a low post trap system in the defense.

Using a "live man." A team may use its smallest man, or quickest man to be ready to trap in the low post whenever he thinks he can do it profitably. He can be called the "Sandman," throwing sand on the fire. Or, it can be set up so that whoever is guarding a certain poor- shooting opponent will be "live," the Sandman.

Being "live off of a cutter." A defender going through the middle with his man as he cuts may be designated as a "live" man, or Sandman. In diagram 4, 3 has passed to 5 and cut to the goal. It is actually easier for the defense to trap if 3 cuts. Scouting reports will tell us a team's tendencies.

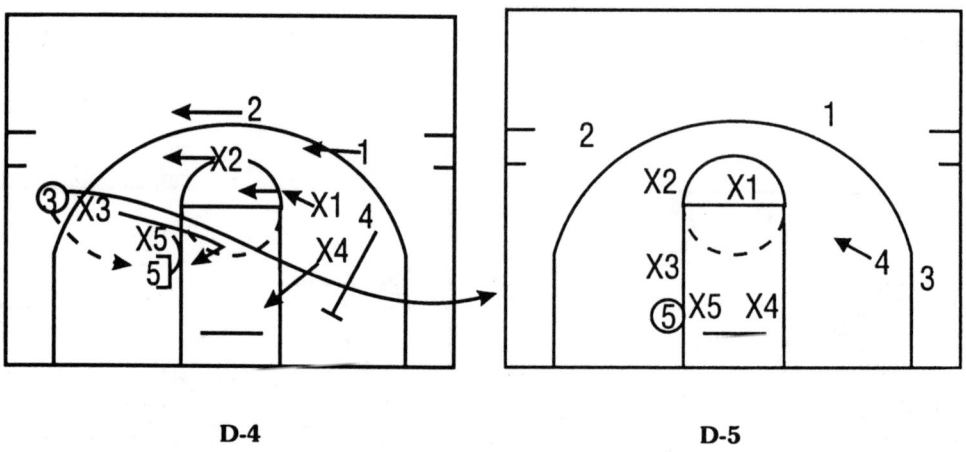

D-4   D-5

X3 must go part way with 3 as he cuts to prevent the easy give and go pass. When X3 hits the middle of the lane, he is "live." He is free to go back to trap the ball with X5. 3 is absorbed by the weakside defense, but X3 and X4 must talk as X3 "hands off" 3 to X4 and goes to trap the ball. X3 attacks the angle left open by X5, the top side in D-5.

Trapping with the nearest small/big player. In certain situations the nearest small player or the nearest big player to the low post can be designated as the man to set the trap, regardless of whether that man is on the wing, the top, the weak side, or the baseline.

Trapping with the first/bigger/smaller man from the weak side who can get there. Again, a designation can be made to have a man from the weak side come to trap and it can be the first one to read it, or it can be the smaller or bigger of the players on the weak side, whichever is preferred.

When players understand the concept of how to trap and rotate, it will not matter who traps or where the trap comes from, the team will know how to adjust. The following explanation of rotations will make it more clear how the team must adjust when a trap is set in the low post.

ROTATIONS

This word is talked about a lot, but is not understood all that well. An easy, common sense approach is to teach that rotating simply means one teammate is put in a position whereby he must attack an opponent other than his own man. Therefore, the team defense must rotate to cover the man he leaves open.

There are three reasons a man will leave his own assignment to attack another player, causing a need for a rotation:

- He may want to trap the ball for profit or for need (to prevent a fire or to put one out).
- He may read that the ballhandler is beating his man on a penetration move either to the middle or the baseline.
- He sees an open man and decides to rotate to prevent an easy shot by him, or to steal a pass that may be coming to him.

PLAYER MOVEMENT IN THE LOW POST TRAP

Please note first of all: as a player or coach reads and studies the following rotation system he must realize that in the diagrams, X1 and X2 are always out front in the guard positions, X3 and X4 are on the wings and X5 is in the low post. This is done for illustration purposes. In the course of a game, any player may be posted and any player may be on either wing area, or out front, or on the baseline.

Furthermore, a "live" player may come from any direction into the low post to trap; everyone will have to adjust to cover for him. Therefore, it's necessary to drill with every player being in every location when a trap occurs. Players must understand the whole picture, the concept, and then they can make the system work. The understanding of filling the zone spots and of rotating to the weak side opposite the pass are absolutely essential to executing these traps and rotations from more than one angle.

FILL THE TWO ZONE SPOTS

The two "zone spots" must be filled as soon as a low post trap is set, just like for any trap that is set anywhere except in the middle lane of the court. Naturally, two players will be involved as the trappers. That leaves three other players for which to designate duties. One will be a floater to play the pass out from the trap, and to play his own man if he cuts.

The other two men must get to the two weakside "zone spots" in the high and low post as in D-6 and D-7. To continue the fireman analogy, it can be said that one covers the upstairs and the other gets the downstairs. It is better if the smaller of the two players gets to the high zone and the bigger one to the low zone, if that is possible (another big in-little out situation). In D-6 X2 is smaller and gets the high zone and in D-7 X3 is smaller than X4 and takes the high zone.

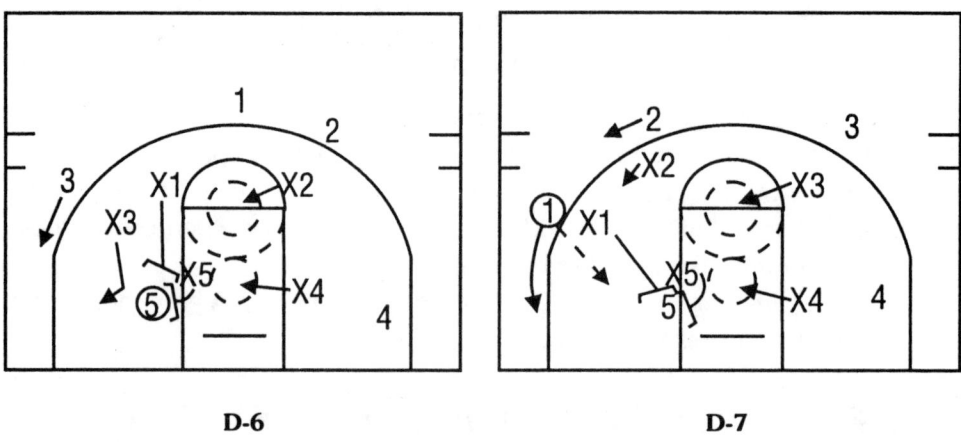

D-6   D-7

The concept of the two zones is explained by looking at the dotted lines that depict the zones in the diagrams. As soon as the trap is set, these two areas must be filled immediately and the two zone men will play against three offensive players while the ball is in the trap. They will continue to zone up against these three men even after the ball is passed out of the trap until the Sandman who trapped can rotate off and take one of the open men.

HOW TO ROTATE FROM THE TRAP

The general rule for the man who goes to trap is to *go to the weak side and find an open man* as quickly as possible, when the ball is passed out of the trap. While there is an exception to this rule when the trap is set from the wing (Fire 1), it is better to learn the rule despite the exception.

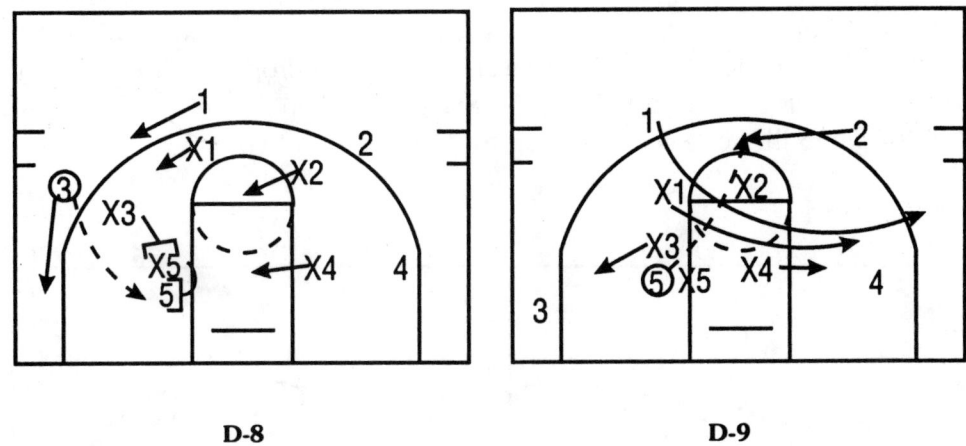

D-8   D-9

FOUR ANGLES FOR LOW POST ROTATIONS

On the Trap from the Wing (Fire 1)

In D-8 3 feeds 5 low and X3 traps 5. The weakside players X2 and X4 shift immediately into the zone spots and X1 floats to help play the pass out to any area above the wing. If 1 cuts, X1 will go with him.

If 5 passes out to 3 in the wing or corner area, X3 must recover back to 3. X3 easily can read the direction 5 kicks the ball back out, and pursues it in that direction. To help X3 do this he cannot turn his back on 3 as he harasses 5. He must turn only halfway so he can slide quickly back out to the wing or corner. No one else is close enough to be able to rotate to the wing or corner, so in this case X3 cannot "go weak side and pick up the open man" when the ball is passed out. This is the exception to the low post trap rotation rule and it is a logical one.

When X3 recovers back out to 3 he must be alert to prevent 3 from faking and driving past him. X3 must be under control and not leave his feet until 3 leaves his feet to shoot. Then he can go at the shooter's hand. He can be allowed to run on out to the offensive end on a "run-out" for a fast break after the shot.

It is important to prevent 5 and 3 from playing the in and out game by passing the ball back and forth. As soon as the ball is passed out to 3, X5 must fight to get in front of 5 in the low post in order to prevent this in and out game.

Regardless of the movement of the offense, X2 will move up to cover whoever is in the front area if the ball is passed out there; however, if it is thrown out front to 1, X1 will be responsible for him (D-9).

On the Trap from the Top (Fire 2)

Trapping from the top will normally give cause for a rotation. In D-10 X1 yells "Fire" and traps at an inside angle in order to take away inside penetration by 5. X5 slides baseline to take away 5's baseline move. X3 drops and is ready to go with 3 if he cuts and to get to him if 5 passes out to 3 in the corner. Players X2 and X4 get to the zone spots as soon as X1 goes in to trap 5.

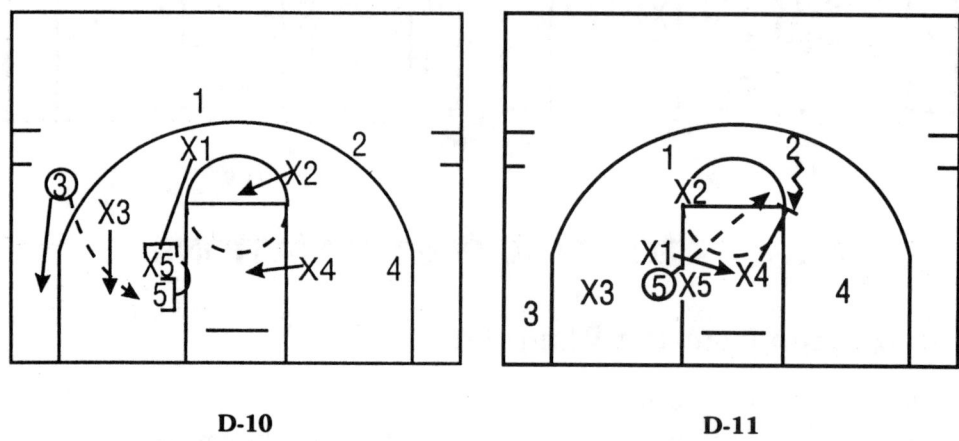

D-10   **D-11**

After X1 has trapped, the high zone man (X2) will be ready to make a commitment to the strongside elbow; but he is still aware of his own man that he just left. He is zoning the area and is ready to play the pass that comes out to the top. In his zoning technique, he can vary his positioning:

1. He may play half-way and read to go to the ball if it is passed to either 1 or 2 (D-10).

2. He may commit completely to 1 and force a rotation. He will either be hoping to get a steal or to prevent the ball from going to 1 in the event 1 is a great scorer. If X2 has committed to 1 and the pass goes out diagonally to 2, X4 will have to rotate to him and X1 will rotate on to cover 4 (D-11).

It is important that X1 rotates quickly to the weak side and picks up the open man, which may be player 2 or 4. In D-12 X2 rotates to 1 when 5 passes to the top. X1 will go to the weak side and find an open man. Whether X1 rotates to player 2 or 4 will depend on communication between X4 and X1. If 2 is a good scorer and X4 thinks that X1 will not be able to rotate fast enough to prevent him from getting an easy shot, he will yell out to X1, "I've got up!" If the pass out from 5 to 1 at the top is a slow, high pass or if player 2 is not a good shooter, X4 can yell to X1, "You take high!" or, "Go up!" Players should talk and point as well; the more communication the better (D12).

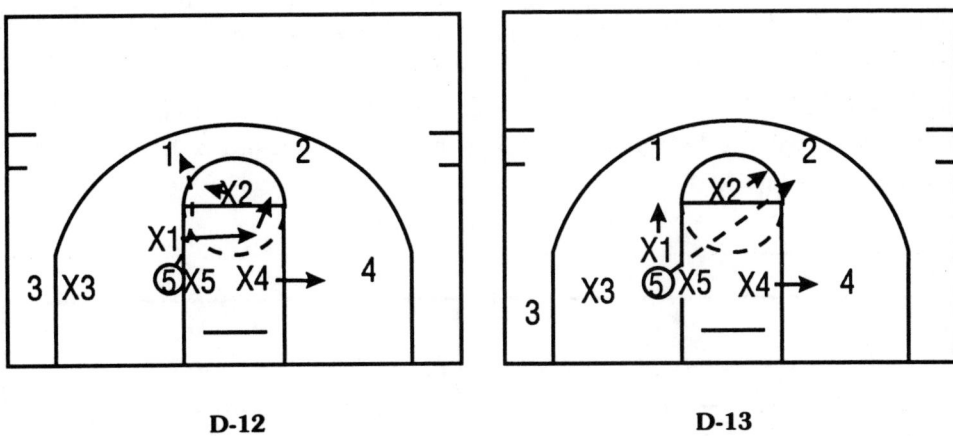

D-12   **D-13**

If player 5 had thrown the ball out diagonally to 2, X2 would pursue the pass and X1 would rotate back to 1 — which is still "going weak side and picking up," since the weak side is always the side of the floor opposite the ball as in D-13. Since 2 has the ball, X1 is on the weak side.

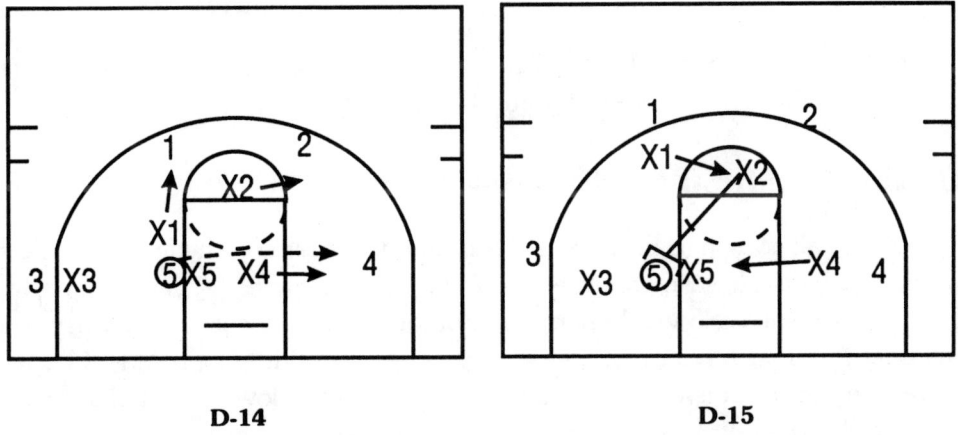

D-14   **D-15**

If player 5 passes the ball over the top to 4 along the opposite baseline, X4 should be able to get to him and X2 would shift back to the same side and X1 would get back to 1, who is now opposite the ball as in D-14.

On the Trap from the Weakside Front (Fire 3)

In D-15 X2 yells "Fire!" and traps the ball in the low post. Immediately, X4 gets to the low zone and this time X1 has to get to the high zone. X3 must defend 3 if he cuts or floats outside. Player X1 and X2 have just changed jobs from those described in Fire 2. Now X1 must play the pass out to the top from 5 and X2 must rotate to the weak side opposite the pass. If the pass goes to 2, X1 will follow it and X2 will rotate to 1.

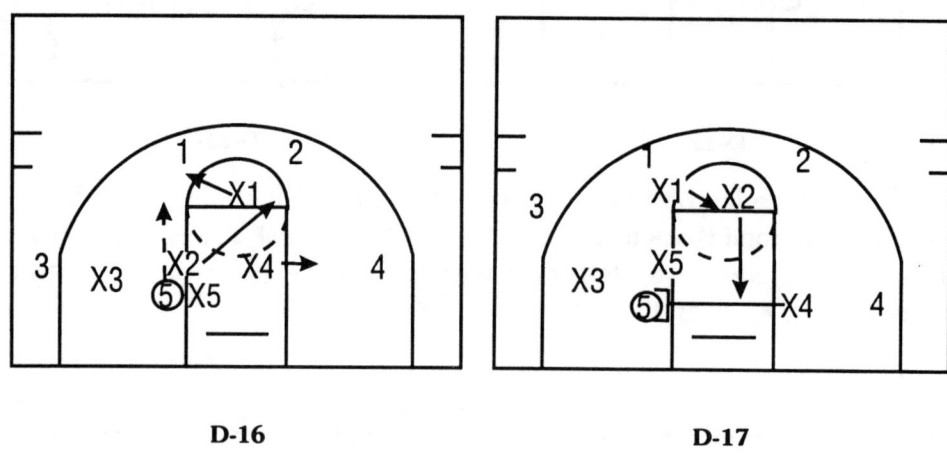

D-16   D-17

If the pass from 5 is to 1, X1 will recover back to 1 and X4 will communicate with X2 as to which of them will go up high to get 2 (D-16).

On the Trap from the Baseline (Fire 4)

As the ball goes in to 5, X4 yells "Fire!" and traps with 5. The angle X4 takes will usually be the baseline angle as D-17 shows. Sometimes X4 can slide under 5 for a nice steal. If X5 would happen to be on the baseline side of 5 when the ball goes to him, X4 would of course trap on the top side. As soon as X4 goes to trap, the zone spots must be filled. This time X2 gets low and X1 slides over to the high zone.

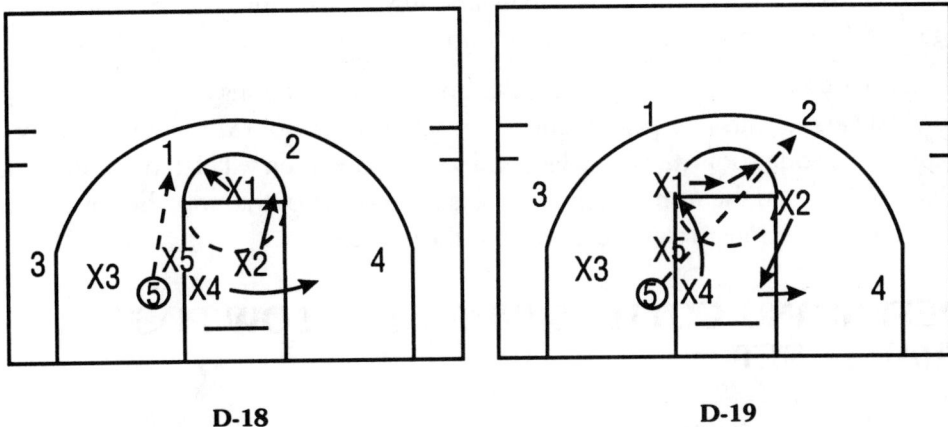

D-18   **D-19**

If the ball is passed out to 3 or 1, everyone can recover back to their own men easily (D-18). If the ball goes to the weak side to 2 or the baseline to 4, X1 and X2 will cover the ball side and X4 can rotate up to the new weak side to defend 1 (D-19).

Note that since a pass from 5 to 4 will probably involve a mismatch, X4 may want to follow the pass to trap with X2 to get him out of the mismatch. If he forgets, X1 can come down and trap with X2 on the mismatch.

It's easy to see that the rebounding can be a problem if this trap is overdone. Of course, in the process of playing a game, the defender on the baseline where X4 is in the diagram will not always be X4 as mentioned at the beginning of this section. It could be any player. Therefore, it is good for all the players to know how to get the zone spots filled and to rotate when a trap is set from the baseline angle.

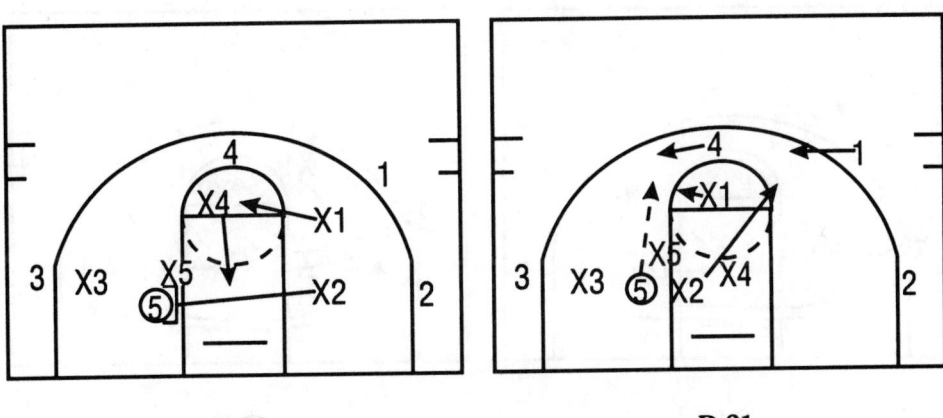

D-20   **D-21**

If X1 or X2 were on the baseline when the ball went in to 5 as X2 is in D-20, it would be a very good option for him to sneak under 5 to deflect the ball away. Player X4 is out front when this occurs and would slide into the low zone spot. Again, X2 would go weak side opposite the pass when 5 outlets it (D-21).

It is easy to see how a team that drills on low post rotations will be able to trap from any angle with any player, once they all understand: (a) that two men will trap; (b) the zone spots must be filled; and (c) the zone men will defend three men while the ball is in the trap. When the ball is passed out of the trap, the zone men and the trapper must rotate to cover the three men.

DEFENDING CUTTERS WHEN THE LOW POST TRAP IS SET

While it's vital to know how to do all the items described above in executing trapping, many defenses take it no further than this. Those teams still get burnt quite often by cutters who receive passes for easy goals as they cut through the defense during a trap effort.

Playing a cutter from the wing. The defender on the wing is responsible for his man if he floats in the wing or corner area as already mentioned and must go with him if he cuts through to the basket, regardless of who is trapping inside, including himself.

In D-22 X3 is trapping in a Fire 1 and 3 cuts through to the goal. X3 must release from the trap when 3 is a step in front of the trap and prevent him from getting a pass from 5. X3 has already done a good job of preventing a quick scoring move by 5. After 3 and X3 clear on through, if 5 starts to make a good scoring move, a player from the top or weak side may want to make a second trap on him.

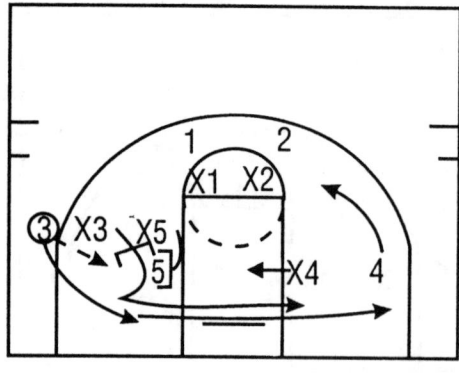

D-22

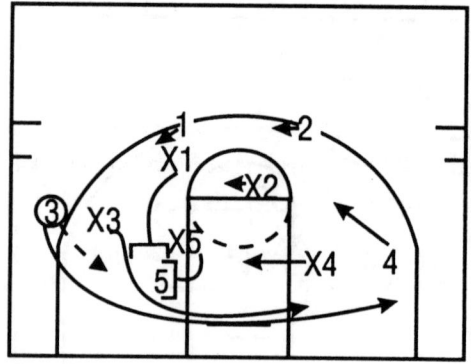

D-23

D-23 shows a Fire 2 and 3 cuts to the basket. Again, X3 is responsible for him and must stay with him. The other four men are all involved with specific tasks: X5 and X1 are trapping while X2 and X4 must fill the zone spots.

Playing a cutter from the top. If a cutter goes into the lane from out front during a low post trap set from anywhere, the players in the two zone spots work together to absorb him.

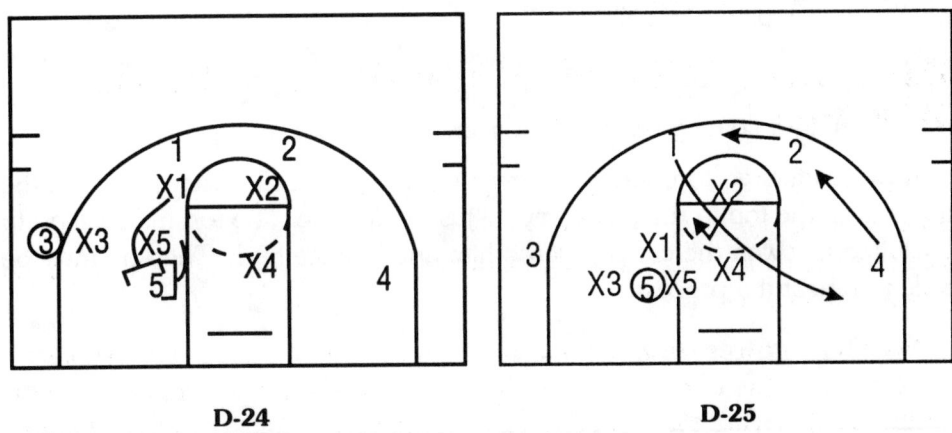

D-24   **D-25**

D-24 and D-25 show a Fire 2 with player 1 cutting to the goal as X1 sets the trap. X2 and X4 get to the zone spots and must execute the cutter defense rule. X2 in the high zone will yell "cutter!" and must either get between the cutter and the ball or he must get into a position to force him to cut through so close to the trap that a pass cannot be made. The latter is more likely to be the case.

At that point the job is half done. X2 will continue with the cutter until the dotted line of the free throw circle and then release him to X4. X4 will say "I've got him!" or "Get back!" and at that point X2 must bounce back up quickly to the foul line to reassume his zone positioning. Another player will definitely be cutting in to fill the spot vacated by cutter 1 (D-25).

Knowing this technique and practicing it will set a good rotating team apart from the average or lesser ones. The top man in the zone checks the cutter, hands him off to the low man in the zone and recovers back to the high zone spot; that's the rule in short form. Talking and pointing are vital, as always.

SPECIAL NOTES ON DEFENDING CUTTERS FROM THE TOP

When the trap is set by the wing player (Fire 1), and a cutter goes through from the top as in D-26, there are two players who are defending at the top of the defense in many offensive formations. It is still best to rule it the same way as when the trap comes from Fire 2, 3 and 4 and there is a cutter from the top. X2 in the high zone will still check the cutter to make sure he does not get an easy pass. What X1 does is up to the philosophy of the coach. X1 is the floater in this case (X3 and X5 are trapping while X2 and X4 are the zone men). X1 can be told to be responsible for his own man and go through with his man as we prefer in the NBA due to illegal defense rules. Or, he can be told to drop in as X2 does, let the cutter go and stay in a floating position out front. Each has its merits.

If two cutters go through, one after the other, it is still better to defend the cutters from the top in the same way — just do it twice. The top man will go to the dotted line with the cutter, release him and bounce back. Then he must be ready to repeat the process.

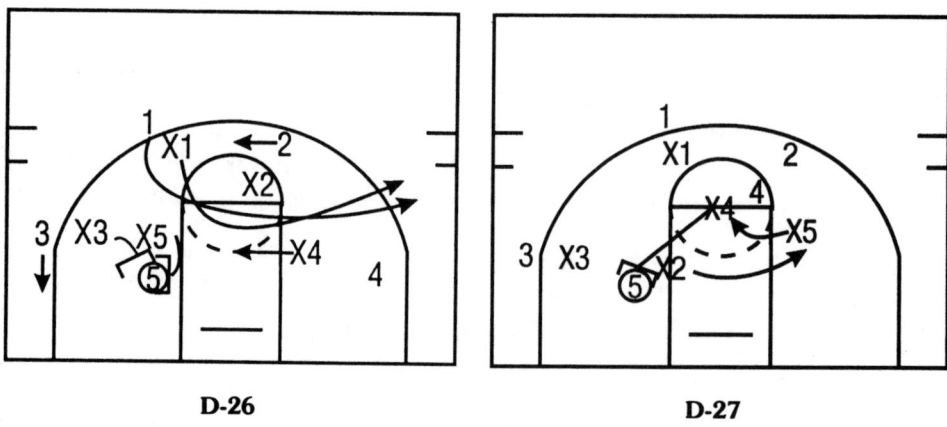

D-26   D-27

AUTOMATIC LOW POST MISMATCH TRAP

We have already had cause to mention the importance of having an automatic mismatch trap rule for both the inside and the outside mismatches. It bears repeating here in this context for emphasis and clarity. Whenever the switching system (or an error) has put one of the small defenders in the low post against a big man, the nearest teammate should trap the post as soon as he sees the ball go in as X4 does for X2 in D-27. This will preferably be a big man. When the ball is passed out, the bigger man in the trap will stay and the smaller man will rotate off. This is called "trapping out the mismatch" and goes along with the thinking of preventing any easy, embarrassing scores. If no one comes to trap, a hard foul by the small player while the offensive players hands and arms are down that prevents a layup/dunk is better than a two-point gift.

DEFENDING THE "ELBOW DRIFT" ON FIRE 1 TRAPS

A unique situation presents itself when the wing-feeder's defender traps in a Fire 1 and the wing man drifts to the strong side elbow after passing in to the low post. Remember that the wing man is responsible for his man when the low post is trapped if he cuts, or if he drifts to the corner, or the regular wing area. However, in D-28 3 passed in to 5 and drifted right to the elbow area. It is not likely that X3 can get low enough to bother 5 in the low post and still get back to 3 at the elbow in time to prevent 3 from having an easy look at the basket. When it becomes known that a team uses this move, an adjustment must be made. It is necessary for the nearest front defender to rotate to the open man at the elbow. X3 then will go to the weak side opposite the pass and pick up an open man when the ball is passed out of the trap (D-29).

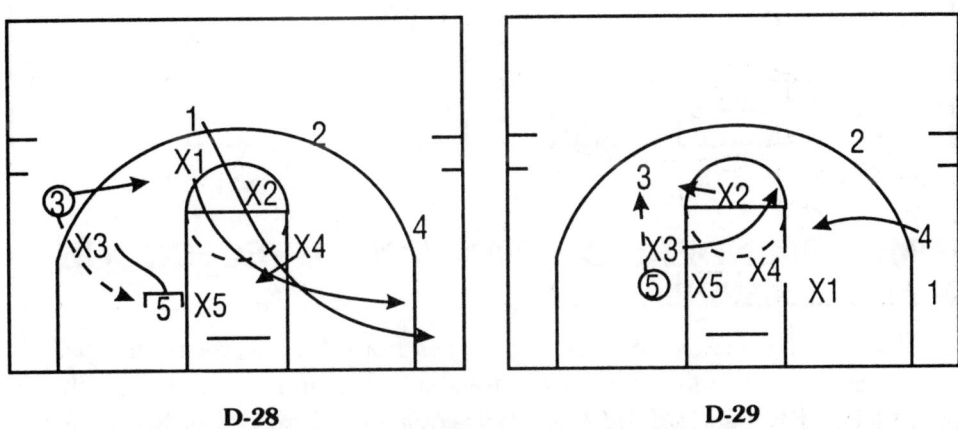

D-28   D-29

Note that X3 will go to the weak side and pick up an open man, unless a rare event occurs in which some other offensive player fills to the strongside corner or wing area where his normal coverage is. If someone does, he simply covers him as if 3 had stayed there.

SHOULD BIG MEN BE ALLOWED TO TRAP IN THE LOW POST OR NOT?

With the exception of the low post mismatch automatic trap, some coaches will not allow their big men to trap during parts of a game or even at all. The reason for holding the big men away from trapping is that it tends to hurt the rebounding pattern. On the other hand, many coaches like to trap with the big men because they present a difficult wall from which to outlet the pass from the trap. Sometimes a 5-10 man has no effect on a big 7-footer when trapping in the low post, for example, but a 6-10 man would.

Both of these thoughts are legitimate and it is up to the coach to evaluate how successful his own team is at trapping, rebounding, rotating, etc., with the various combinations of trapping that the team attempts.

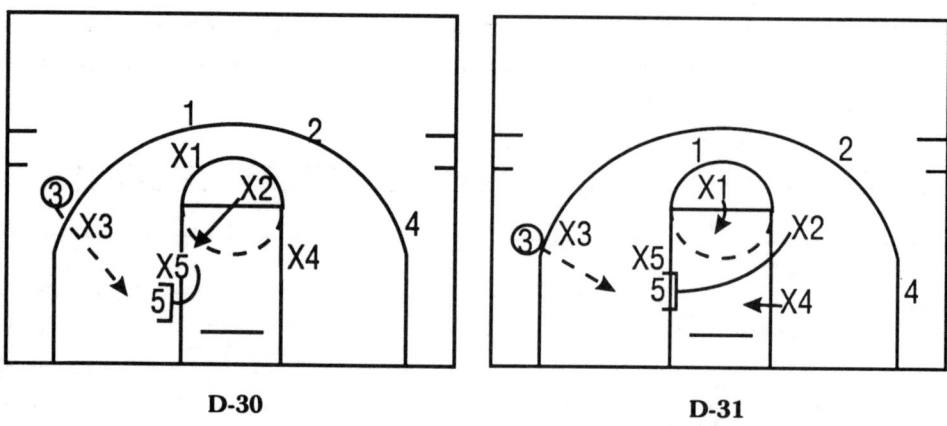

D-30   D-31

SOME REMINDERS ON INDIVIDUAL TECHNIQUE IN LOW TRAPPING

1. The trappers must take away two angles from the man being trapped. In general the defender who goes to trap as 2 does in D-30 and D-31 should attack at the open angle adjacent to the one his teammate has. X5 will always drop back to break contact when he sees his man is going to catch a ball in the low post in order to play between his man and the basket anyway. When X5 hears a man coming down from the top to trap, he will slide down a little more to be sure to take away the baseline spin by the posted man. If X5 had been extremely high on 5, X2 could have trapped to the baseline side from the weak side as in D-31, especially if he had come to trap quite early as the pass was in the air. If he does, he should communicate that he is trapping on the baseline side. It is a mistake to have both trappers defend the same angle.

2. The trappers should always close the gap by putting their adjacent feet together. They do not want the trapped man to be able to duck his body through the middle of the trap (no splitting of the trap).

3. The trappers should body up to the ballhandler to nudge him off balance, but should not reach in.

4. Never foul in a trap. He's in a bind, do not bail him out.

5. Do not try to steal the ball in a trap unless the man virtually hands you the ball. The job of the men trapping is to stop a quick, easy score and to force a weak pass out of the trap. In the best of worlds, a trapper who is staying in good position with active hands extended up (not out) will get a finger-tip on the pass out. This deflection may allow a teammate to pick up a steal. A deflection is a far better objective for trappers than a steal.

6. Rotate hard and fast off the trap if you are the rotate man (almost always the man who trapped). Do not turn to see how successful the pass was — that is time and space lost. Run off immediately opposite the pass and find an open man. (Remember the wing trap exception when the wing must get back out to his own corner or regular wing area when the ball is passed there out of the trap.)

EXTENDING THE ROTATING DEFENSE BEYOND THE LOW POST AREA

In order to break up an opponent's offensive rhythm or to wake up the defense to create steals and generate some offense. A team can use the number "22" to call for any half court traps not in the low post or use the calls Fire High, Fire Wing, Fire Corner, Fire Elbow, Fire Read, or Fire Live. All may be called by other names or numbers, of course. These labels are simple enough for our purposes here since "Fire!" means to trap and the second name indicates where the trap will occur in general.

THREE-STEP RULE

When applying a trap of any kind, but especially an extended trap, it is good to utilize the "three-step rule," which means that if a trapper cannot get to the ball within three steps or less, he should wait, since the surprise effect will have been lost. There may be occasions when the coach will want to force any kind of trap, but the three-step rule is a good general guideline for most traps from any type of defense.

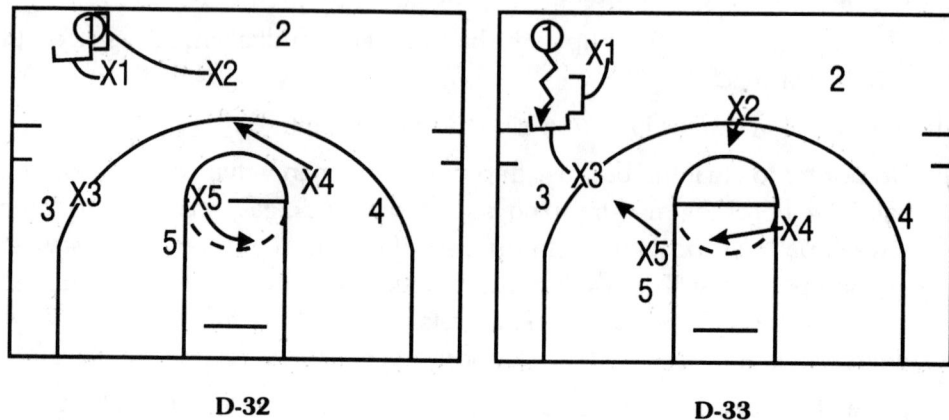

D-32   D-33

FIRE HIGH — 22 UP

D-32 shows X2 going to trap the ball in the high backcourt area, and it may be that he will even cross the halfcourt line to set the trap in the event that 1 comes right up to the line and stops.

This trap may also be set by X3 as 1 enters the front court, being especially effective if applied quickly when the ball is between the hash mark at 28 feet and the foul line extended (D-33).

ROTATING FROM THE TRAP

A coach may rule that the trapper rotates off as the ball is passed or that the trapper stays on the ball and have the original defender run off in the rotation. Any one of several systems can be used. Because of the amount of material our teams have had to learn, we've had success by telling the trapper himself to rotate on the extended traps and follow in the direction of the pass. This keeps a consistency with the low post trapping by having the trapper rotate. There is a difference, however, in that the low post trapper will normally rotate to the weak side opposite the pass out instead of in the direction of the pass.

The advantages of having the trapper follow the ball are that it reduces mismatches, and it is easy to learn. If the ball is passed on down toward the basket on the strong side of the floor as in D-34, the trapper can chase it right on down and get another trap or possibly two. Again, the standard method of having the trapper stay and rotating the original defender has its merits as well. Each one works with hustle and execution.

If the ball is passed cross-court as in D-35, X2 will probably not be able to get into another trap right away, since more distance must be covered. When X4 comes up to defend in the high zone spot as the trap is set, X2 should be able to rotate to cover for X4 in the corner. If 4 gets X2 posted up, X4 can come down and give a low post trap to get rid of the mismatch.

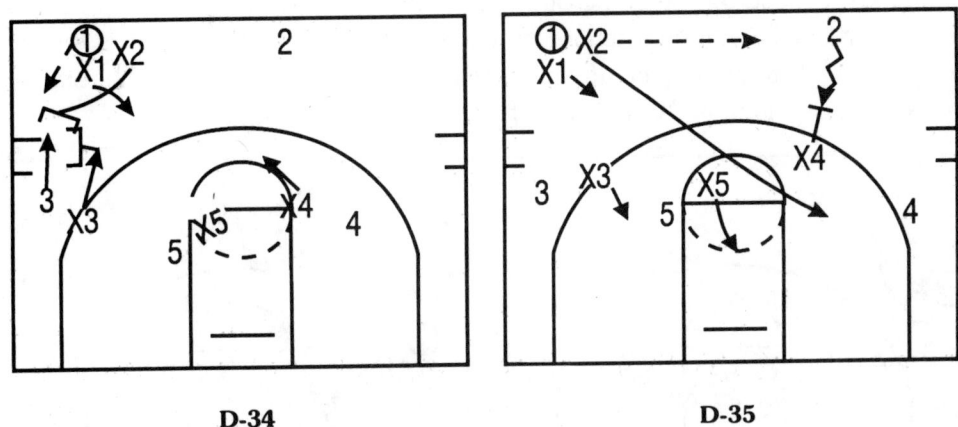

D-34 **D-35**

In general, the defense is figuring that the Fire High will give only one trap, but they are ready to get another within the confines of the three-step rule. If the purpose is to break up the offensive rhythm/set play or to stimulate movement in the defense, that will have been accomplished with a one-trap and done exercise. On the other hand, if it is a desperate situation or an all-out aggressive attack is preferred for whatever reason, the signal "roll it" can be called out to indicate that the defense will try to get in as many traps as it can that possession.

Against teams that are able to attack the half court defense from the middle lane, a 22 trap called "Fire Middle" can be used by trapping at the center circle and rotating to trap the next pass. At that point, it becomes like any other 22 high or wing, depending on where the ball is thrown. An exeception would be if it is thrown into the high post — a defensive error. In that case the ball is jammed by the nearest defender and the basket is protected by the baseline defenders until the ball is passed out from the high post.

When an offense depends heavily on its ballhandler to run the offense, a good strategy is to trap the ballhandler high and then have the original defender deny the ball back to the man as forcefully as possible. This can be very time-consuming and disruptive to that kind of team.

Fire Wing — 22 Side

The philosophy is generally the same as the Fire High, only the location of the trap is changed. The rule is that the nearest outside player (normally a small man) will trap the ball as soon as it gets to the wing. The three-step rule still applies.

In D-36 X1 leaves to trap, taking a "banana" route to set the trap in an effort to help close the angles to prevent a split. This is a good technique for all trappers, as it tends to close off the angle of penetration. If the ball goes to the corner or low post, X1 will continue to chase on down to trap (D-37). If the ball is thrown laterally, X1 will rotate to pick up an open man such as 2 or 4. Again, the rotation to trap can be made by X3 instead of X1.

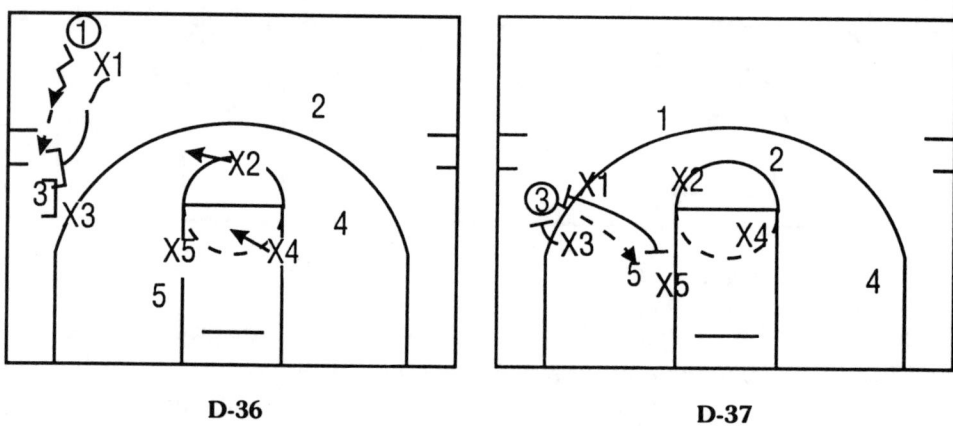

D-36   D-37

Fire Corner — 22 Down

The location of the trap is the only change. The nearest outside man will trap the ball when it goes to the corner (D-38). If the ball is thrown into 5, X1 will continue to trap, but if it is passed out front, X1 or X3 will rotate to the weak side and look to find an open man as in all the foregoing extended traps (D-39).

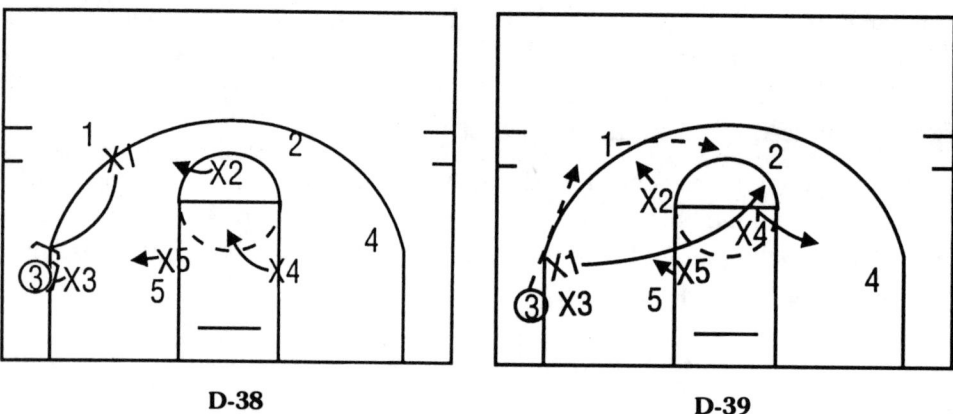

D-38   D-39

Fire Elbow — 22 Up (Bent Elbow)

Because the elbow can be such a vulnerable place for the defense to allow the ball, it may become necessary to trap the ball when it gets there. When a player has the ball there and a player like Charles Barkley, Kevin McHale, Karl Malone or Clyde Drexler is in the low post, a lot of things can happen and not many are going to make the defense happy. One tactic is to trap the play with the nearest man and follow the ball. In D-40 X1 traps 4 at the elbow and continues on down to trap posted man 3. If 4 passes to 1 instead, X1 will have to get help from X5 and scramble back, possibly rotating men with X5 in the process. Hopefully, X5 and X1 can recover to their own men, but the mismatch is better than giving open shots (D-41).

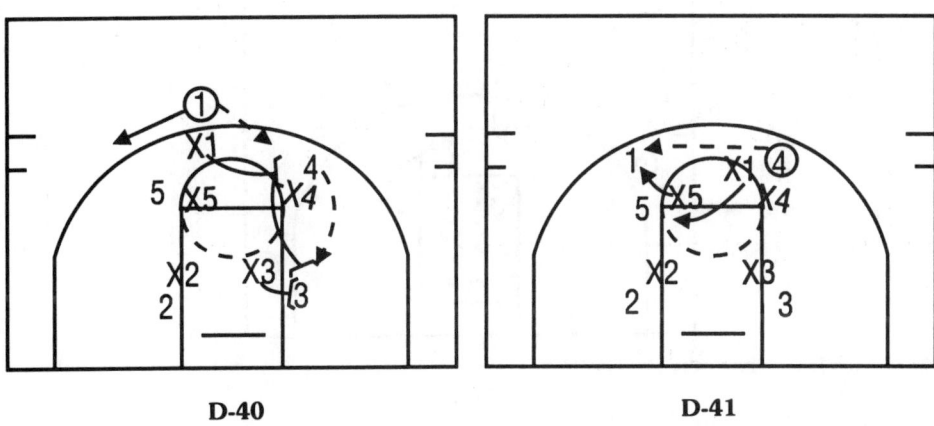

D-40   **D-41**

Fire Read — 22 Read

When players get good at executing the defense, they can be allowed to be in a "Fire Read" from a timeout. In this fashion, they enjoy the same rights that they have in the "Fire 5" low post defense option. They are free to use their own judgment as to when they can set an effective trap. The three-step rule applies, but a player can trap high, wing, corner, etc., when he thinks he can accomplish something positive by trapping. His best bets are to trap a hot player, an off-balance player, apply a sneak trap from the blind angle, trap a poor passer, etc.

Fire Live Man — 22 Live

In this call we can appoint one defender to feel free to trap the ball anywhere, but especially in the wing and corner areas. A player has to earn the right to become this kind of defender, or else be so bad a 1-on-1 defender that we think he can help more by being aggressive in a team defense.

Fire for the Outside Mismatch Automatically

This has been alluded to, but it should be confirmed here. When a good 1-on-1 player has one of our bigger players isolated outside, the nearest small player automatically traps him off to get rid of the mismatch. The big man will run off to the weak side and find an open man (D-42).

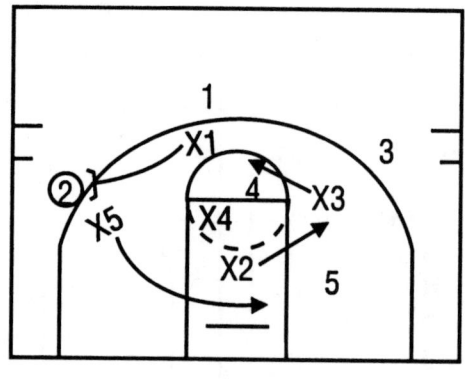

D-42

Using a "high-risk" or "low-risk" call. We have used a thumb up call after our defensive signal to indicate that we want our defenders to be very aggressive when looking to set a particular defense such as "Fire High," "Fire Wing," "Fire Corner," etc. A thumb down would indicate that we want to be conservative and be sure we have a good look at a trap before we decide to set one.

SUMMARY NOTES ON EXTENDED HALFCOURT TRAPS

1. Observe the three-step rule in setting traps.

2. Avoid fouling in a trap.

3. Prevent the split through the trap by the ballhandler.

4. When the prime purpose of trapping is to get the ball out of a particular player's hands, be sure to deny him the ball back once he passes it.

5. The one who rotates out off of the trap must run hard when the ball is passed. It's easy to follow the pass on down toward the basket, but crosscourt passes require extra effort.

6. It is good to vary the speed with which extended traps are set. By coming fast, a surprise trap may result. By coming slowly, sometimes the ballhandler can be influenced to get rid of the ball too soon. This will tend to break up the offensive set play or rhythm and still not necessitate a rotation by the defense.

7. It is helpful to vary the timing with which a trap is set. The trap can form when a player catches the ball in a general area, or after one or two bounces, or when the ball gets to a certain spot on the court, or when the ball gets to within a designated distance from the goal.

8. Using a signal to indicate the risk level desired when extending the defense can be helpful at the decision-making level for players.

9. It is useful to have a signal or call to indicate when the defense should continue aggressively to pursue further traps after one has been broken. We have used the "roll it" signal for this purpose, by rotating the hands.

A defense can be very multiple by adjusting with these trapping techniques. There are many points that will fit a given team each year. This approach will cause a lot of problems for the opponent, when all five defenders stay alert. Each player must be willing to give enough to each other and to the team defense. This takes teamwork, pride and commitment — but so does winning.

USING ROTATIONS IN OTHER SITUATIONS

Besides the low post and extended traps that require the defensive players to understand the concepts of rotating, there are other times that it's necessary for a defender to leave his own man to attack another, hoping that the team defense will rotate to cover up for him by absorbing the man he left open.

Defending Baseline Penetration

Considerable mention was made earlier of the necessity of attacking all penetration. Since the basic defense is to influence the ball away from the middle in the fanning overplay, there are bound to be some baseline penetration attempts by the offense. In order to be ready to meet this, it is good to practice "building a baseline wall" to fend off this penetration.

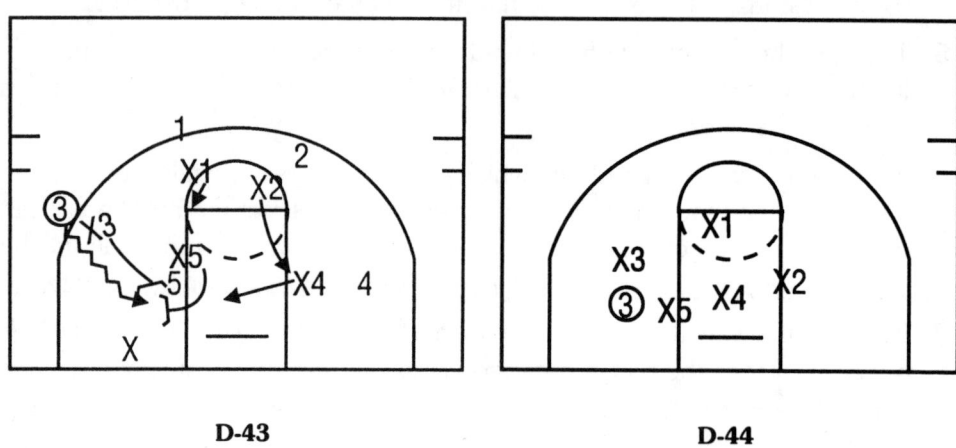

D-43   **D-44**

D-43 shows the offense attacking baseline when the defense has a man in the low post on the strong side. Player 3 drives for an advantage against X3 and X3 pursues him with the hope of cutting him off at the baseline before he can get into the paint. X5 must commit to "wedge in" 3 at an angle with X3 at the baseline spot marked with an "X" in the diagram. This is where X3 hopes to be able to cut off the penetration with or without 5's help. X5's job is to make sure that 3's trail ends right there, before he gets into the paint.

When X3 and X5 converge on the penetration, two more big jobs must be taken care of in order to complete the building of the baseline wall (D-44). Someone must move to the front of the goal to cover for X5 and in the diagram X4 makes that move. The second spot to be filled is the weakside post area vacated by X4; X2 runs a V-back to cover that spot.

The fifth man, X1 in the diagram, will float in the foul line area, looking to jam the lane and steal a pass out. Naturally, if there is time for a choice to be made, it is better for the man who covers the front of the goal to be a big man, but the spots must be filled to get the wall formed in any case.

Building the Wall When the Low Post is Open

In D-45 the offense has no man in the low post and so the baseline is more vulnerable. The high post man should yell "High post!" to the wing defender so that he will understand that he is in jeopardy on a quick baseline drive. This kind of situation is where the defense will sometimes want to change to a funnel overplay as mentioned in the discussion of overplays in Part One.

Regardless, if penetration occurs and X5 cannot get to the wedge spot, X4 on the weakside baseline must come quickly across the lane and work with X3 to wedge in the penetration. X2 drops back to cover the weak side vacated by X4 as always and X5 must get to the front of the goal. X1 will jam the lane and be ready to play the pass outside from the trap.

Obviously, X1 and X5 are aware of 5 and must jam up any pass lane to him (D-46).

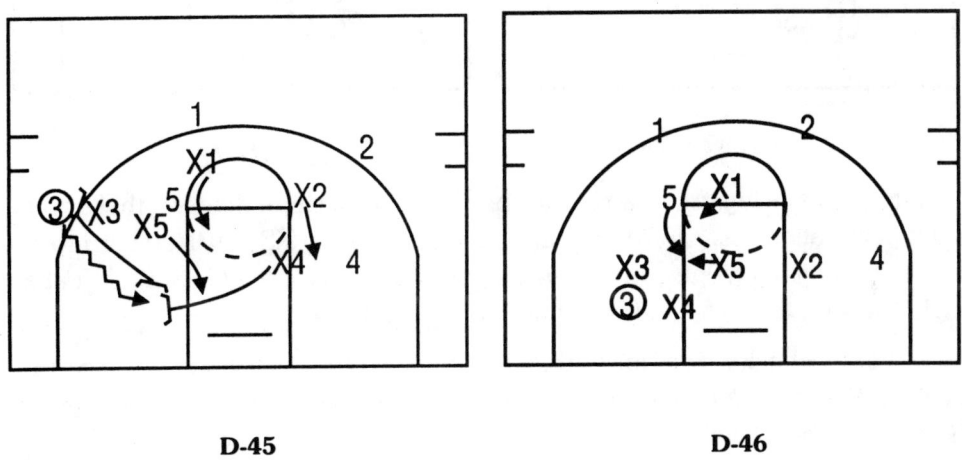

D-45   D-46

Rotating Back when the Ball is Passed Out

If the ball is passed into the interior of the defense, everyone must jam into the middle to get it out. If the ball is passed outside because the penetration and the inside pass angles were shut down, X1 (who was floating in the foul line area) will go to the pass as in D-47. X3 will stay with 3 and the trapper will usually be able to get back to his own assignment. The V-back man will complete his move by coming back out off the baseline looking to pick up the open man. If the pass went outside to 1's man, X1 would get him and X2 would be able to get back to 2. If the pass went to 2, X1 would probably have rotated to him and X2 will pick up 1 for X1 (D-48).

The simple ruling to remember on forming the baseline wall is: the player on the ballhandler tries to cut off the driver and "wedge him in" at the baseline "X." He expects help in the "wedge" from the nearest baseline man. The second nearest baseline man must move to cover the front of the goal and the weakside front defender must V-back to cover the weakside low post for the rebound. The man nearest the ball out front drops to zone up for the pass outside. Rotation generally involves scrambling back to original assignments. Go for the blocked shot!

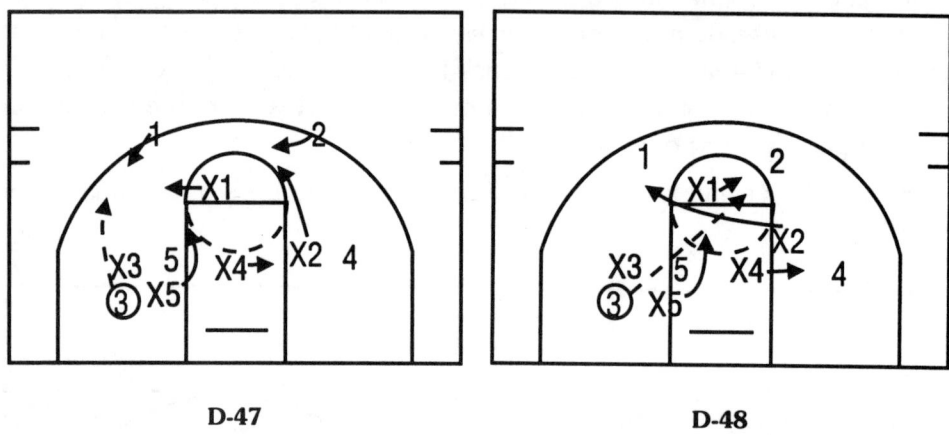

D-47   D-48

If the penetrating drive can be stopped by good position defense, that's great. But if penetration was allowed to happen too quickly by X3, it will be hard to get to the "X" spot to wedge 3 in. When it's possible to go for the blocked shot at an angle like this, the defense is obligated to do it (D-49).

If the first attacker goes for the block and is faked out by the shooter, a second attacker (the man who is assigned to get to the front of the goal) should go for the blocked shot. Oftentimes this second blocker has a better chance at the shot because the shooter has lost his ability to elevate, since his rhythm was broken. In D-50 X5 was faked out, but X4 attacks 3 for the block.

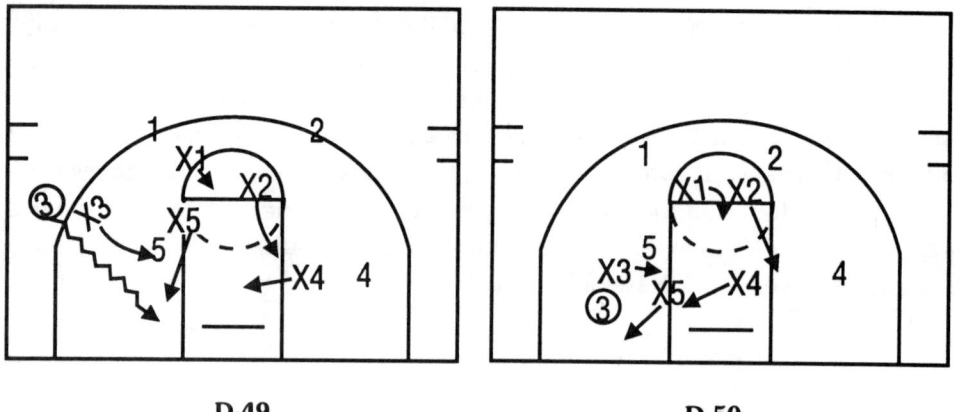

D-49   D-50

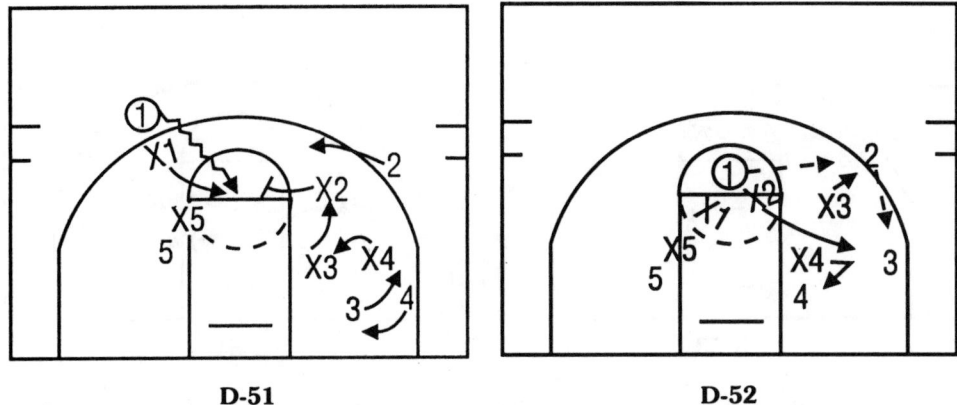

D-51   **D-52**

Rotating to the Middle Penetration

While a defense that fans the ball to the outside is dedicated to prevent deadly inside penetration, even the best of teams will make errors and allow it. This is a major breakdown and must be answered with near panic. In D-51 player 1 beats X1, so the nearest man who can identify it must attack the ball. Here X2 is able to get to 1 and as he does, X3 has to read that 2 is left wide open for a prime elbow shot. X3 must rotate up off the baseline to cover for 2's rotation. If 2 catches the ball and moves it on over to 3, he must be covered by X4, unless X2 can rotate quickly enough off the trap to get out to 3 (D-52). X4 and X2 must communicate. If X2 sees that he can get there, he can tell X4 to stay inside. But if X4 has to go out to cover 3 to prevent an open shot, X2 will rotate to front up on 4 inside. If the ball ultimately goes to 4 against X2 down low, X4 or X3 can trap with him.

Players attacking penetration must approach under control and with an inside angle (banana route) that prevents further inside penetration. If X1 were beaten badly by 1, he can rotate in the direction of the pass, but this rarely occurs with good teams.

In D-53, 3 penetrates from the wing. X1 on the strongside is denying 1 and cannot attack 3, but X2 on the weakside front does. He tries to keep 3 out of the lane and attacks aggressivelly, hoping to catch 3 before he can gather for a shot.

In D-54, 3 penetrates and neither the front strongside nor weakside can get to him. Whichever can attack first from the inside, X5 or X4, must step up to the penetration. Here X5 stops 3 while X4 and X2 rotate to jam the lane area.

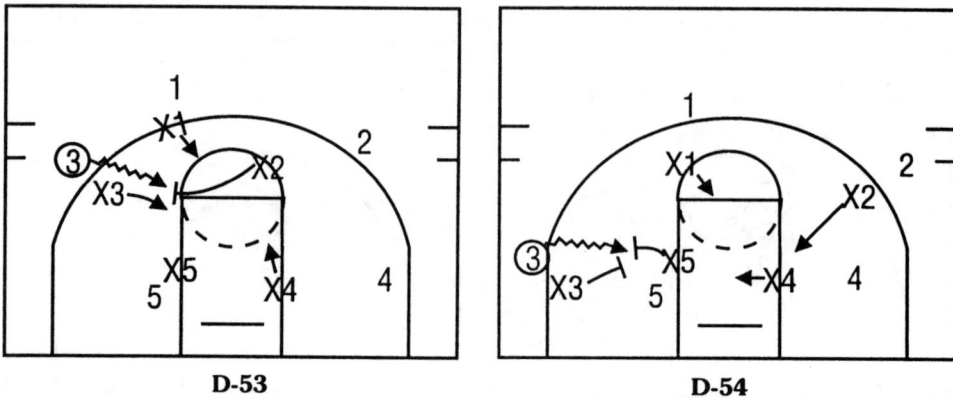

D-53   D-54

While some players may be reluctant to come up off the baseline to attack penetration or open shooters at the elbow, they must do it to force the offense to make the extra pass. Good rotations will cover up quickly enough when everyone works together. This is defense; daring a good player to make an open seventeen footer is not.

Teams should drill against this penetration as well as the baseline, learning to stop penetration from the various positions will emphasize the importance of maintaining vision of the ball for weakside defenders.

Rotating Against the Pick and Roll

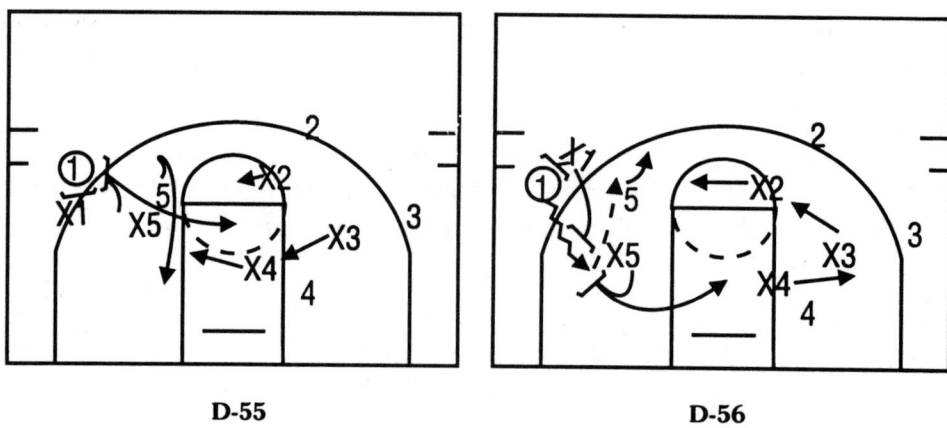

D-55   D-56

A quick look ahead to pick and roll defense technique (covered in Part Three) will be helpful here, but to put it in the proper context, diagrams will be included here as well. In D-55, X5 trapped with X1 and player 5 is open on the roll. The other three defenders not directly in the pick and roll had already moved a step or two toward the action as it began to occur, anticipating a rotation low to the roller or high to the pop-out man. Since 5 rolled, X4 leaves to absorb him. X3 rotates to 4 and X5 runs off of the trap to find the open man in the lane. He will try to release X3 so that X3 can slide on outside to cover an outside player, either 3 or 2. X5 must talk as he comes into the lane off the trap. X2 jams back and anticipates covering any drop-off or kick-out pass.

Rotation to Pop-out Shooters and Open Men

Whether it's in the process of running a pick and pop or if it's just a "lost man," there will be times when the opponent will have a man pop open within his comfortable shooting range. Whenever this happens, the nearest man must sacrifice and rotate to him. Again, he has to feel that a teammate behind him will see him attack the open man and will rotate to cover for him. The original "lost" defender on the man left open must cut back into the middle of the defense and pick up an open man.

In D-56 X2 rotates to cover 5 who popped open while the defense was trying to fan a pick and roll down to the baseline. X3 had to come out to cover for X2. Player X5 quickly cuts into the lane and talks with X4 so that they can match up with the open men. X4 would take 3 and X5 would take 4. (If 5 cannot shoot at all, this whole rotation can be avoided, with X5 getting back to 5.)

In D-57 X2 fell down and was late getting into the halfcourt defense. 1 finds 2 open at the elbow and passes to him. X3 reads the danger of allowing the open shot and rotates to cover for X2. X2 must not now continue to go at 2, as so many players automatically do. He must communicate with X4 as they work out how to cover up for X3. If X2 can get into the play soon enough to get to 3, he will. If not, X4 must leave the baseline to take 3. Then if X2 cannot get to 4, X5 will slide over, etc.

Every player will rotate to cover the open dangerous man — more aggressively to the good shooters and slower in a more containing half-way approach to poor offensive players (you must know your opponents). Hopefully, X2 will eventually get there to find an open man. If he never gets there, the four men must continue to rotate and help each other without willingly giving up penetration or an open shot to anyone in his range.

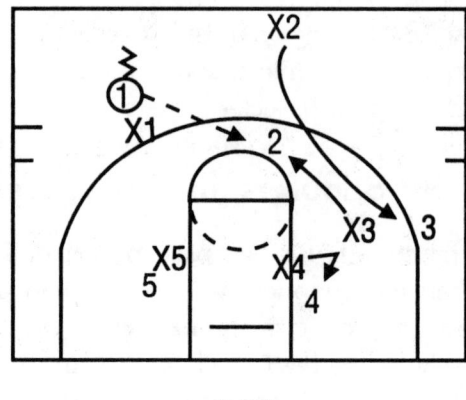

D-57

SUMMARY OF PENETRATION DEFENSE

1. A good defender should always be in a "read" position to help teammates and by leaving his own man to trap or cover open shooters. Each man must have the confidence that when he leaves his man to attack the ball, a teammate behind him will rotate to cover for him.

2. When a ball is passed out of a trap, the man who is designated to rotate off must remember to run hard to pick up an open man. His goal is to find an open man before the ball can get to him.

3. When a defender has lost his man and his teammates have covered for him, he is obligated to find an open man quickly, just like the man who rotates off of a trap does.

4. If all defenders are in a good "ball, man and lane" position, it will be much easier to attack penetrations outside and inside and to close down open players.

If a team does a good job of reacting consistently to the baseline drive by being ready to build the baseline wall, it will give the defender on the ball more confidence to play in position to curtail most middle penetration.

Part Three

Multiple Defenses to Defend Basic Two and Three Man Plays

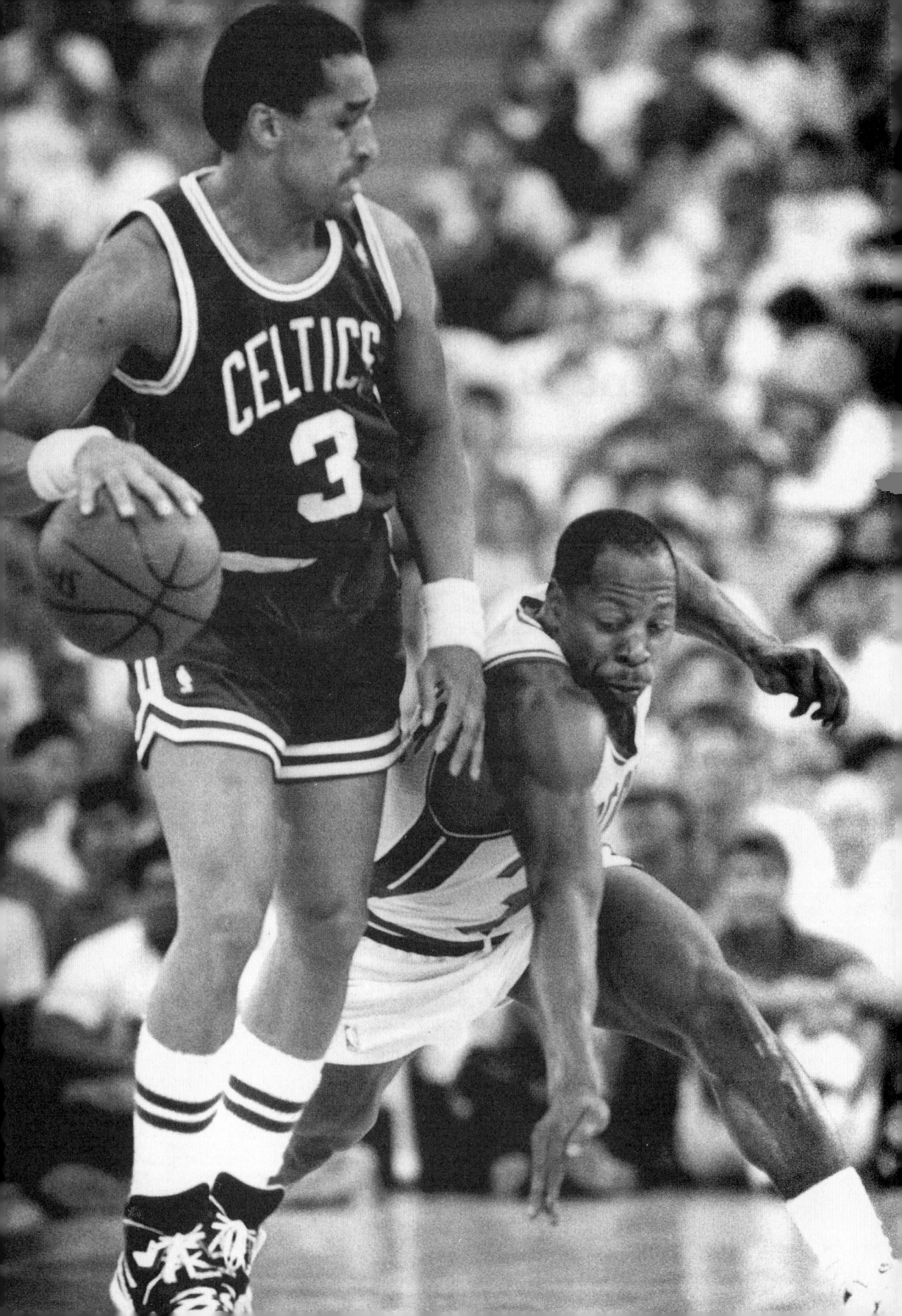

Introduction

Basketball teams at every level commonly use a number of two-and three-man play actions such as back-picking, down-picking, screen and roll, flex, pick the picker, and others. Most NBA players execute these moves so well to get open that defenders often find knowing only one defensive technique per action is not adequate to defend their assignments.

In order to have an effective NBA defense, players must first of all do their best to learn the strengths and weaknesses of every opponent in the league. While it is easier to get to know players whom one sees play a number of times per year as NBA players do, any player at any level can learn a lot about each man he has to defend if he will concentrate and study his foe's moves as a season or even as a game progresses.

How quickly a player can get to know his opponent's tendencies will go a long way in determining the success he can expect to have at crunch time. Under pressure, a player will normally try to use his best tools, his favorite moves, and he may not even be aware of it. Many smart NBA players can tell an opponent his tendencies better than the player himself. As Yogi Berra once said, "You can observe a lot just by watching." An alert player at any level can pick up on his assignment's preferences, if he starts at the beginning of the game and makes it a priority.

Compounding the issue is the fact that offensive players not only have their own pet individual moves, but will learn how to use certain two-on-two or three-on-three moves with their teammates. To have the best chance of defending these actions, defensive players must be able to identify and understand these team moves. Then they have to communicate with teammates to help each other defend every two and three man screening/cutting/passing situation they have to play against.

It's necessary to drill these basic two- and three-man play actions often in order to get defensive execution. This also helps the offense by practicing good offensive execution in these exercises.

Success on defense will depend quite a lot on how well each individual and the team learns to defend the actions on the following pages.

COMMUNICATION IS A MUST: FIRST AND FOREMOST, TALK ON DEFENSE

There can be no outstanding defense played by an individual or a team without constant communication. Any talk about defending two- and three-man play actions has to begin with this reminder. We could mention talking on every page of this book and it would not be wasted space. While talking is essential to every phase of defense, it becomes more vital as defense expands from one-on-one to three-on- three and five-on-five.

PICK AND ROLL DEFENSE IS VITAL IN THE NBA

One of the first two-man plays devised was the screen and roll, now more commonly called pick and roll. Other early play actions such as the give-and-go, backdoor cut and splitting-the-post have remained a part of every team's offense since the day they came on the scene. But the pick and roll has had an up and down history in the game. It almost disappeared from the high school and college game in the 1960s and '70s and was not a main staple of most lower-than-NBA-level teams as basketball entered the '90s.

Strangely enough, the pick and roll has recently seen a tremendous resurgence in the pro game. While it never disappeared entirely from the big league game (the Celtics were always excellent practitioners of the play), it would seem that the Detroit Pistons of Chuck Daly were mostly responsible for its renewal as one of the most feared actions in the pro game.

As the game enters its second century, it's interesting to note that the best NBA teams are also the best pick and roll teams. Teams at the college level are just beginning to revive the pick and roll into their game as a result of seeing the success of the great teams and the great players in professional basketball. Plus, the 3-point shot has brought back man-to-man defense to the college game. It should become an even more used tool as the years go by.

One reason why the pick and roll faded from all but the pro game is that zone defenses tended to neutralize it. Coaches felt that the teaching time required for the proper offensive execution was not worth it, if a zone or a trap could negate it. Perhaps a more significant cause of its near-demise was that so many motion game coaches insisted, as many still do, that all picks should be made away from the ballhandler. That strategy has accomplished certain positive results in terms of movement and spacing, but has also had the effect of throwing the baby out with the bath water. Something very worthwhile has been discarded.

Certainly the NBA's success with the exercise makes it appealing for other levels to use. But even more importantly, the growing tendency to use the three-point shot as a standard offensive tool, instead of a gimmick, has had the effect of causing teams to forego playing as much zone defense. The three-point threat also makes the proper execution of the pick and roll (or pick and pop back) a deadly weapon. The reason the pop back technique has become more in vogue is the increased ability of players to be able to make a nice percentage of three-point shots. If a power forward or center can shoot a three-pointer (or even just a 17-foot shot), it puts tremendous pressure on his defender to do the three things required of him in this situation:

1. To help his teammate on the ballhandler.

2. To protect the middle against the roll by his own man.

3. To be able to get back out to the perimeter to defend against his own man's shot, if he elects to pop out instead of roll.

And switching is not always a good alternative because that puts a big man on the ball handler and a small man on the big guy rolling inside. While trapping is a good option, clever teams can make the extended defense pay, if they know when its coming and everyone responds properly to spread the court, pass the ball out of the trap and attack quickly below the foul line.

Using the pick and roll in the three-point area increased the value of two well-established NBA players in the late 1980s and early '90s: Jack Sikma of Milwaukee and Bill Laimbeer of Detroit. Sikma had made only seven three-pointers his first eleven years in the league, but in his last three seasons, he established himself as the best long-range, seven-foot bomber in the history of the game. Already a great foul shooter, having shot .922 to lead the NBA in 1987-88, he extended his range the next season and connected on nearly 200 threes in his final three seasons. He made over 35% in those final years, playing much of the time with an injured back.

Laimbeer virtually matched his 8-year three-point production when he connected on 30 of 86 in his ninth season (1988-89) and then practically doubled it the next year with 57 of 158. While these three-point numbers are not as significant as Sikma's, Laimbeer made most of his field goals from the 18-to 21-foot range on the pick and pop. He teamed with Isiah Thomas, Joe Dumars and Vinnie Johnson to terrorize defenses and cause the league's coaches to devise various ways to defend them.

No one method would work all night against the Pistons. As they developed their pick and roll game, they became adept at setting the action at every workable angle on the court — the wings, the top of the key, the elbows, the corner and in transition toward both the middle and the sideline.

If Laimbeer were involved, the Pistons would use a lot of pop action. If it were James Edwards, Dennis Rodman or John Salley, the roll was utilized more. In any case, defenses had to worry about the ballhandler first of all. Then, if help were given to the two defenders most directly involved in the pick-roll action, the clever guard ballhandlers would find an open man against all but the most perfectly executed defensive counter-attacks. Coaches who thought they could beat the Pistons with just one or two pick and roll defenses soon found themselves back at the drawing board or behind a microphone.

As other teams watched the Pistons' success, they copied several aspects of their game, not the least of which was the pick and roll. If you were going to beat the Pistons, you had to defend that action; and to learn to defend it, a team had to work hard to learn to execute it on offense in practice.

As a result of that offense/defense practice, most teams got so good at pick and roll on their own offensive end that the players wanted to use it as a part of their offense as well. Thus, it proliferated. This same thing happens at every level. UCLA's zone presses of the 1960s, Dean Smith's run-and-jump defense of the '70s and Bobby Knight's passing game of the '70s and '80s all had profound effects on the game world-wide, just to name a few easy comparisons.

The foregoing gives good reason for high school, college and international players to incorporate pick and roll/pop into their offensive arsenal. An even better reason is the fact that their three-point line is so much closer than the NBA's.

If players at all levels utilize the pick and roll a lot more and become proficient at it, teams will have to become more sophisticated in defending it. While some levels of play will not want (or need) to get into the defense at the depth that will be explained in this section, we will show many options from which to choose. Installing one or two of these methods as a change-of-pace against a particular opponent could make the difference between winning and losing a key game.

In the four years between 1987 and 1991 when the Pistons were the dominant team in the NBA, the Milwaukee Bucks were the only team to play .500 basketball against the Pistons. One of the reasons for this success was that the Bucks were outstanding at pick and roll defense.

To simplify our discussion, bear in mind that there will be four men directly involved in the pick and roll — two on offense (the picker and the ballhandler) and their two defenders. *But it takes five men to defend the well-executed pick/roll successfully.*

The four men in the direct action. When we talk of the four men directly in the pick and roll action, the ballhandler will always be referred to as the "first man." If his defender goes over the top of the pick as X1 does in D-1, we say X1 is going over the pick or simply "second man," knowing that the ballhandler is the first man.

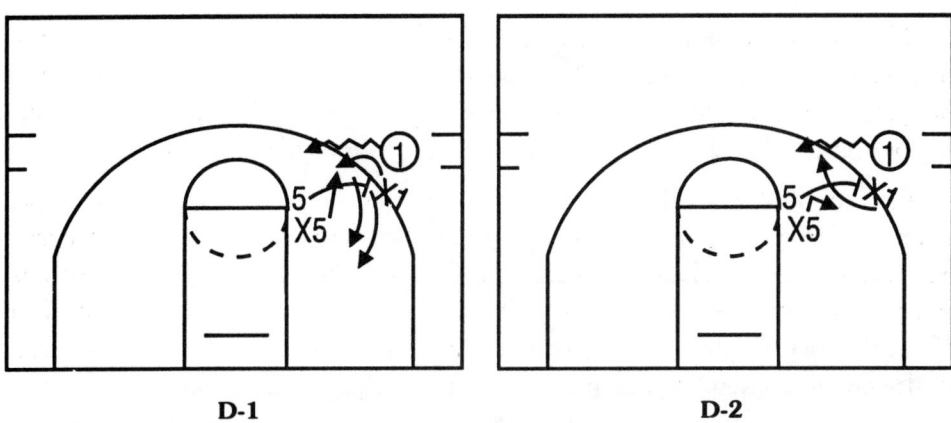

D-1   **D-2**

In D-2 the defender 1 goes under the pick as "the third man" while X5 offers help as he did in D-1. This technique is safe if the pick is far out on the floor, not within easy shooting range, or even in closer if the ballhandler is not a particularly good shooter. In both cases X5 tries to cut down 1's angle of penetration until X1 can get under the pick by 5. Then X5 recovers back to 5. X5 can help pull X1 through by using his hands to help him.

Diagram 3 shows the defender executing the option of "going fourth man" under the screen and the screener's defender. This used to be considered a "no-no" by coaches, but since the Bucks started using this technique against middle lane pick and rolls to defend against Bill Laimbeer of the Pistons, many teams have begun to use it on picks that are not set too close to the prime scoring area on the wing.

It is a good tactic to use when the picker is a primary receiver, especially if he is a good outside shooter. The defender on the screener must put his body right up against his man as he sets the pick and "squeeze him up," as we call it. If he is strong enough to move the picker on out a step or two from the goal by doing this, so much the better.

The defender on the ball handler must go under (fourth man) the squeeze-up action. He must hustle quickly to get under the pick and to greet the ballhandler on the other side of the pick in time to bother a long shot and to take away his angle to the middle. If he should forget and trail the ballhandler over the top of the pick (second man), he will have no chance of being able to prevent a shot or penetration by the ballhandler.

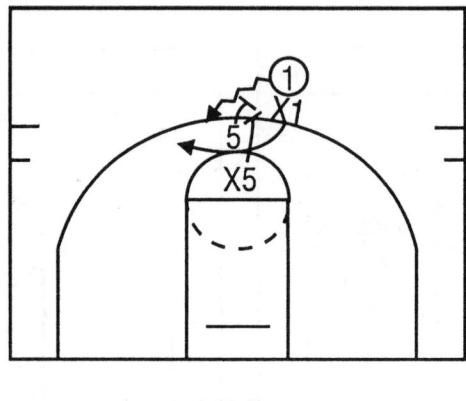

D-3

This technique eliminates the pick and pop play because the picker cannot get a pass from the ballhandler. The difficulty lies within the ability of the defender on the ballhandler to be able to contain his own man with this method. Against the Pistons it was usually more effective against Vinny Johnson and Joe Dumars than it was against Isiah Thomas due to Thomas' greater quickness and range, although Dumars had nights when his range was very good.

THE VARIOUS ANGLES OF PICK AND ROLL

There are four angles from which most pick and rolls are run: the wing, the top (middle lane), the corner and the elbow. At the elbow, the pick and roll may be used with the ballhandler seeking to get to the outside or to the inside of the lane and one is a little different from the other. The various angles present different problems to the defense, so people who say there is only one way needed to play the pick and roll have not coached against NBA players.

The wing pick and roll (D-4). The defense must be aware of a good "roll down" man as the picker. If he is also a good outside shooter, he can cause another problem, because it is hard to rotate anyone from the weak side in time to get to him, if he "pops" back instead of rolling. The pop action helped extend the careers of Jack Sikma, Bill Laimbeer and James Edwards as effective players in the NBA.

The ballhandler is dangerous from the wing as either a shooter or a penetrator. The more attention that the picker's man must pay to stop his penetration, the more effective the roller/popper becomes. And if the ballhandler attracts weakside help by penetrating, he can open up a lot of good spot-up shots.

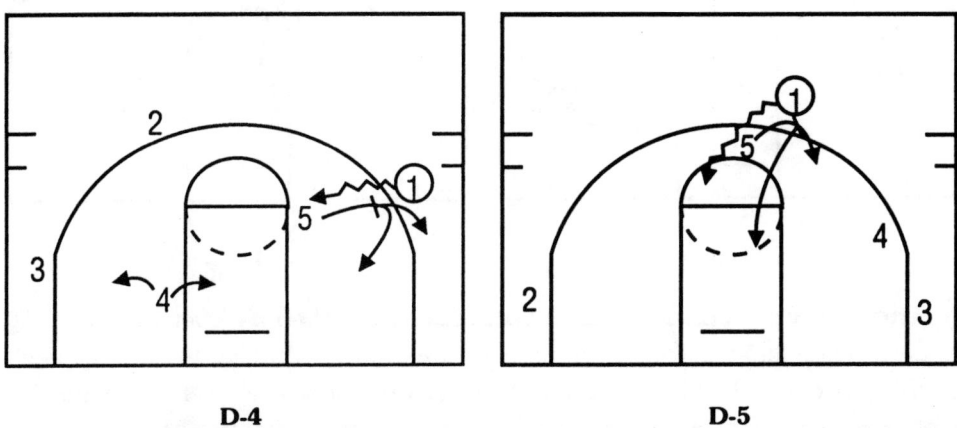

D-4   **D-5**

The middle lane pick and roll (D-5). The picker is more dangerous as a pop man to shoot the ball in this angle, but he can also get involved as a roll-down threat if the offense will empty out the low post area as the picker rolls. The ballhandler has a good angle to penetrate from this pick and will be capable of getting his own shot or creating a shot for a corner man as well as the picker/popper.

The corner pick and roll (D-6). If the ballhandler is allowed to get into the middle of the defense from the corner, he has a lot of options with which to hurt the defense. Again, it is hard for anyone else to get to the picker if his defender cannot get back to him.

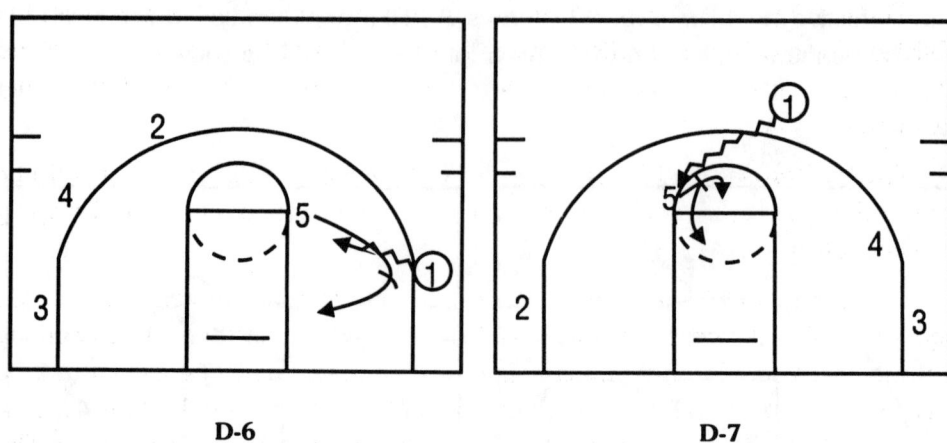

D-6   **D-7**

The elbow pick and roll to the outside angle (D-7). Player 1 is especially dangerous as a jump shooter from here. Michael Jordan and Scottie Pippen each use this move as a deadly weapon in their personal offensive arsenals, mainly for an elbow jumper. The picker can be a threat as a roller or a popper, as his defender has to give major help to the shooter's defender in most cases.

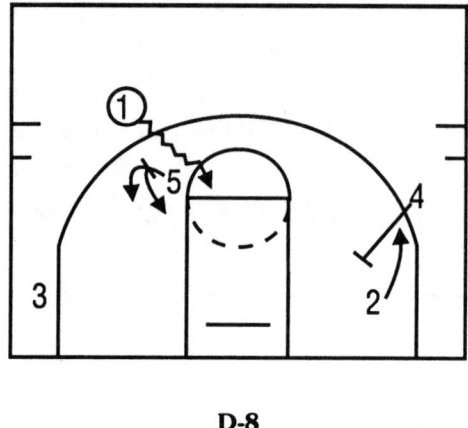

D-8

The elbow pick and roll toward the inside angle (D-8). From this angle, the ballhandler can actually choose to go either direction off of the pick. It can be a tough assignment for a defender on a good player such as Jordan, Thomas or Dumars. And the picker can be a huge threat as a pop man.

KNOW THE INDIVIDUALS

There are pick and rolls and there are pick and rolls. It all depends on the abilities of the two main participants as to the choice of the best way to defend the action. It can also depend on the outside shooting abilities of the other teammates as well.

The ballhandler. If he is a shooter with range, he will usually have to be attacked aggressively in order to break his rhythm, the major objective. Trapping is often called for.

If he's a jet-quick penetrator, he may be able to beat a defense that is too aggressive. The objective will be to contain this man and make him take something from the outside. Not that an aggressive approach can never be used, but if he has the quickness, ballhandling skills and judgment of a Mark Price or Isiah Thomas, it's necessary to be able to give a different look from time to time. The object in playing the good penetrators is to keep them from turning the corner and getting inside the defense. The help from the defender on the picker will try to take away any sharp angle of penetration and to make him go out wide.

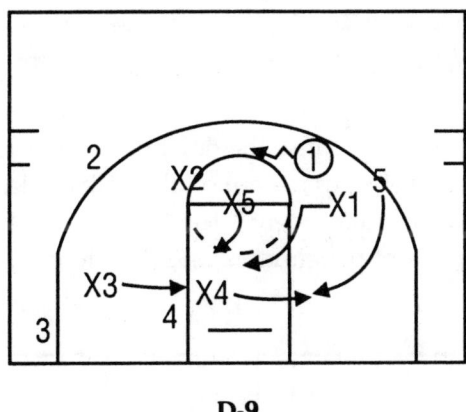

D-9

The picker. If he is a big target as he rolls down and the main threat in the action, his defender must recover very fast to him after helping. Sometimes that cannot be done effectively because the ballhandler's ability demands too much attention. That is when a help defender has to be able to rotate quickly from the weak side to pick up the roller (D-9).

If the picker is a good outside shooter and pops back to catch and shoot after screening, the defender on him will have to stay close to the picker's body as in the "squeeze" method alluded to, or else the team defense must rotate to him at about the same time the pick is being set on the pick and roll. Knowledge of the tendencies of the opposing team is vital.

In setting a game plan it is important to consider whether:

- The ballhandler usually/seldom looks to shoot right behind the pick.
- The ballhandler looks to shoot after 1, 2 or 3 dribbles.
- They look to feed the roller.
- They look to pop the picker back for a shot.
- They try to get the ballhandler into the middle for a scoring move of his own or to create a shot for a perimeter player or an inside player.

FOUR BASIC DEFENSIVE ATTACKS

Hard help and recovery. This is the most commonly used method in defending the pick and roll and is shown in D-10. The defender on the picker is X5 and he steps out to "show" his body right away to the ballhandler at the outside shoulder of the picker to influence him to take a wider path around the pick. The purpose is to make him take a wide angle instead of a direct angle toward the goal so that the ballhandler's defender, X1, can get over or under the pick to regain position on his man. When X5 sees that X1 has gotten through, he can recover back to his own man.

This is called "hard help" because the defender on the picker takes a hard 90 degree angle and aggressively tries to shut off the ballhandler's penetration angle. The objective of hard help and recovery is to stop an early shot by the ballhandler as well as to alter his angle of penetration, and then to get back to cover his own man, if possible.

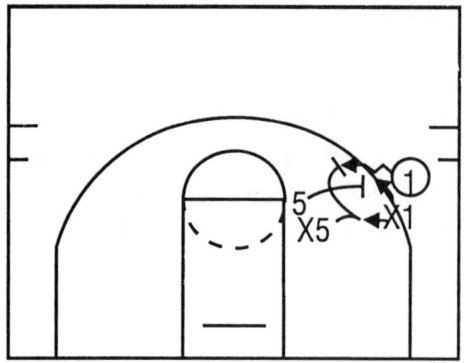

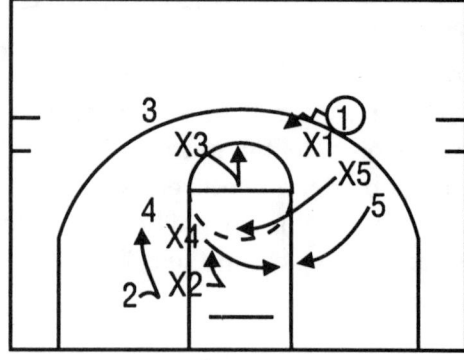

D-10   **D-11**

To execute properly as in D-10 and D-11, X5 must call out the pick as he sees it begin to materialize. Immediately he gets into a position close to 5 so that he can be in the "hard help" mode as soon as the pick is set. At the same time the defender on the ballhandler, X1, must jump over to the baseline side and funnel the ballhandler into the help that X5 is offering. X1 must not allow the ballhandler to beat him to the baseline side, because everyone is now set to help the action that is coming toward the middle.

X1 will try to go over the top (second man) in hard help, and particularly so if the screen occurs within easy shooting range. However, years of experience have taught that players must have the option of going under the pick (third man), if they cannot get over the top.

X5 can push 5 up into the ballhandler's path with a nudge of the nearest hand (right hand in D-10), not violent enough to get a foul called, but enough to upset some timing.

It takes five men to stop the good pick and roll. All the other defenders must immediately move a step or two toward the pick and roll action and watch the pick/roll develop in order to be in a position to help out or possibly even rotate to the roller or ballhandler if one of the two breaks open.

X5 will quickly recover back to 5 when X1 gets through 5's pick. The pick in D-10 occurs in the prime scoring range, so the shot by 1 is a threat and this is a good reason to use hard help. X5 will try to avoid letting 1 split between him and X1. Although he is aggressive in his help, he cannot give 1 a short cut to the basket.

X5 will stay as long as he must to contain 1 and let X1 get through. X1 is obligated to keep on coming, even if he slips or gets picked really well. If X5 has to commit to 1 for so long that 5 is open for a catch, the nearest back man must rotate to keep 5 from going to the goal on a free ride. Diagram number 11 shows X4 rotating to 5 and then X5 drops back to pick up the open man on the weak side, probably 4.

Soft help and recovery. All of the action is the same as in hard help and recovery except for the angle of help that the picker's defender takes. Instead of getting up early and high in a 90 degree angle, X5 plays a softer angle (about 45 degrees) as he offers help to X1 in D-12.

D-12

The reason for the difference in the help angle is that the defensive objective is to contain 1's penetration angle and to allow X5 to be able to have a better opportunity to jam up the passing lane to 5 on the roll. The lower angle allows X5 to recover more easily, obviously.

Soft help is good to use when the pick occurs outside of easy shooting range or when the ballhandler is more of a penetrating threat than an outside shooter. Again, it is an option to use if the roller is the chief option.

X1 can usually go under the pick (third man) when soft help is given. X5 will be loose and may even be able to help pull or push X1 under the pick to help X1 get through.

TEAM COVERAGE IN BOTH HELP AND RECOVERY METHODS.

Wing angle. D-13 shows how all five players are involved in defending the action. We already know what players X5 and X1 must do. The players nearest the weakside baseline must be watching the action and it is better if the bigger one of the players is ready to rotate to the open roller. X4 moves to roller 5 in the diagram and X3 "V's" back down to cover for X4. If X3 had been inside instead of X4, he would have had to have made the rotation to 5.

X2 is on the weakside high position and he is watching to see if he will have to help jam up the middle in case 1 beats the defense and gets into the middle. X2 does not want to have to leave his man, 2, because he is probably a good shooter. However, in D-14 he must react to the penetration and force the offense to make the extra pass. X3 is ready to rotate up to cover 2 if X2 must leave. How aggressively X3 rotates depends on 2's shooting ability.

The defender in the pick and roll who must have help from a teammate by a rotation will go to the weak side immediately as he sees someone has rotated to his man and he will pick up an open man on the weak side. Therefore, X5 would pick up 4 or 3 in D-13 and X1 rotates to pick up 3 in D-14.

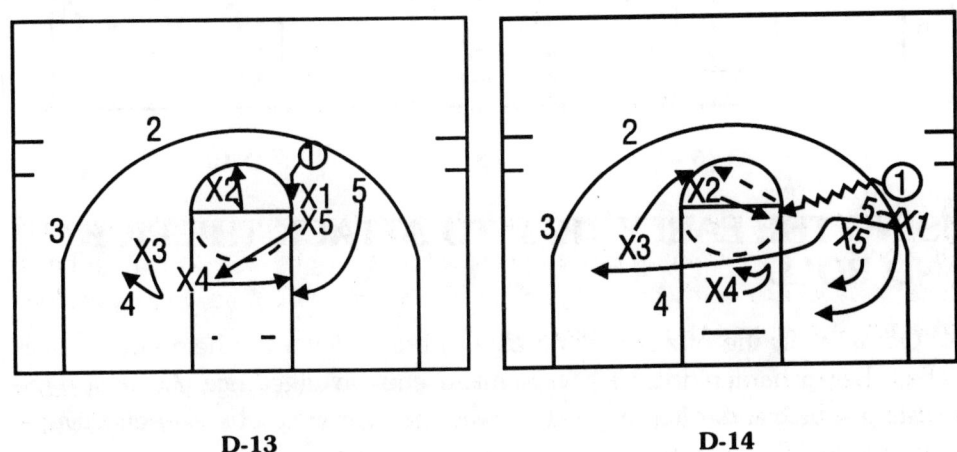

D-13   **D-14**

Top angle. D-15 and D-16 show how the team might respond to help a breakdown in the pick and roll coverage from the middle lane. In D-15 the strong side corner is filled with a shooter, 2, and X2 must be ready to help. If X2 commits totally to 1, X1 has the best chance at running to 2 to contest a shot.

In D-16 the strong side is cleared, so the weak side must be ready to help. If 1 should break loose, ideally a smaller weakside man would try to rotate to him. If 5 rolls down open, a bigger weakside man would try to absorb him.

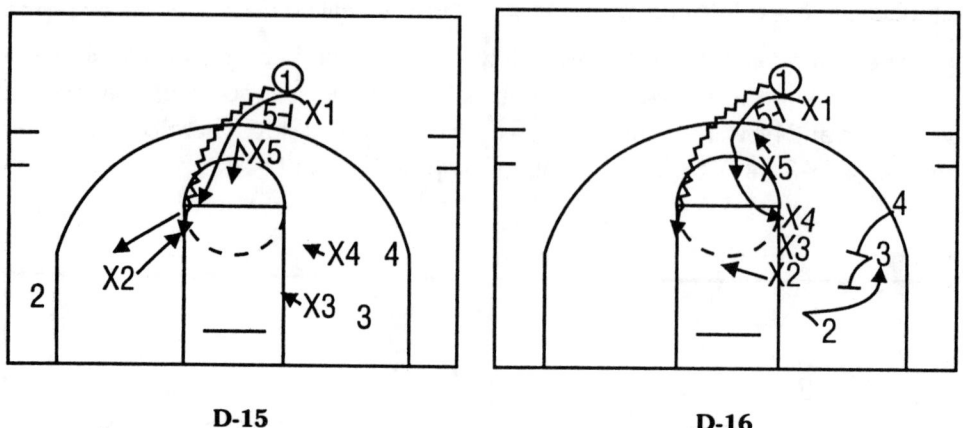

D-15   D-16

USING THE EARLY TRAP TO ATTACK THE PICK AND ROLL

Occasionally the offense will be able to break down the help and recovery tactics. Trying harder doesn't always make enough difference. At those times adjusting strategies is often a good answer, and a trap can be very effective.

The trap can be set early or late or it can be set from a player coming to the action from the weak side. Trapping can be used against all the various angles of pick and roll, but the entire team has to be even more alert, because it is more imperative that all five get involved when the trap is set.

The Early trap. As soon as the defender on the picker sees his man move toward the ballhandler to set the pick, he calls out "Fire," or any other desired key word to indicate trapping, and X1 on the ballhandler must quickly jump over to the baseline side to funnel the ballhandler into X5. In the "early" trap, X5 quickly accelerates and sets the trap with X1 before 5 can actually set the pick. This response to the pick and roll eliminates the pick (D-17).

There are two things that 5 can do to get himself open: he can roll to the basket quickly anyway, as if he had picked, or he can pop up high and ask for a release pass from 1. Player 1 can try to pass to 5 in either one of these moves, or he can elect to dribble his way out. If the trap is executed poorly, he may be able to split the defense. Otherwise, he can pull or stretch the trap by dribbling up toward the halfcourt line. This technique will open up pass lanes, particularly if the two trappers continue to pursue him, but that is a defensive mistake against a good team.

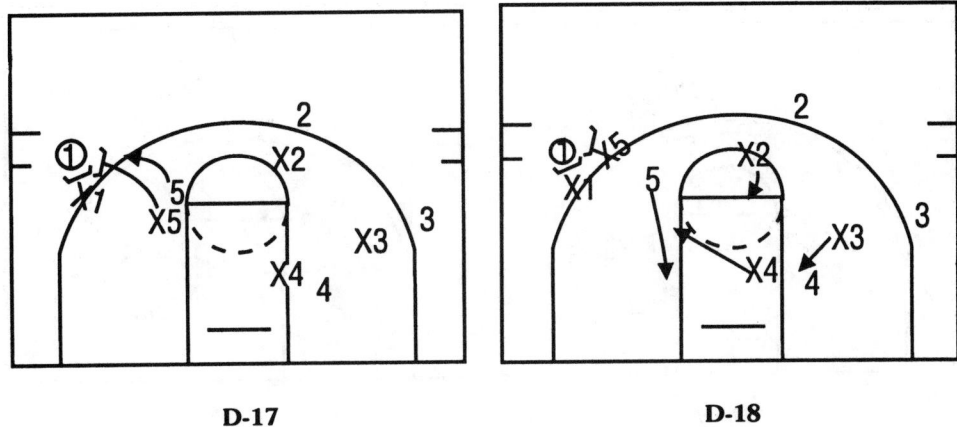

D-17   **D-18**

Team response in the early trap. As always, the three players not doing the trapping move a step or two toward the action as soon as it begins and try to read the situation to determine their next response. In D-18 player 5 decides to roll to the goal as soon as X5 sets the trap. The baseline defender (the bigger one if there is a choice) must be watching the play and as soon as he sees 5 make his move to the goal, he rotates to him, hoping to intercept a pass. The area vacated by X4 must be filled, so X3 V's back to fill for X4. X2 zones the area, ready to react to the next pass.

In D-19 player 5 pops up to offer a short escape pass for 1. Since all three defenders who are not in the trapping action itself have moved toward the action and are reading the play, X2 reads that 5 is going to stay up high. Obviously, X4 cannot rotate to him in time and so it is the weak side front defender's job to rotate to the popper. If he can get there in time for a steal, that's great, but he must at least get there in time to contest a shot or penetration. The other weakside players respond by rotating to cover up for X2 as X3 does in the diagram.

In both cases, X5 has to rotate off the trap quickly and go to the weak side to find an open man as soon as the ball is passed. Note especially the fact that the trapper should not pursue the ballhandler, if the handler decides to stretch the trap by dribbling back toward the halfcourt line. He should immediately release and get back to his own man because his job is completed — he broke up the pick and roll. If he forgets and continues to chase the ballhandler, X1 should yell at him to go.

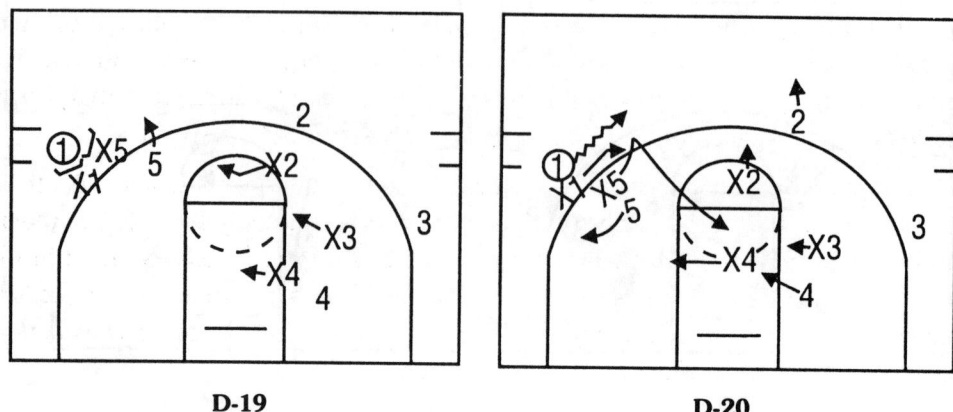

D-19   **D-20**

X1 then tries only to contain the ballhandler's angle to the goal. He does not try to chase him, since he is going away from the basket (D-20).

The late trap. The difference between the early and late trap is simply a matter of timing. All the other fundamentals of the early trap remain the same. X5 calls out "Fire!" and X1 jumps to the outside to prevent any baseline drive; but the difference is that X5 trails 5 as 5 goes to set the pick as in D-21. The trap occurs right at the point of the pick, instead of prior to it.

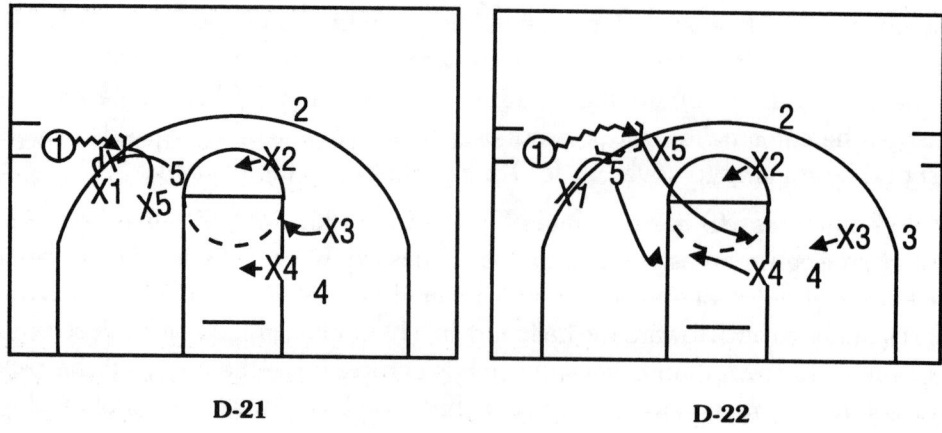

D-21   **D-22**

Team response to the late trap. Everything remains the same as in the early trap above. The baseline defender must be ready to rotate to the roll and the front defender has to be ready to defend against the pop. X5 rotates to the weak side to find an open man. (D-22)

ALTERNATIVE COVERAGE AGAINST THE PICK AND ROLL

Switching. This hardly needs an explanation. Normally the offense will not use equal size players in the pick and roll because an aggressive switch can usually neutralize the action. In the event that the defenders are "switchables," that is the easiest and normally the best course of action for the defense to take.

In a case mentioned earlier, the Bucks began to defend Bill Laimbeer with a small forward in order to be able to switch the middle lane pick and roll. Laimbeer and both of the Pistons' guards in their championship years were too good most nights against the help/recovery and trapping defenses for them to be effective consistently, so the switch was a good change of pace. Laimbeer rarely took the smaller man into the low post after the switch.

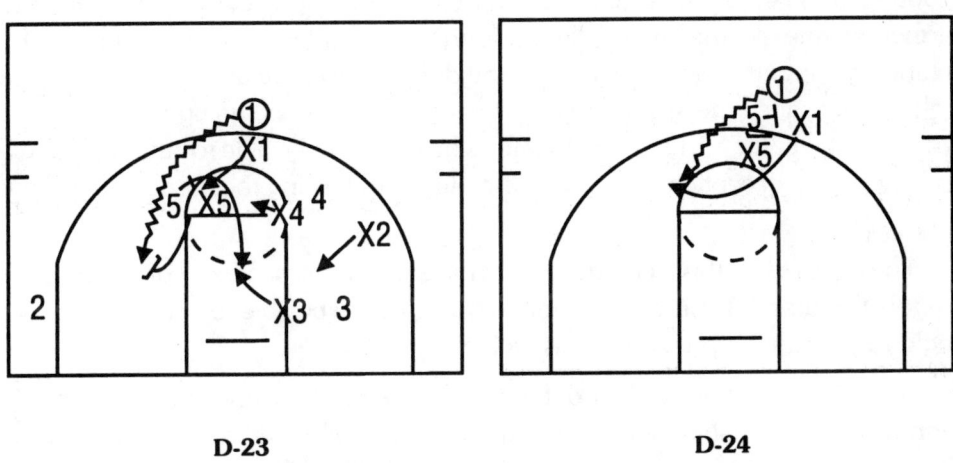

D-23   D-24

Picks at the elbow angle often call for a switch or at least a temporary switch. D-23 shows the elbow pick and roll. If player 1 is coming into this action with any speed, X1 will have a hard time staying with him, even when X5 steps out to show for a help and recovery. Since X5's job is to give help until X1 can regain position on 1, he may have to stay an extended period of time on this play.

This could accurately be called an "extended help and recovery," but we have called it a "temporary switch" since X5 had to stay as long as necessary. The weakside defenders must move toward the action right away and be ready to rotate to 5. If 5 rolls, the low man near the baseline checks him until X5 can recover back. If 5 pops back at the elbow, the front defender tends to him until X5 can get back (or X5 may rotate weakside to an open man).

Any way you look at it, this pick and roll angle can be tough to defend. Mainly X1 will try to go second man over the top of the pick, because nearly every good player will be able to score from this spot. Since this makes X1 an easy target to pick, X5 must be up and ready to do whatever it takes to challenge an easy shot. Even a switch to a big mismatch is better than an easy shot. The weakside defense can always help with the mismatch.

The squeeze method. We made a brief mention of this technique earlier in the introductory discussion of going "fourth man" in the pick and roll defense. This method can be very effective with middle lane picks and is acceptable on wing area picks that occur out of the ballhandler's easy shooting range. It is an excellent technique to defend the team who is using the picker as the main target, either as a popper or as a roller. Once again, we can thank Chuck Daly, the master of the pick and roll, for causing us to come up with this method of defense.

To keep a quick shooter like Laimbeer from beating us with the catch and shoot, the man on 1 would body up hard on the side opposite the ballhandler to let the defender on the ballhandler go fourth man under the pick as in D-24. By getting right into the picker physically, the defender may be able to push the pick higher and reduce the space the ball defender gives up by going fourth man. It decreases the traffic X1 has to negotiate as he hurries to be able to cut off 1's angle and gives X1 a decent chance to prevent him from turning the corner toward the goal before he can recover.

The key to using this technique is that the action must occur out of 1's shooting range. Of course, X1 must have enough quickness to be able to get to the proper angle to prevent 1's penetration as well.

A reminder is that the ball defender must always go under the action. He cannot chase the ballhandler whether the pick and roll is out front or on the wing. To do so guarantees good penetration for the ballhandler.

Fanning the pick and roll. In all the other coverage discussed previously, the ball defender had to shift to the outside (baseline side) to funnel the ballhandler toward the defensive help. However in this method, no shift is needed and that in itself is a plus.

D-25 shows a wing pick and roll with the "fan" coverage. X5 must call the play and he *has to be in a position between the ball and the basket* in order to execute the defense. As he calls out the pick and roll, he should remind the defender on 1 to fan him out. Notice that X1 gets an exaggerated fan overplay on 1. X1 cannot let 1 beat him to the middle where there is little help. He must turn 1 down into X5. If 1 dribbles toward X5, as he usually does, X5 will come up and trap him. He should be able to get to 1 within two or three quick steps, preferably two. The trap should happen quickly (D-26).

D-25   **D-26**

The team response in the fan. The picker will either roll or pop up to catch and shoot. If he rolls, he may simply cut right into X5, but usually the bigger player near the baseline on the weak side will have to rotate qucikly enough to pick him up. If 5 pops up, the front defender on the weak side will have to rotate to cover him. This is normal coverage, just like when the traps are set that were discussed earlier.

If X1 and X5 actually set a trap, the picker must be rotated to as the trap is set. Again, the three defenders not involved in the trap will be moving toward the trap to read the coverage anyway. The low man must take 5 if he rolls, and the front man must rotate to 5 if he pops back as X2 does in D-26.

Weakness/strength in this coverage. Fanning the pick and roll is not a good option for actions occurring in the middle lane, because the picker is left wide open. But it *is* the best way to play a corner pick and roll. The defender on the ball should overplay the ball toward the baseline automatically; and the defender on the post man/screener should be positioned on the baseline side when defending a post man with the ball in the corner. Thus, he is in a line between the ball and the basket as is necessary in the fan coverage (D-27).

The Philadelphia 76'ers were the best practitioners of this defensive technique when Jimmy Lynam was coaching Charles Barkley there. They used the fan method almost exclusively on the wing and corner pick and rolls the last couple of years they were there and did it very effectively. It is a most ideal technique if the defender on the picker is a shot blocker. When Manute Bol was involved, it gave them just that and it was about the only way Bol could defend, since he had poor mobility.

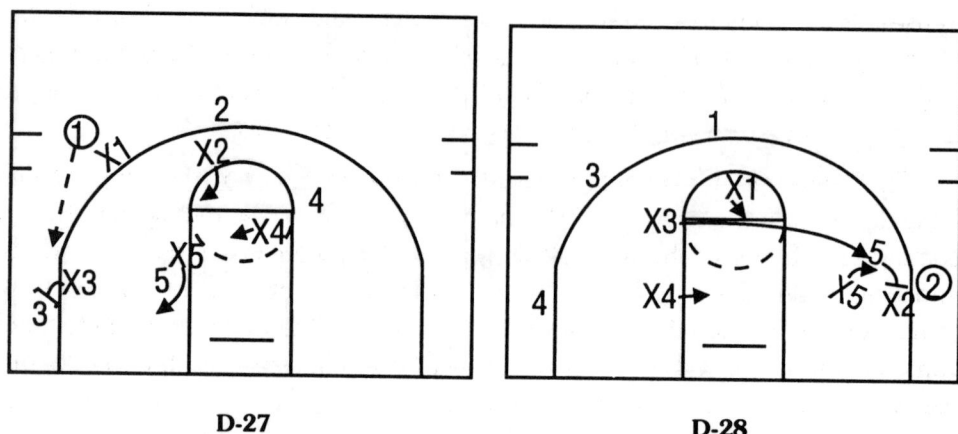

D-27   D-28

Trapping from the weak side. Sometimes the pick and roll will be run with the two players isolated away from the rest of the team. Any one of the methods already mentioned may be used, but a good twist is to send a third man into the action from the weak side to help break up the play. The reason for using this tactic is that it is hard to rotate to one of the two players in the pick and roll if one breaks open when the three other players are isolated far away from the play.

In D-28 player X3 is instructed to set the trap. He may be told to set it early or late. In the early trap he tries to get to the ballhandler as soon as possible, even before the pick is set. In the late, he will set the trap just as the ballhandler comes off of the pick. This method allows X5 to stay with 5 and to eliminate him from the play. The ballhandler must beat the trap or pass to the weak side to one of his teammates.

Response of the team to the trap from the weak side. Players X1 and X4 on the weak side must zone up until X3 or X2 can rotate off the trap to pick up the open man on the weak side. It is up to the coach to decide which of the defenders should rotate off, the trapper or the original defender, but we prefer to stay consistent by selecting the trapper to rotate.

Slow or fast trap option. The first time the Bucks tried this on the Detroit Pistons it was against a low wing area isolation pick and roll in the playoffs during Detroit's first championship season. The Bucks were up against the wall, having two starters out with injuries in a series that would ultimately end up with five Bucks players unable to play the final game. Undermanned, the conventional ways of defending were ineffective and so this method was used in game 1.

Prior to game 2 of the series the head of NBA operations, Rod Thorn, called to say that from what he had been able to see on television, we would not be able to use this method anymore because it was against the NBA illegal defense rules. He had the chief of NBA referees, Darrell Garretson, meet me before the game to go over it to see if it was, in fact, illegal. At the meeting he agreed we were legal, and we continued to use it, and it was utilized by many teams later.

The biggest point of contention was that we sometimes had the trapper come fairly slowly from the weak side with the hope that the ballhandler would see him coming and get rid of the ball quickly. This served to break up the pick and roll and it eliminated the need for a rotation, because our trapper could scramble back to his own man. The NBA has since better enforced the rule that trappers need come to trap aggressively or it is illegal. With the oldest team in the league, our plea was that our team was so slow we *were* being aggressive — it was just that no one could tell!

A more advanced technique is to allow the players to call their own coverage. In order to influence our players to talk, think and react, we would drill the pick and roll from the various angles and give the players a choice of two, three or ultimately four options to call out to use. If the team can get good enough in practice, it might possibly be carried over into a game situation. The verbal signals we use are as follows:

1. "Hard" for hard help and recover.
2. "Soft" for soft help and recover.
3. "Early" for early trap.
4. "Late" for late trap.
5. "Switch" for switching.
6. "Squeeze" for the squeeze method.
7. "Fan" for the outside overplay.
8. "Fire" for the trap from the weak side.

To be able to do this the defender on the picker must identify the pick and roll as early as possible and call out the coverage immediately and loudly.

While this may not be something that a team would want to try in its totality, some variation of it has certain obvious advantages. It keeps the opponent guessing, it is hard to scout and it allows a knowledgeable player to read a situation and play smart. Despite its perhaps limited utility in a game because of crowd noise, it is a very good practice tool.

Summary of pick and roll defense. Regardless of the method used to defend the pick and roll, there are some fundamental priorities common to each method:

- No easy open shot.
- No middle penetration.
- Everyone on the weak side must be ready to rotate to open people.
- If someone rotates to your man, quickly rotate to find an open man on the weak side.

DEFENDING BACKPICK AND CROSSPICK ACTION

The old expression that the most dangerous man on the court is the man who just passed is only partly true. In today's game a player of at least equal danger is the man who has just set a screen and opened up to the ball. Therefore the following discussions are of vital importance to individual and team defense.

It's easy to switch equal size players, and to do so aggressively in order to deny both the ball. With unequals involved, the man on the picker should give help and "see the unequals (mismatches) through." It is always important to allow the "emergency switch" option for the time when a man really gets nailed, especially close to the goal. It's better to have a mismatch than an open man, of course.

If the backpick involves unequals and we are not wanting to switch, the proper execution of the defensive technique is as follows:

1. The picker's defender calls out the pick as early as possible.

2. The defender on the cutter must immediately get to the cutter's body and go with him as he cuts over or under the pick as in D-29. It's better if the defender, X3, can get to the ball side of the cutter so he can keep his body between his man and the ball. He aims for the ball side shoulder of the cutter and gets his inside (nearest the ball) forearm up at the 45 degree angle and is ready to muscle right through the backpick with the cutter. This is very good defense against the lob to the cutter and it also allows the defender on the picker to be able to close up earlier on the picker to prevent an easy step-up catch.

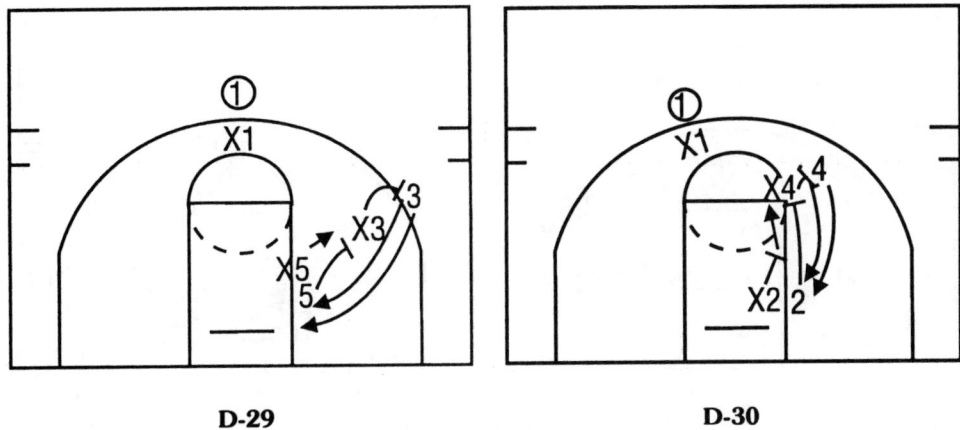

D-29   **D-30**

The man guarding the cutter should be physical and get right into the cutter's body on the ball side and not worry about finding the picker. He will want to body right through the pick. He will keep coming even if he gets hit.

The traditional method of backing up and feeling the picker only helps the picker to set a better pick and puts more pressure on the picker's defender to give help. Our method is different than most coaches teach and is different than a player's natural response, which is to try to "feel" his way through.

The defender on the picker must loosen toward the goal in any case and should stay high toward the ball to be in position to give help to the cutter's defender. "See your teammate through the pick" and quickly close back up on your own man in order to stop the step-up move as X2 does in D-30.

Pressure the passer. Try to prevent any lob or easy reversal pass in the action.

Wing Backpick on the Passer

This action is a typical passing game maneuver and involves picking the passer. The man defending the passer normally will jump back from his man in the direction of the pass as he passes, but if a backpick is called out, it is necessary for the defender to try to get to the passer/cutter's body as quickly as possible.

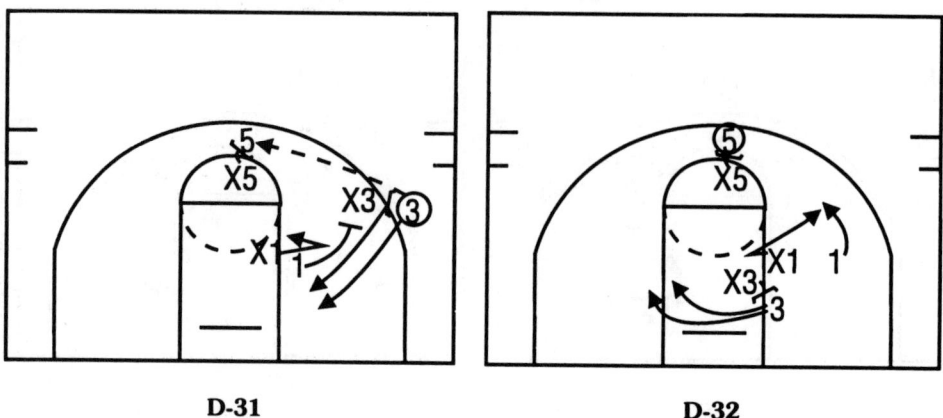

D-31   **D-32**

In D-31, 3 passes to 5 and receives a backpick from 1. This is not an easily switchable play, so X1 calls out the pick by 1. X3 moves up to the ball side shoulder of 3 and prepares to muscle through the pick set by 1. X1 must loosen and stay on the ball side (top) of 1 and see X3 through the pick. As soon as he sees X3 has gotten through the pick, X1 quickly closes back up to 1 to prevent an easy pop and catch by 1 (D-32).

Flare Picks

This pick is used often as an entry pass to get into motion or for a quick-hitter shot. The move has been around the NBA many years. Dick Motta and John MacLeod made excellent use of it for many years. Paul Westphal was a master at using this screen to his advantage as a player. Many college teams have maximized and popularized the action in recent years, most notably the Indiana Hoosiers of Coach Bob Knight.

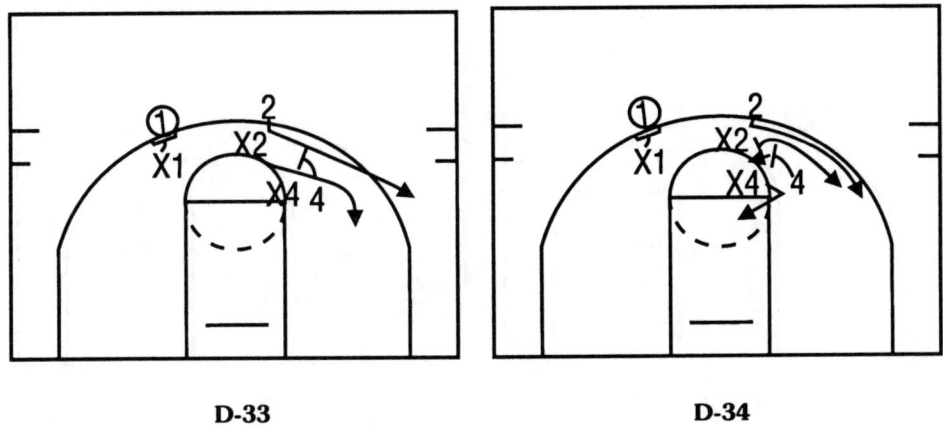

D-33   **D-34**

In D-33, player 2 cuts off of 4, looking to receive a lob-over from 1. X2 can go under the pick (third man), or over the pick (second man), depending on the skill of the offensive player. This coverage happens most often. Player X4 can help pull/push X2 through on this and still be able to stop 4's step-up move after the pick.

If he is defending a great shooter, X2 can go over the top of the pick (second man) and can get to his body as in a regular backpick. However, it is easier for 4 to pick X2 off if he knows he will try to go over the top. X4 has to be aware to give help on this and that exposes the middle for 4's step-up (D-34).

The play could be switched (depending on personnel) especially when we are denying the pass from 1 to 2, or if we get caught by surprise. If X2 is a big guard physically, the switch to 4 is easier to justify as well.

X4 is responsible for defending the lane and has the inside responsibility for his own man leaving early and going to the basket. Bob Love of the Bulls made many baskets stepping through into the lane on this in the late '60s and early '70s.

There is another option that can be effective, which is the squeeze-up move. X4 squeezes up on the picker and lets X2 go under (fourth man). If 4 is a good catch and shoot man, this can be a good change of pace tactic (D-35). Ball pressure by X1 on 1 will help make the play more difficult in each coverage.

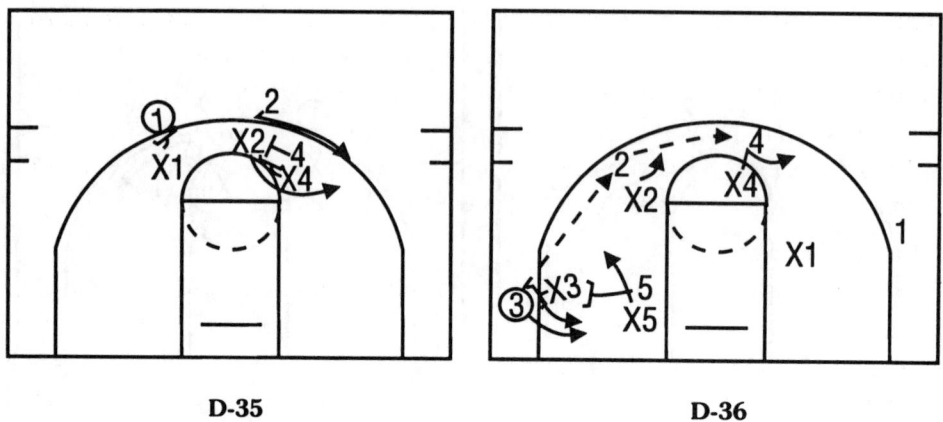

D-35   D-36

Flex-corner Backpick

This is a part of the flex-action offensive system and is used in both the passing game and in some transition secondary attacks as well (D-36). The corner backpick is covered like the wing backpick. When the ball is reversed, the defense should react with X3 getting right to 3's body to carry over or under. X5 loosens to see X3 through and gets back fast to 5. As usual, X2 and X4 put pressure on the ballhandlers 2 and 4. It is best always to prevent the pass from 2 to 4, the elbow to elbow pass.

UCLA backpick at the elbow. Special note should be taken of the coverage here, because it is a little different than the standard coverage. The play is frequently used at all levels.

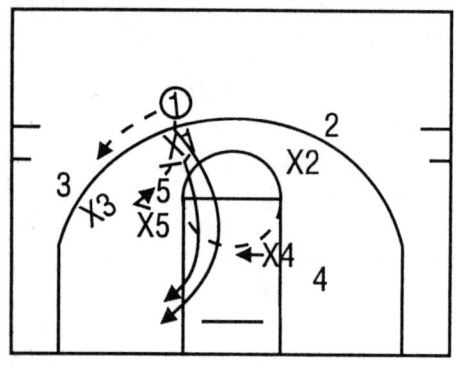

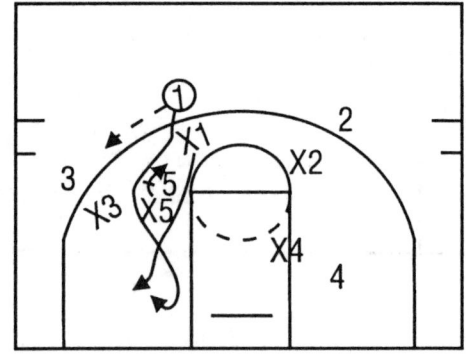

D-37   D-38

Diagram 37 shows the action that is basically a backpick. Instead of trying to get to the cutter's body and going on the ball side of the screen, he must go under the screen and through the lane to prevent the lob pass option. He quickly picks up his man on the other side of the pick. In order to be able to do this, he must get help from the defender on the picker. So X5 steps out toward the ball side of the pick to bump 1's cut and hold him up a little bit (or make him take a wider route) in order to give X1 more time to get to 1 under the screen. Naturally, if 1 cuts under the pick, X1 is in an easy position to maintain coverage. X1 is also able to get back to 1 in the event that 1 fakes a cut and pops back to look for a jumper in front of the pick.

The key to the coverage is for X1 and X5 to work together. X1 has the weak side cut and pop-back, while X5 bumps the strong side cut to hold 1 up until X1 can recover to 1. X5 must quickly get back up to his own man. The harder X1 works, the quicker X5 can recover back to his own man to prevent an easy elbow shot (D-38).

Weak side front backpick (shuffle cut). This has been a standard cut in offenses at every level for nearly forty years and still gives fits to defenses due to the angle of the cut and the floor position occupied by three key players (1, 2 and 4 in D-39).

To defend the pick on 2 by player 4, equal-size players can switch. But normally this pick is a mismatch situation. One option is to play it like the UCLA cut previously discussed. X2 will take the low cut and the pop-back move and X4 will play on the ball side of the pick and bump to hold up 2, if he cuts over the top of the pick as in D-40.

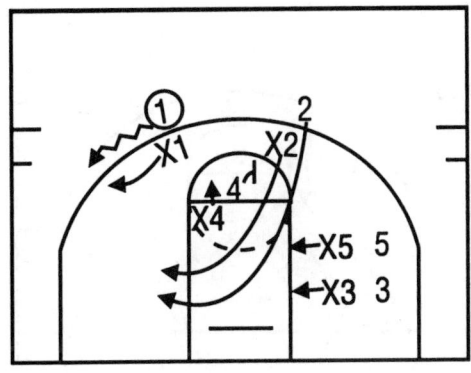

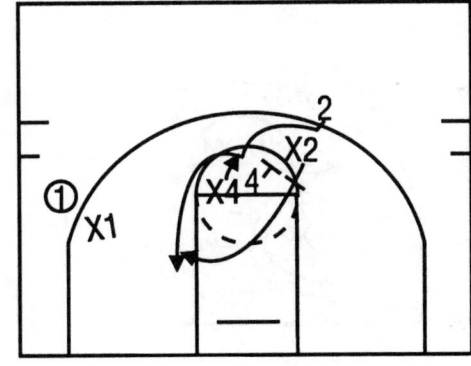

D-39   **D-40**

On this angle X2 does not have as much worry about 2 flare-cutting to the goal for a lob, so X2 has the option of getting to 2's body and carrying over or under the pick, if he feels he can play 2 better in this physical manner. It is good to allow X2 this option because it does make it easier to defend the pop-back option by 2.

A main aspect of this play and the UCLA cut is that the cuts off the backpick often allow the offense to get the ball to the picker at the elbow. A live ball at the elbow is a dangerous offensive tool and not one that a good defense wants to give up. Therefore, the defender on the picker must hurry to get back to his man to prevent the elbow pass, if possible.

Reverse Zipper — Elbow Backpick

Diagram 41 shows this variation of the common "zipper" move out of the box set. As the action begins, X2 is three- quarters on the low post player, 2. X5 moves to three-quarters on the strong side of 5 as 1 dribbles over to the wing.

X2 gets to 2's body and tries to lock him down to keep him from cutting up the lane to set the pick, or at least to break his timing. He calls out the backpick on X5 and loosens up to help get X5 through the pick. X5 will get to 5's body on the ball side to bump him and hold him up from using the pick easily. X5 wants to make 5 cut into the lane behind the pick so he can stay on the ball side to prevent an easy direct pass from 1. X5 can usually muscle right through the pick by being with 5's body because 2 is a smaller player (remember that equals would switch).

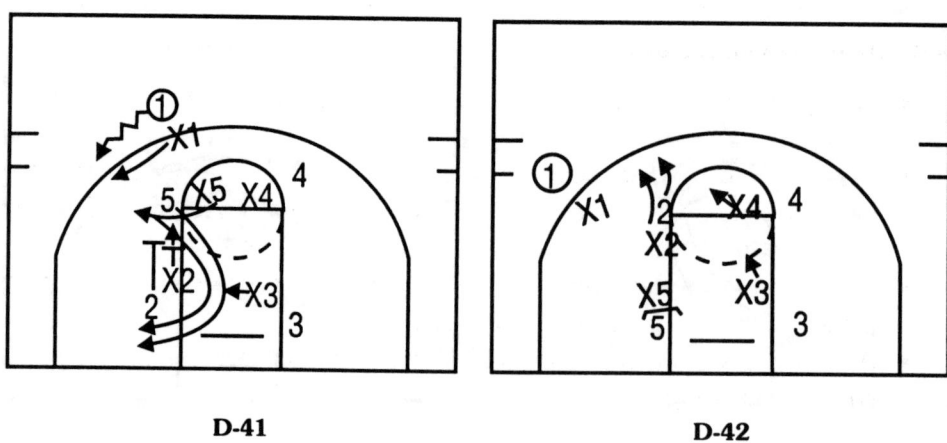

D-41   D-42

X2 must be alert to his responsibility to be in position to bump 5 to prevent an easy score in the event 5 gets free of X5's body. It will not happen often, but X2 must be ready. This may cause X2 to be a little late getting out to recover to his man after the pick, but it is better to allow the catch by 2 than the easy post catch by 5 (D-42).

If 2 starts scoring on this play, adjustments must be made. The weakside defenders can be very supportive on this action. The low man can help X5 on 5's cut and post up. X4 will be in a "live" position to be able to run at the open shooter, 2, if X2 fails to get out fast enough as in D-43. Occasionally X4 can get a steal on this pass; X2 can rotate on over to 4.

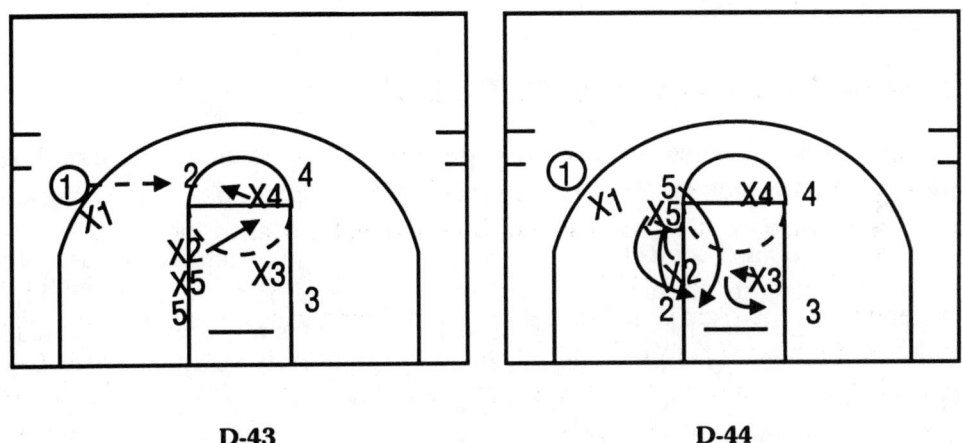

D-43   **D-44**

The squeeze-up method can be used by X2 if 2 gets open too often on the pop and is making shots. X5 would break contact with 5 (X3 must stop the lob) to let X2 stay with 2 (D-44).

Summary on backpicks. The most important fundamentals to remember in defending backpicks are:

- Get to the ball side of the cutter's body immediately, if there is to be no switch.
- The defender on the picker must call out the pick and get into a loose, ball-side position on his man. He is obligated to "see his teammate through" and quickly get back to a good ball-side position on his own man.
- Ball pressure on the passer will help the defenders directly involved in the picking action to be able to get their jobs done.
- An emergency switch to the world's worst mismatch is better than an open shot in easy range.

Horizontal Post Crosspicks

This is another of the most-used NBA offensive actions and a common occurrence in passing games at all levels. There are four variations that are viable options for the defense: high-high and switch; high-high and stay; high-low and switch; and high-low and stay. Notice in each of the strategies the word "high" appears first. The reason is that it's necessary to play on top (ball side or high side) of the man setting the pick. To play low on him would set him up to be able to turn and lock his own defender, plus it does not put the defender in the best position to give help to his teammate on the cutter.

Furthermore, the defender on the ballhandler should put good pressure on the ball in all the coverage to discourage an easy pass. If the ballhandler tries to break his man down off the dribble, that man must call out quickly for help, because his teammates defending the crosspicking action will be occupied and may lose vision of the ball momentarily.

High-high and switch. This technique with equal defenders has both defenders getting to the high side of their assignments' bodies as in D-45. The advantage is that the proper position of both defenders is to be on the high side as the play is initiated. As X5 calls out the impending pick, X4 moves right into 4's body and is ready to body over the top if 4 tries that avenue, since there would be no need to switch. If 4 chooses to go away from the overplay and cut low to the baseline, X5 switches to deny him a low post position. Again, X4 has the difficult task of whirling to get on top of 5 when the switch is used, since 5 can pin X4 and step open to the ball (D-46).

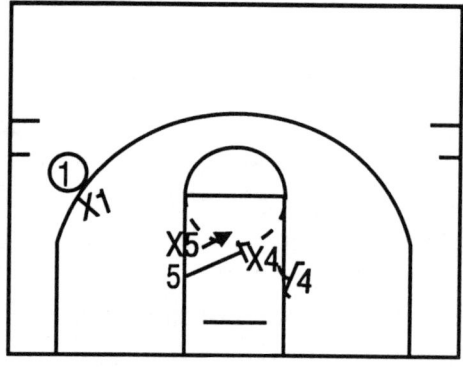

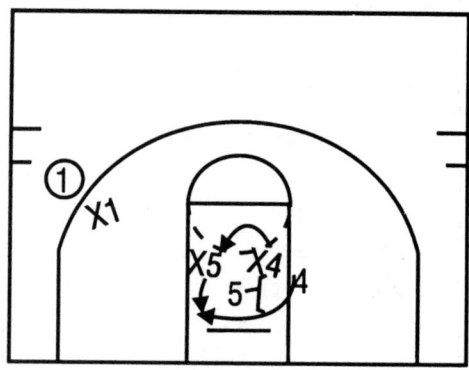

D-45   D-46

High-high and stay. With the mismatch (or if switching is not desired), playing and staying on the high side is a good option. It tends to allow the defenders to flatten down the cuts of the two players involved in the picking action.

In D-47, 5 picks across on 2 and X2 gets on 2's high shoulder opposite the baseline and tries to get through the pick and maintain body position between his man and the ball. X5 must loosen enough to see that X2 gets through, because if he gets hung up by a hard pick, 2 will be wide open under the goal. As soon as X5 sees X2 is through safely, he has to get to 5 immediately with his hands high. 5 is in a great position to receive a lob from 1 if X5 cannot recover quickly. That is the greatest danger in this coverage (D-48).

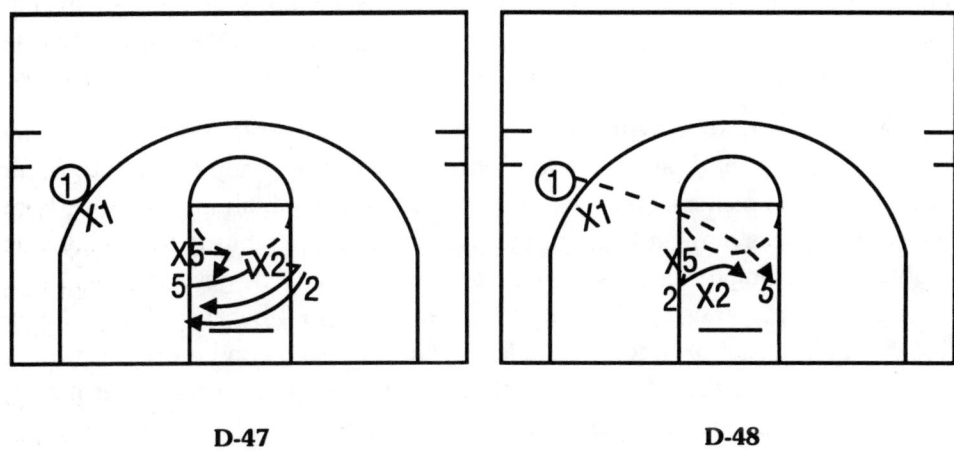

D-47   **D-48**

High-low and switch. When equal defenders are involved such as 4/5 or 2/3, it's easy to play high on the picker and low on the cutter and switch if the cutter comes over the top (D-49).

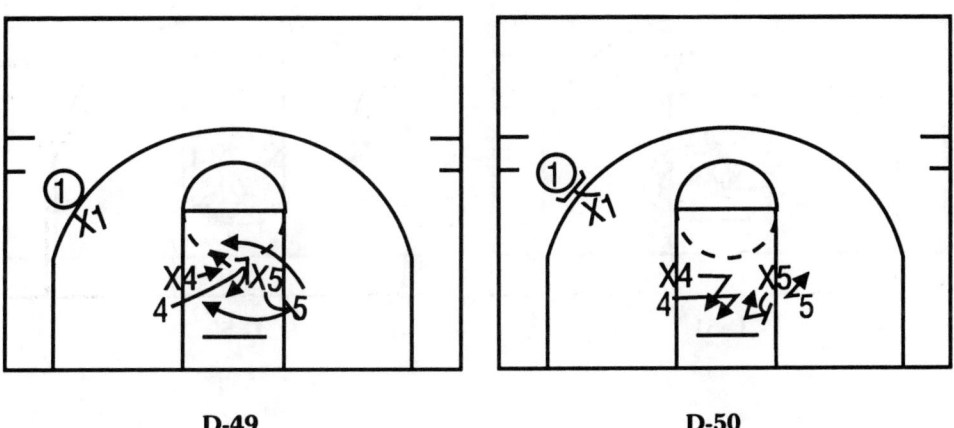

D-49   **D-50**

There is no need to switch if the cutter tries to cut low right into the direction of his defender's overplay. The defender can carry right on through with him. But if the cutter goes over the top, the picker's man is ready to body right up on him. Then the defender on the cutter must work hard to get into a position between his new man and the ball. He will have to go over or under, but he has to work hard. The danger on the switch is that the picker will pin the man he picks and open back up to the ball and be wide open.

The defenders have to be alert for the fake pick action where the picker will immediately step back and be open to receive the ball, if he sees his own defender get ahead of or even with him as he goes across the lane to set the pick. The defender on the picker must be near his man, but must be a step closer to the ball to prevent this step-back move as X4 does in D-46. At the same time 5 can pop back and signal for a lob pass on the same fake-pick action, so X5 has to be ready for that possibility.

High-low and stay. When a mismatch is involved, another option is to play high on the picker and get to the low side of the cutter, ready to body through with the cut. The picker's defender, X2 in D-51, will stay high and will give help to X4 until he sees him get through the pick. He will give a bump to 4 if X4 gets caught and is trailing the cut. X4 has to keep coming even if he gets screened hard. The hardest part comes on the stay if X2 has to bump 4 because that makes it difficult for X2 to get back to 2. If he is slow to do this, 2 can be open for a lob as in D-52. After covering the crosspick, X2 will need to be alert to get picked himself, because a common action on this is to pick the picker.

D-51   D-52

Which coverage is the best? Our experience in the NBA has been that there is a place for all of them at one time or another. The scouting report will indicate the strengths and the tendencies of each individual and team. Therefore, if a team is good at using the weakside low cut, our defender on the cutter will jump to the low side as soon as the play is identified.

Naturally, if a player tends to do best by cutting over the top of the screen, we continue with the high-high initial positioning. The overplay will be in the direction of the strength whether we are telling our players to switch, stay or just switch when there is a good hard hit on the cutter's defender. If there is an area where the individual gets open, we want it to be at his second choice of cuts, not his favorite.

Even armed with the best of scouting reports, it is possible that the game flow will indicate that the selected coverage is not working. This is where the advantage of having at least a second option becomes an advantage. The good bench coach will be flexible enough to have an alternate plan when one of his players needs more from the coach than just the words, "Try harder."

Summary on defending crosspick actions. It is important to drill this defensive exercise. It should be worked on from the parallel block to block position and also from the non- parallel — with the cutter being both higher and lower than the position of the picker. Players will let the coach know ways they are more comfortable with, but they must be exposed to more than one way to play the action. Good defensive technique will have at least the following elements:

1. The picker's defender must call out the pick loudly and early. He will always stay on top and near the picker's body, yet loose enough to be able keep his own man from pivoting around and being open for a quick pass on a fake pick. He must be loose enough to help see his teammate through (if there is no switch) and close enough to give a bump to the cutter when absolutely necessary and still be able to get back to his own man.

2. The cutter's defender must get the cutter's body (high or low) and be physical instead of trying to back off and feel his way around the picker. The latter method only helps the picker get to his body, as in a regular backpick.

3. The defender on the ball should threaten the ballhandler. Do not allow easy looks into the lane area. He must call out for help if the ballhandler drives him. Consideration can be given to funneling the ballhandler inside on this, if the ballhandler is a quick driver. The crosspicking action tends to jam up the middle of the lane, but the baseline can be vulnerable because the screening moves divert the attention of the low post men from their normal "ball, man and lane" thinking. This was a special threat when Philadelphia ran this action with Hersey Hawkins on the wing with the ball, a man who could shoot and

drive. The defense had to worry about Barkley in the cutting action so a baseline drive could cause problems. The Lakers with Magic Johnson and James Worthy presented gigantic problems as well.

4. If a switch is made, both men must deny the men they switch to.

5. If the defense intends to avoid the switch, the cutter's defender must keep on coming to recover, even if he gets picked. The picker's defender is obligated to give help until his teammate can get into decent position after the pick.

6. In case of an emergency (the defender falling down, for example), always look to put out the first fire, the man in the most threatening position.

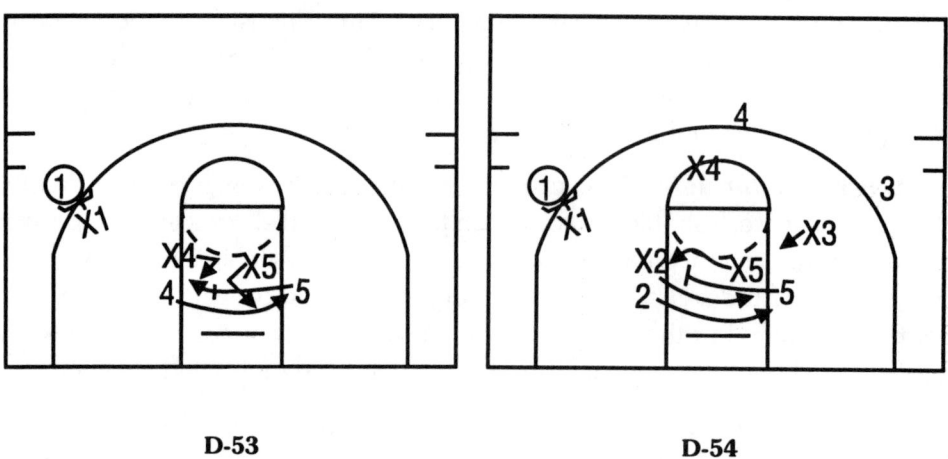

D-53   D-54

Reverse Crosspicks

On the reverse action in which the ball-side man receives a backpick from the weakside man as in D-53, it is best to switch and deny equals, because this puts the defense right in between the strongside posted man and the ball. It basically eliminates the strength of the play.

The move is quite dangerous when unequals are involved, the picker being the main threat. To defend it, the defender on the cutter must stay on the ball side and trail the cutter through the pick as close to his body as he can, with one or both hands up to discourage a lob. The defender on the picker will be unable to drop to give help; to do so will allow the picker to be absolutely wide open in front of the goal. He must fight over or under the picker in order to get a front position on him as quickly as possible as X5 does in the diagram (D-54).

Weakside defenders must be alert to give help regardless of the rest of the coverage because the picker's defender cannot give the normal help.

Non-parallel Crosspicks

There are many coaches who do not want both blocks covered at the same time. They insist that the weakside player line up higher or lower than the inside player on the ball side. When these men use cross-screening, the angles become more diagonal up or down with resulting angular cuts as opposed to flat horizontal cuts. These cuts are not as easily defended as the more often used flat screen/cut action of parallel players.

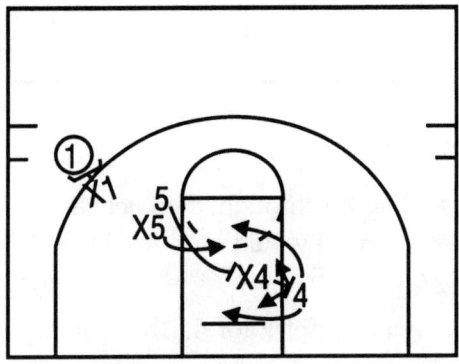

D-55

In general it is still more effective to switch equals and to avoid switching unequals, if possible. And ball pressure remains an essential.

A team can still use the four methods shown in defending the parallel cross-cuts. However, the high-high positions put the defense in better defensive angles for the diagonal downpick and high-low is better for the diagonal uppick (whether switching or staying).

In D-55, 5 sets a diagonal downpick for 4. If X5 and X4 are to switch, X5 is in a good position to check 4's cut. From the high position, X4 can roll to get on top of 5 or can perhaps slide in under him. 5 would be able to lock X4 down easier if he were low on 4's baseline side and set himself up for a lob from 1.

If X5 and X4 were not switching, both are still better able to maintain body position from a high-high start regardless of the direction of 4's cut.

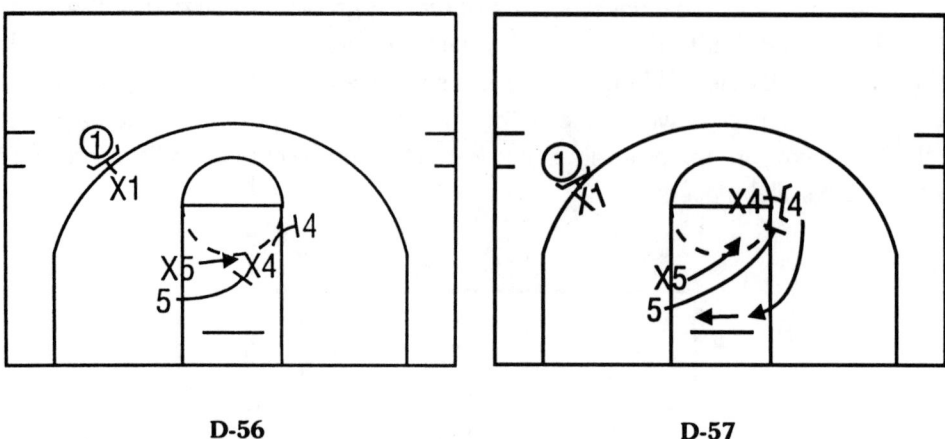

D-56   **D-57**

X5 can loosen up and let X4 through, then get back to his own man quickly. However, from a low position X4 would have trouble with a high cut by 4 and a possible curl cut — even with X5's help.

In D-56, 5 sets a diagonal uppick for 4. The high-high positioning is still all right unless 4 gets up as high as a step below the foul line. At that point the high position on the cutter fails to pay dividends, whether the players are switching or staying. On the switch, X4 can get sealed off by 5 and on the stay, he can give up a possible lob pass at the weakside corner of the goal since he can be picked off easier by X5 for a lob or post up (D-57).

On this coverage if X4 plays *low*, he can stop the backdoor lob play. If 4 cuts over the top, X5 can give help by bumping him, as in the case of the UCLA/shuffle cut defense, and allow X4 to recover if they are not switching. If they are switching, X5 is still in great position, while X4 should be able to get his body in front of 5 by rolling over or slipping under on the baseline side of 5 (D-58).

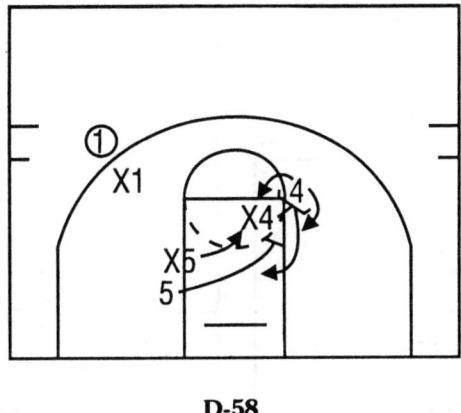

D-58

Baseline Picks — Single and Double

As frequently used in the NBA as the pick/roll, backpick and crosspick is the baseline pin-down or pinch-pick action. Every NBA team uses a variation of the play due to its simplicity and general effectiveness. When used from a 1-4 set or from a stack on one side of the post, it is commonly called "single-double action." One reason for that is that the target shooter normally has a choice of cutting off of one side that has a single pick set for him or the other side which has a double pick waiting.

CUTTER OUT THE SINGLE PICK SIDE

In D-59, player 2 cuts out off the single side where 5 is setting a pick. There are several defensive factors to consider:

- The first order of business is for X2 to keep 2 from catching a direct pass in front of the basket from player 1. Dick Motta was able to get Rolando Blackman this pass about once every game due to Ro's big size and the passing ability of Brad Davis when they were with the Dallas Mavericks.
- It is essential to decide whether to switch the equal size players (X2 and X3 usually) if they cross. Since X2 and X3 are usually of near equal size, most NBA teams choose to switch the action. While it is convenient to do so for many reasons, it is not automatically the best tactic to employ. Lazy switching can cause a defender to lose contact with a good shooter. Against some of the great shooters, it becomes better to avoid switching in order to try to keep a defensive body on the shooter. That way the defense can sometimes influence his cutting route and also hinder his timing. He may

not prevent a catch by the target shooter, but he can usually end up being in a better position to challenge the shot than when switching is employed. This decision will have to be made and adjusted depending on the results in any given game. Both methods must be practiced.

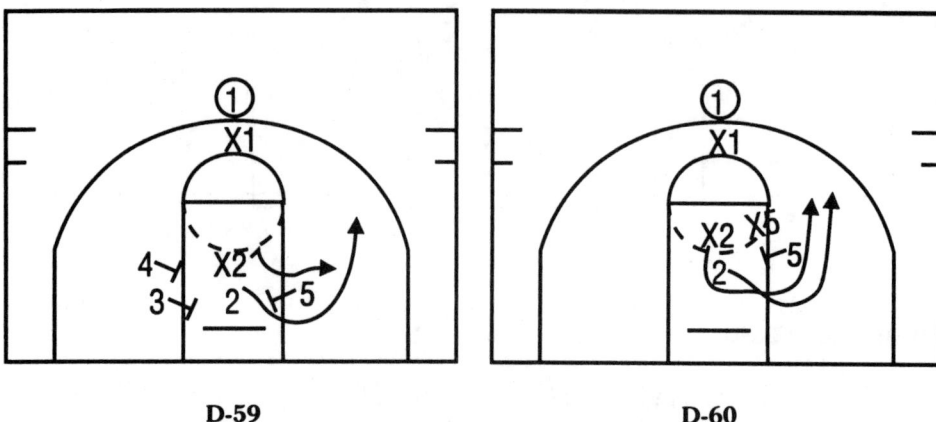

D-59   D-60

- Another decision is whether to have the defender try to get over or under the baseline pick on the single side. On the double pick side the defender on the cutter/shooter must go *under* the picks, if there is no switch. Teams who allow the defender to go over the top of a double do not have as much success in defending the play, though many keep allowing it. An unchallenged shot will result in most cases.
- Going over the top of the pick. When the picks are set very low near the baseline as in D-59, it is easier for the cutter's defender to go over the top. The cutback for a lob is not as big a threat since there is inadequate space. The duck-out cut to the corner is not as big a threat either, because the cutter is so close to the baseline. This method eliminates the curl cut as well, since the curl cutter would cut right back into his own man.
- Going under the pick. When the picks are set higher above the blocks as in D-60, it is better to go under the pick and stay with the cutter/shooter's body. Going over the top when the picks are set high allows space for possible lobs and duck-outs to the corner for the shooter/cutter. The biggest drawbacks to going under the pick are that it allows the curl or half-curl and permits the picker to get a better angle to set a pick on the defender. To counteract this, the defender on the picker must be ready to step up and body-check the curl-cutter as in D-61.

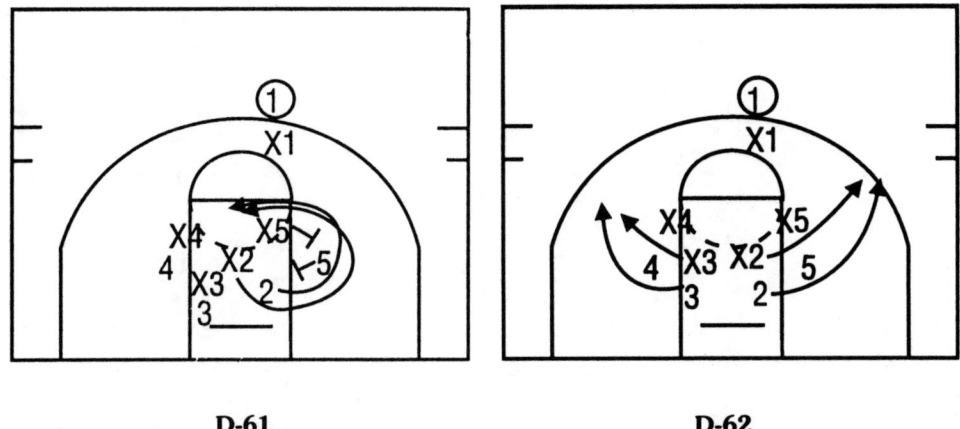

D-61   **D-62**

- This technique can help equalize the problem of the curl cut. The difficulty presented by the better picking angle is eased if the defender on the cutter/shooter will trail behind the cutter's outside shoulder until he clears the screen. He can then angle cut to a denial position on the cutter as X2 does in D-60.

- A decision also must be made as to whether the defenders on the pickers should play high and loose on their men or body up and squeeze down on their men as they pick.

High and loose. We often choose to play the down pickers this way in order to give the men guarding the shooter/cutters the room to make a choice to cut out over or under the pick (D-62).

By being active with the hands and feet, the defenders on the pickers can be in a position to give temporary help, or switch out to shooters, or step up to body-check curl cutters and still be able to defend their own men against posting up. It also puts the inside defenders in a position to attack a quick penetration by the cutter after catching the ball on the short wing area (D-63).

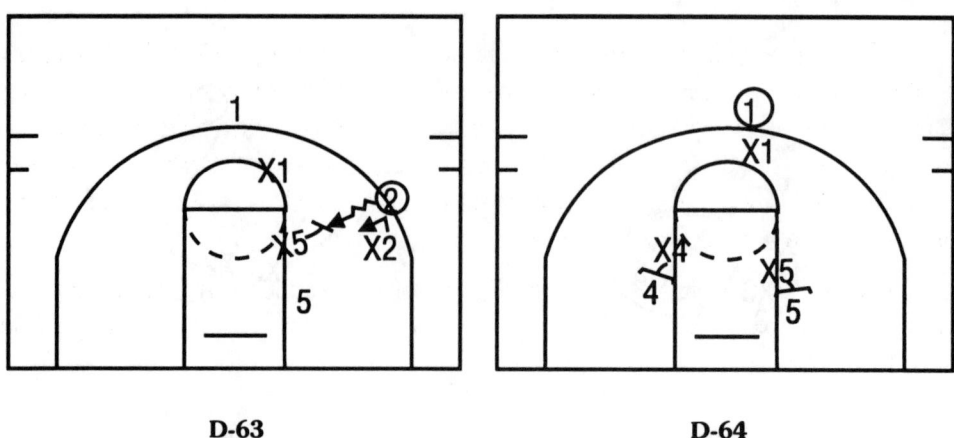

D-63   **D-64**

Tight and squeeze down. Sometimes we are not successful with high and loose, because it tends to turn the pickers loose. It also allows the pickers to set moving picks. By bodying down on the pickers we can push them low toward the baseline (D-64). In this position the defender on the picker is on top, where he can defend a step-up to post more easily.

The defender on the cutter/shooter may still be able to go over or under the pick as with the high and loose method. He just has a bigger obstacle over the top with two men close together as 5 and X5 are in D-65.

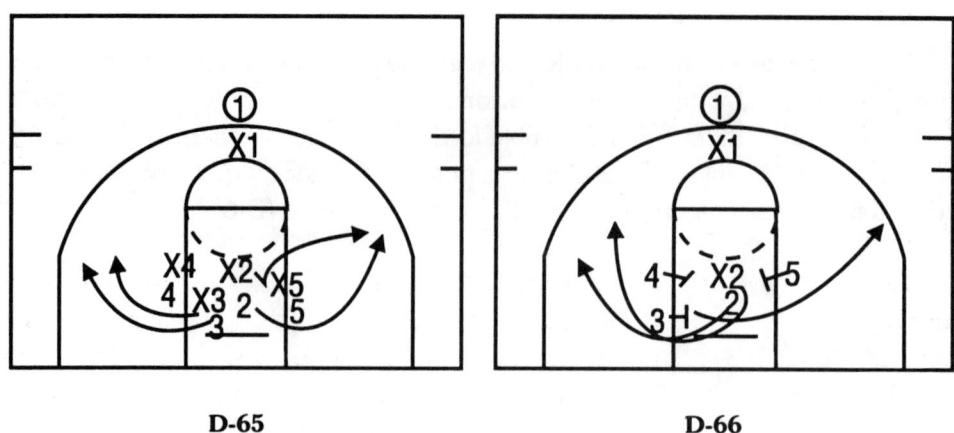

D-65   **D-66**

WHEN THE CUTTER COMES OUT THE SIDE OF THE DOUBLE PICK

In D-66, player 2 cuts out under the side of the double pick. X2 will get right behind 2, a half a man closer to the baseline than the cutter is so that he can stay with the cutter and still avoid being picked (in this position the picker would have to hit his own man in order to pick the defender). If the defender tries to go over the top of the double pick, the shooter/cutter can cut back to the basket for a layup or duck into the corner for an open catch and shoot.

X4 defending on the top of the stack must still step up to bump the curl cut of 2 or 3, a major responsibility. He must make contact with the curl cutter to slow him down enough to let the defender regain position (D-67).

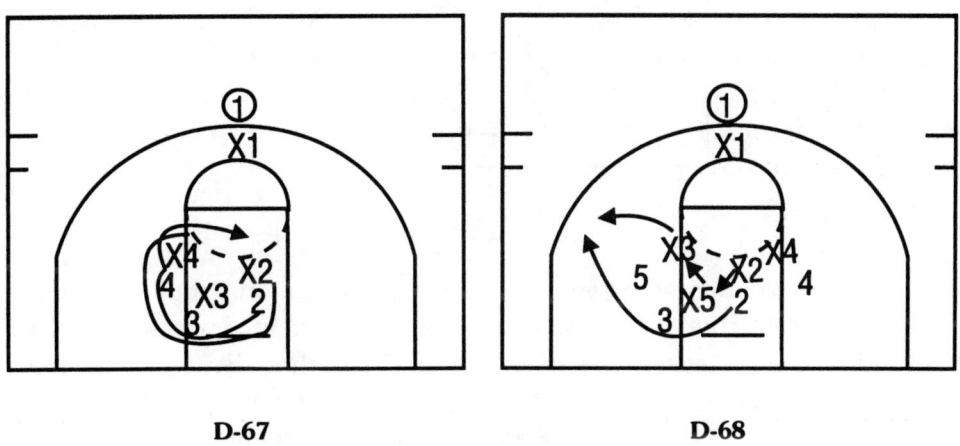

D-67   **D-68**

In the event that the stack contains a big and a small man, the small man can switch out on the cutter as an option. In this case, when there is time to get it set up, the defenders on the stack can "invert" their defensive assignments. By inverting as X5 and X3 do in D-68, X3 is able to switch out more easily to shooter 2. X2 then takes 3 and X5 moves up the line to get back to his own man.

Against teams with a point guard of lesser talent, the defense may be able to turn him in the direction that a scouting report says the offense shoots poorly from. In the NBA this is difficult to do because of the tremendous skill level of the point guards; still ball pressure is helpful and necessary in defending the single- double.

Step up to defend wing penetration. Regardless of the side that the cutter/shooter selects to cut under, the threat of the cutter catching the ball and quickly penetrating into the middle is a real one. It is more likely to occur when the defender trails the cutter out or if there is a lazy switch. D-69 shows 2 catching on his cut under the stack and quickly turning the ball to the middle. The man defending the post, X5 in this case, must step up and attack the penetration or 2 will have an easy shot. X5 tries to be aggressive to attack 2 and X3, who switched, must continue to pursue 2 to catch back up and release X5 to get back to his own man. X2, X1 and X4 must jam up the middle when X5 gets involved in helping X3. X5 will be active with his hands as well to make it as hard as possible for 2 to make an easy inside drop-off pass.

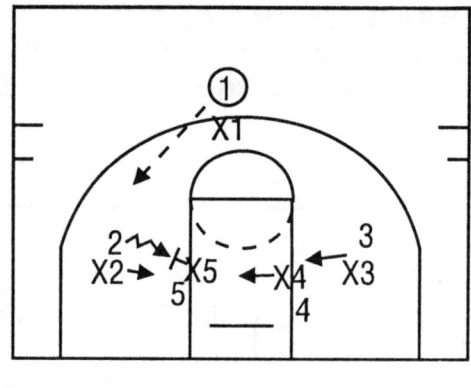

D-69

The post defender must give help to this penetration on both the single and double pick sides of the offense. Many big men are reluctant to make the play, but it is consistent with attacking all penetration and open shots. By forcing the tough short pass play into a jammed up area, a good team defense with active hands will gain more than it loses by employing this strategy. Big men must remember to make this commitment to penetration.

HELPFUL REMINDERS IN DEFENDING BASELINE PICKING ACTIONS

- It is good to switch when big men can be kept inside and small men can be switched to the outside. It is best not to switch the big men out, but if it is done so in order to prevent an easy open shot, it is better than allowing a shooter a free look at the basket. This is another key emergency switch-out situation.
- Big men on the pickers must remember to be active with their hands to help discourage the point man's pass to the cutter. Still, the inside defender has to get back to his own man to keep him from catching the ball in the post on a step-up after he picks. This active technique is sometimes so aggressive

as to be called "fake-switching." The picker's defender has to be active with the hands and body to force the cutter to go out further and to give the cutter's defender more time to regain position.

- Against a "hot" shooter it is good to change the timing of the play by switching out even the big man to the shooter. If they pass inside because of the mismatch, the nearest big man not on the hot shooter can trap the mismatch and have the small man rotate off right away.

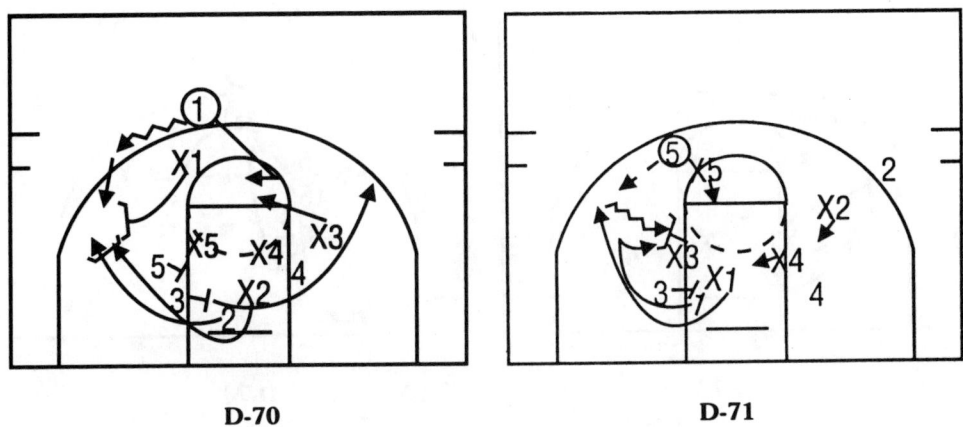

D-70   **D-71**

- Occasionally, a good change-up on defense is to trap the hot shooter with the point man's defender (on the catch or on the dribble) as in D-70. X3 will have to rotate to 1 fully, if 1 is a decent shooter or if 1 penetrates quickly at X3. If 1 is not a big scoring threat, X3 may be able to fake a rotation toward him and allow X1 to recover back to 1. In any case, the defense has made the hot shooter 2 give up the ball. If 2 passes, X2 must remember to deny a quick return pass back to 2.

Defending the pin-down variation of the baseline pick. D-71 shows the pin-down variation used as part of the famous John Wooden UCLA offense still quite prevalent at all levels of basketball. Player 3 throws the ball to the elbow area to 5 and sets a pin-down screen on 1. If equals were involved, the switch would be easy, but this tactic seldom involves equals.

To execute a stay on defense, X1 is on top of 1 in a three- quarters position. X3 bumps 3 on the ball-side shoulder as he cuts down to set the pick in order to break his rhythm and angle, and then loosens (while staying high on the ball side of 3) to allow X1 the option to chase under the pick with 1's body or to go over the top of the pick as X3 lets him through. X1 can usually defend better by trailing and staying with 1's body like is done in playing against the baseline double picks. He should get his inside shoulder in line behind 1's baseline shoulder as he "shadows" out with 1 to avoid the pick.

If X1 trails out, there is a threat of the curl cut by 1 off 3's pick. That is why X3 must stay high on the ball side of 3. He has to be able to step up and body check the curl cut just like the picker's defender on the single-double action does.

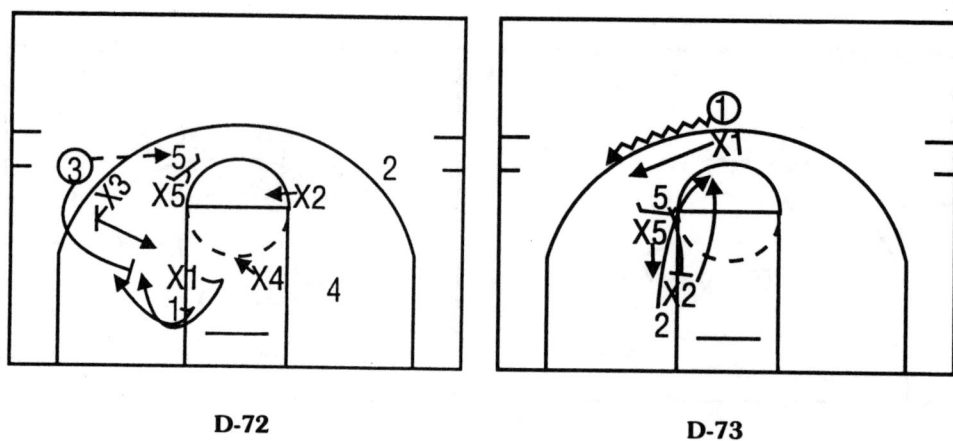

D-72   **D-73**

If player 1 catches the ball off of the pick, and puts the ball on the floor for more than one dribble into the middle, X3 (the defender on the picker) will have to step up to challenge the penetration. The rest of the defense must jam up the middle lane to stop the middle action (D-72).

DEFENDING STRONG SIDE DOWNPICKS

Diagram 73 shows a common offensive action generally called the "zipper" move. Player 5 sets a downpick on the strong side and X5 must bump 5 on the ball side shoulder to break his timing and rhythm, yet maintain position on him in the low post. To accomplish this X5 must let 5 slide under him after the bump and release so that X5 can stay on the high side between 5 and the ball on the wing.

Player 2 is seeking to cut to the top of the key for a catch and so X2 comes up the inside of the lane to defend 2. He does not want to go over the top of the pick to the ball side or he will allow 2 to catch the ball right in the middle of the free throw area. X2 cannot allow 2 to catch in the vertical middle of the court or 2 will be open for a shot, a penetration either way or an easy pass down to the weak- side low post (D-74). This catching in the middle is called "gaining ground" by 2 and X2's defensive goal is to make 2 catch the ball as near the wing on the ball side as possible.

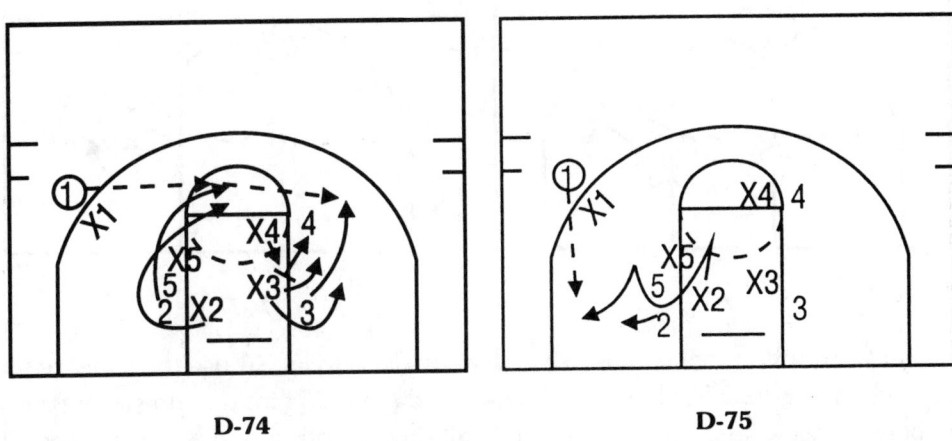

D-74   **D-75**

A risk that X2 runs by going under the pick and up the lane is that sometimes 2 will be able to duck back into the ball side corner for an open catch (D-75). X2 simply has to hustle to get to the shooter when this happens. To give up this option is better than giving up the easy free throw area catch. If X2 will concentrate, he can usually defend 2 regardless of the direction he cuts, though he will not be able to prevent a catch by 2 in most cases.

DEFENDING THE WEAKSIDE DOWNPICKS

There is a lot of difference in defending the downpick set on the weak side as opposed to the one set on the strong side. Of course this is another situation in which equals can be switched and for that reason the action seldom involves equals. If the play is unswitchable or the switch is not desired, the play is treated in a "let me through" manner as X3 does in D-76.

As 4 goes down to pick on X3, X4 bumps and releases on 4, if he can. In any case, he gets off toward the ball to allow X3 the option to go over or under 4's pick. It is preferable that the defender on 3 go ball side of the pick. The problem with trailing under the pick is that the cutter can angle his cut right up to the foul line area for a catch.

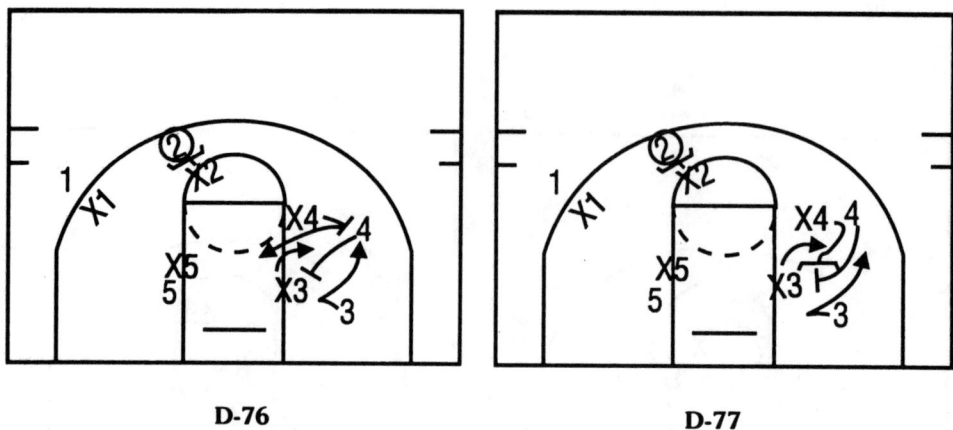

D-76   **D-77**

Another option that can be used occasionally is to let X4 use the squeeze up method on 4 as in D-77. He can get to 4's body to hold him up and stay tight on his body to allow space for X3 to come ball side of both 4 and X4. This keeps 4 from being able to drift open for a lob pass, as when X4 helps on 3, and it still allows X3 to be able to cut off 3's angle to the ball. That leaves 3 with the option of ducking back to the corner for a lob, however. Pressure must be kept on the ballhandler.

The defense must be alert on this kind of action that the offense may change the downpick by 4 to a backpick by 3. It is very important to talk at all times on the weak side and to know the game plan as far as switches are concerned. The defense may have to switch the backpick this close to the goal, even with a mismatch, especially if it happens quickly by surprise before X4 can get to 4's body.

DEFENDING PICK-THE-PICKER ACTION

Much of the pick-the-picker action involves a crosspick followed by a downpick as in D-78. X1 and X3 develop the play as a parallel crosspick as directed (switch or stay and high-high or high-low) as per the discussion of the crosspick defense. In this instance, assume that they are not switching. As 1 goes to pick across for 3, X3 gets to 3's body high in this diagram and X1 loosens to see him through.

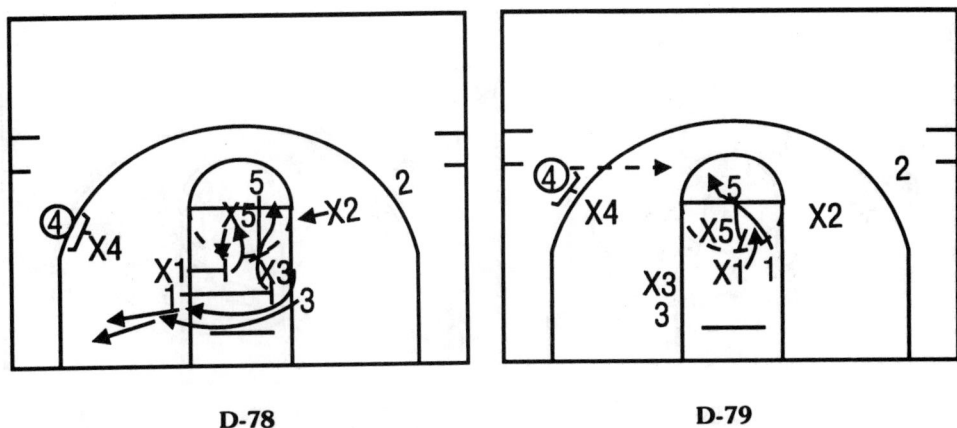

D-78   **D-79**

Then the second pick, 5 picking on X1, is treated as a weakside downpick. That is, X5 bumps and loosens on 5 and helps get X1 through the pick. Again, it is possible to let X5 use the squeeze technique to allow X1 to shortcut between X5 and the ball.

Trailing out with the cutter would allow the cutter to cut right into a nice rhythm-up catch and shoot, the shot the offense seeks with this play (D-79).

An important element in defending the play when the "let through" method is used is to have X5 be active with the hands and feet, ready for a temporary or a full "emergency" switch-out.

WEAKSIDE SWITCH OPTION

In D-80, X2 is in a position to switch out to 1 coming off the pick if 2 is playing as high as the wing area on the weakside wing. If X2 sees 1 coming up free, he can switch to 2 and X1 will then rotate to cover 2 for X2.

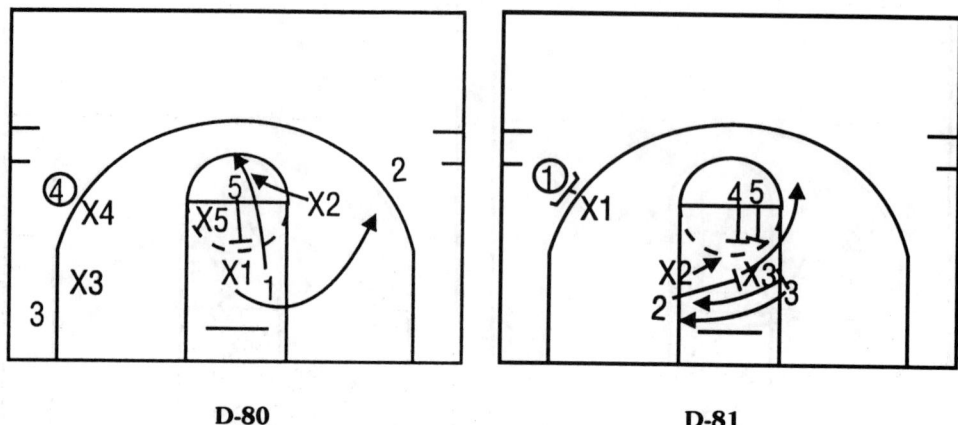

D-80   D-81

DEFENDING DOUBLE-DOWN PICKS

Weakside picks This action is the same as the pick-the-picker play just discussed, except it involves a double-down pick on the picker, so the weak- side helper is not available. X2 and X3 play the crosspicking action as directed in the game plan (switch or stay and high-high or high-low) (D-81).

One option in defending the play is for X2 to split between the double pick and get to the top of the key ahead of 2. However, in the proper execution of the play, the pickers will not let X2 through.

Another option allows X2 to trail under the picks, but 2 will be wide open unless he gets a lot of help from X4 or X5. Still another route is for X2 to short cut the double pick, but this enables 2 to be able to fade to the corner area for an easy shot.

There is a better approach to defending the play. The defenders on the double-down pickers, X4 and X5 in this case, must move immediately into a high-low tandem position as soon as they identify the play. X5 will drop right into the low post as in D-82 and X4 must stay in the high post area. X5 keeps the low post covered and X4 is active with his hands and body to do one of three things:

1. Fake switch. Be active and act like he's going to switch until the shooter's defender can recover, or

2. Switch. Actually switch and stay with the shooter. Try to deny the pass to the shooter if he can, or

3. Temporarily switch (extended help and recover). Make only a temporary switch until the shooter's defender can recover.

4. These actions allow X2 to have a fighting chance to get through the picks and it still keeps the basket/lane protected. X2 must be allowed to get through to the top the best way he can, knowing he is getting some help from X4 (D-83).

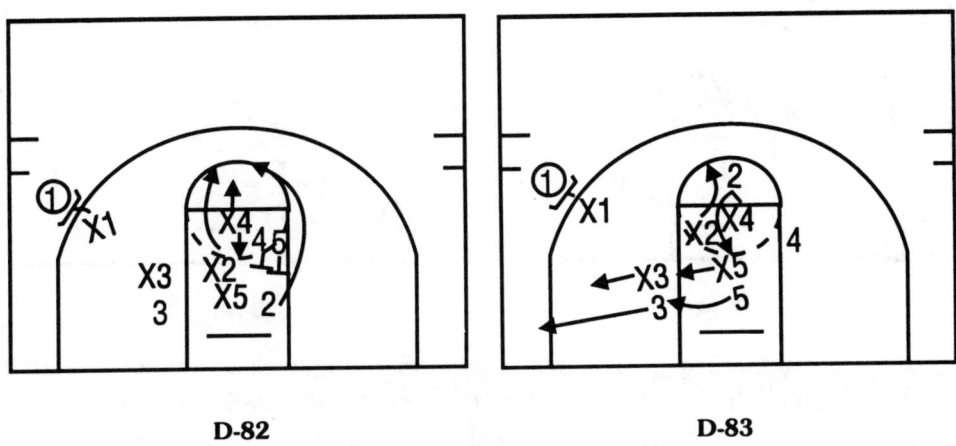

D-82   D-83

STRONGSIDE DOUBLE-DOWN PICKS

In D-84 player 2 comes off a staggered double pick set by 4 and 5. This move is a common one in transition in the NBA, but is also used as a set play for good shooters by several teams. It is best for the defender on the target man, X2 in this case, to try to go under the first pick and to "short cut" between the ball and the picker on the second pick. In the diagram X2 goes with 2's body under 4's pick and this allows him to be able to prevent a lob pass to 2 at the basket. Also, if 2 decides to duck back under the pick to receive a short pass from 1, X2 is there to cover him. X2 short cuts between 5's pick and X5 is active to help see X2 through.

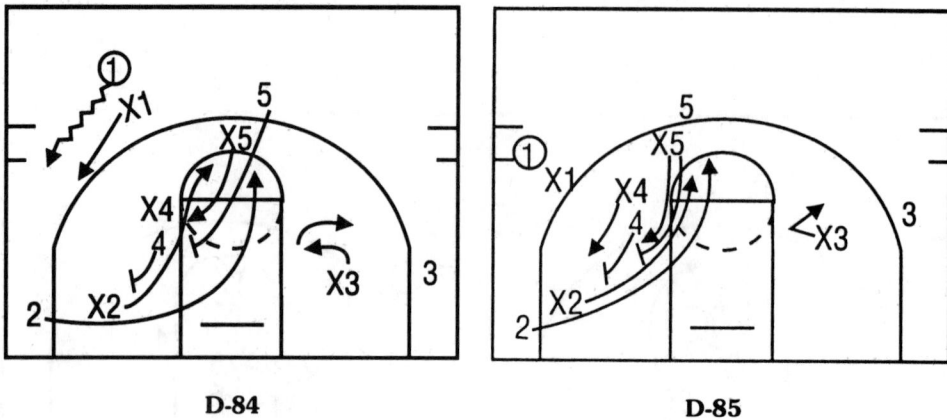

D-84   D-85

In the event that the pick by 5 is set at a sharp angle close enough to 1 that X2 can go behind, it is all right for X2 to take that route (D-85), but generally the short cut is better. It allows a possible steal by X2 and if 2 fades out for a lob pass, a weakside player will usually be in a position to cover the lob pass (as X3 is in the diagram). The lob over the second pick is an entirely different angle than the one over the first pick, where there would be no help.

POINTS OF CLARIFICATION IN DEFENDING GOOD PICKS

1. **Temporary switch concept (extended help and recover).** This method allows the defender on the nearest picker to the shooter to be active with the hands and feet and to get into a halfway switch to intimidate the passer from making an easy pass to an open cutter/shooter. One hand will extend toward the cutter and the other back toward his own man. He will stay until the original defender catches up and then he recovers back to his own man.

2. **When can temporary switching be used?** This may come up at any time because a defender who is in a help situation must stay long enough to see the original defender through. The original defender is obligated to keep on coming through a screen as quickly as possible. The help-out can become extended enough that it becomes a temporary switch, and with communication could be changed into a full emergency switch. The times that the temporary switch may be a part of the actual game plan tend to be more when there are one of the following three offensive actions: double-down picks on a shooter, baseline picking action, or free throw line elbow area pick and rolls.

3. **Emergency switch concept.** Whenever it is necessary to make any switch to prevent an obviously open shot, it is important to commit to the switch, regardless of the mismatch. The player committing to rotate to the open shooter should call out the switch and be confident the nearest man to him will rotate to cover the man he has left open. Everyone covers for everyone.

DEFENDING THE WEAKSIDE POST-UP MOVE

Again, the basketball world is indebted to John Wooden for yet another part of his famous UCLA offense. We have alluded to the UCLA guard down-cut off of the elbow backpick, the pindown pick from the wing to the low post, and now we address the weakside low post up move. While others have used these moves before and after, it was Wooden's great teams which popularized this combination of exercises and who executed them better than anyone before or since.

It is not necessary to run the UCLA offense to use any one of the three exercises mentioned, but D-86 and 87 show the action from the UCLA set-up, with 4 fighting X4 for low post position in order to receive a pass from 5 or 2. The fundamentals of baseline defense require the defense to play on the ball side of all offensive players on the baseline, when the ball is above the foul line extended, as mentioned earlier.

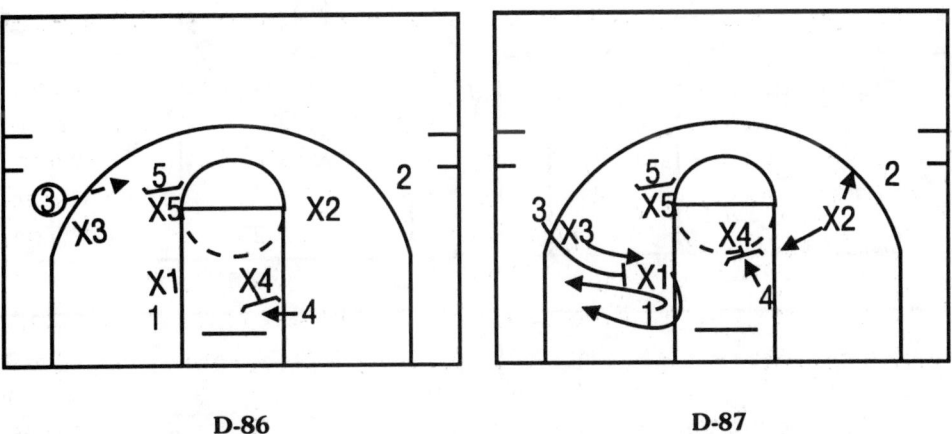

D-86   D-87

X5 will try to deny the elbow pass to 5, but if he catches the ball there anyway, X5 wants to shift to a hard inside overplay to help keep the ball from getting to the reverse side easily. X4 plays facing 4 on the ball side shoulder in a direct line to the ball and tries to muscle him down toward the baseline. The deeper 4 can get into the lane, the harder it is for X4 to defend him, so X4 must do his body position work early and stay strong. He should have his outside forearm (the right one in the diagram) right in 4's upper body and his inside arm and hand extended to deflect a pass. He should have his own body angled in a leaning manner against 4's cutting line. He needs to keep his base broad and use his feet and legs to leverage himself against the direction of 4's cut.

There are two different ways that X2 can be told to play to help X4 on this action. He can get up and deny 2 a pass from 5 and thus keep X4 from having to defend the pass from 2 on the wing. If that fails to work, or if 2 is a non-shooter, another option is to allow X2 to drop right back in on 4 to give additional help to X4. Ball pressure throughout this play will help the low post defender.

DEFENDING SPLITTING ACTIONS

Splitting the post was one of the key strategies of the old Boston Celtics championship teams of Red Auerbach. This tactic was one of the first set plays that players developed, along with give and go, back door ("blind pig"), second guard around, and others. Like pick and roll, it seemed to have its day in basketball only to reappear as a main tool of another championship team, the Chicago Bulls of Phil Jackson. In the meantime, Dick Motta's teams were sure to score a few hoops per game with it. Like all truly sound fundamentals, it always has a place. Splitting can occur in the low post, high post or side post (D-88, 89, and 90). Regardless of the location, there are some basic principles of defense that will apply.

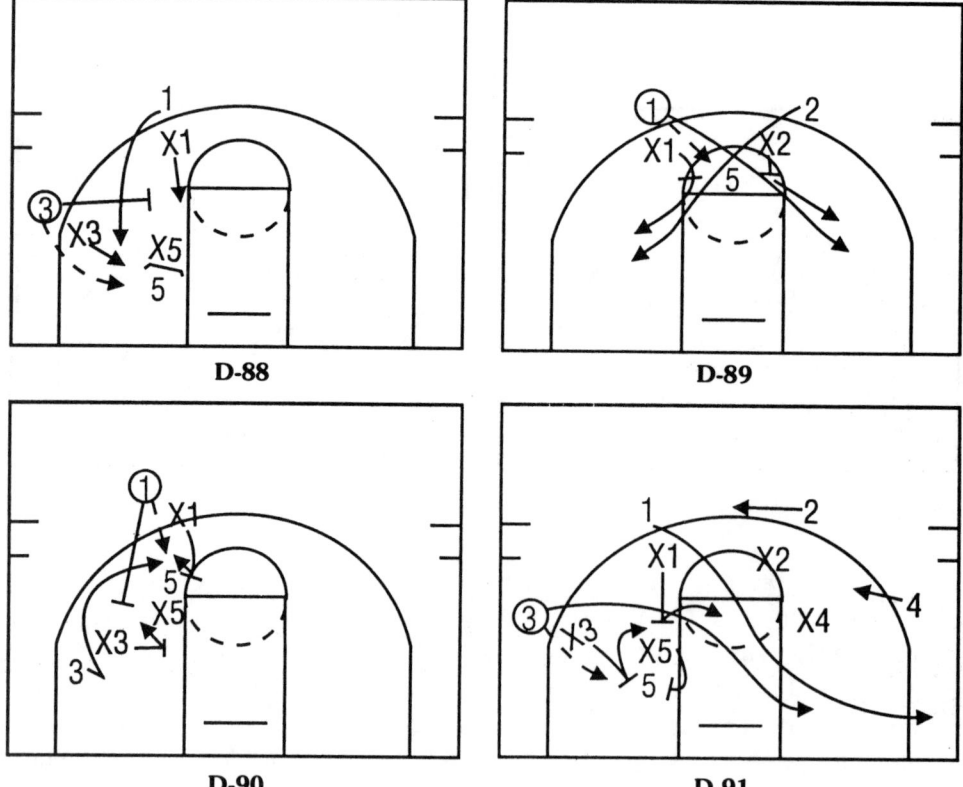

D-88

D-89

D-90

D-91

The basic principles in defending splits are:

- Defenders in front of the posted receiver should drop immediately to about a half a step above the level of the ball as soon as it is passed inside. This quick adjustment allows both defenders to be in position to switch if the men cross in any fashion, and to stay with their own men if they straight-line cut instead of splitting or crossing. It also allows them a better chance to get over the top of the post man if there is to be no switch as when the two offensive players both cut to the same side of the post man as 1 and 3 do in D-91.
- Defenders should be ready to switch when the crossing players come together. It is possible that the game plan will be to avoid the switch, of course. But the proper preparation will put the defenders in position to stay, switch or to emergency switch if necessary.

DEFENDING THE LOW POST SLASH MOVE

D-92 shows the slash cut over the low post man that is effective often in freeing up the low post. Again, the Chicago Bulls were effective with this in their championship seasons and other coaches such as Lenny Wilkens and Bob Hill have used it effectively in the NBA.

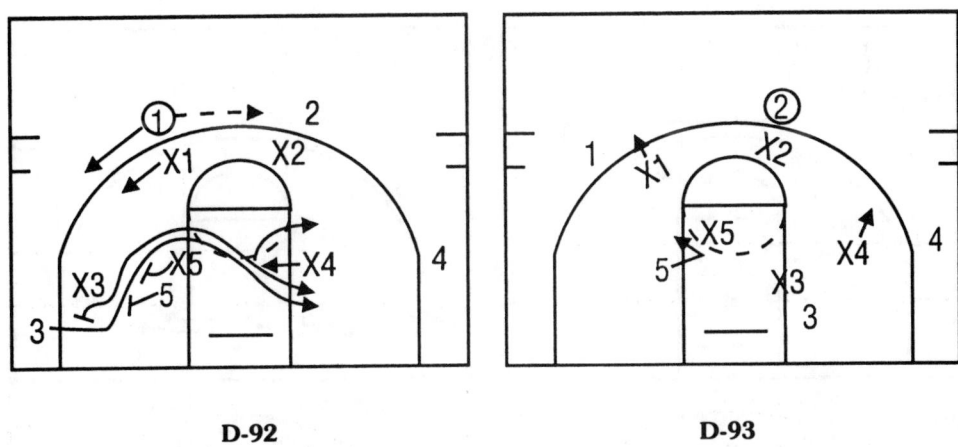

D-92   D-93

Player 3 slash-cuts off 5 as the ball is passed from strong side to weak side. If the cutter is not open, 5 steps up to catch from the top or from the point man on the wing, if the pass is snapped back from 2 to 1 (D-93). In defending the move there are three factors to consider:

1. X3 can body up on 3 and go over or under 5's pick like he would in playing a normal backpick or flex cut. Or, he can play softer and try to beat 3 into the lane. The latter move allows a possible lob on a step-back move by player 3.

2. X5 must stay high on 5 to discourage a pass inside. If X3 plays 3's body, X5 must see 3 through and then close back quickly on 5. X5's main job is to prevent a catch by 5, although he does have to give some help to X3. X4 will give help to X3 by dropping off from the weak side. This allows 4 to be open, but that is the safest option to allow.

3. X1 must deny 1 the snap-back pass from 2; this is a key point in defending the play. It keeps X5 from getting beat in a lock and seal move should the ball get back to 1 for a pass inside as in D-93.

DEFENDING THE CORNER SERIES

Over the years many NBA and college teams have run a series of moves keyed on passing the ball to the corner. Not the least of these have been the Chicago Bulls under Phil Jackson. Gene Shue got a lot of mileage out of the play for many years at Philadelphia and Washington. D-94 shows 3 passing the ball to the corner to player 1 and then running a cut off 5's backpick. If 1 does not pass to 3 or 5, then 5 will step out and set the pick/roll action with 1.

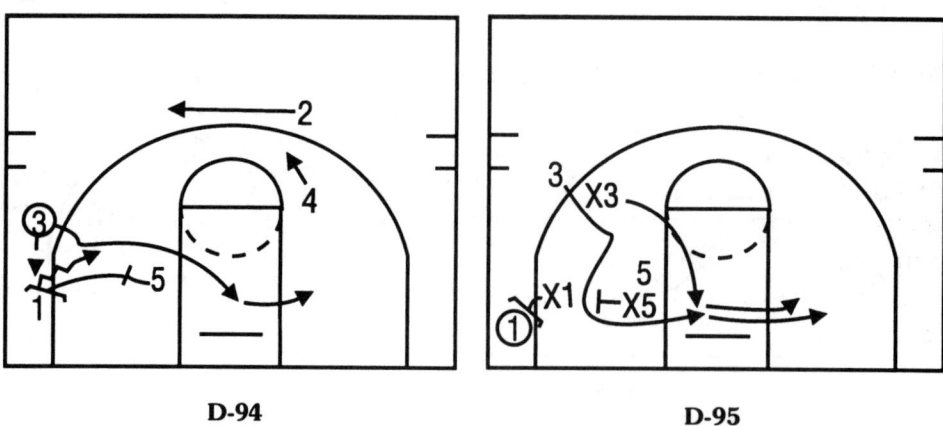

D-94   D-95

One method to defend this action is to deny the pass to the corner as often as needed, and this takes away the play. Most teams do not mind if the ball goes into the corner, however. If the ball does go there, X3 must play 3 on the side of the pick opposite the ball. He must take the free throw lane side to prevent 3 from receiving a lob pass from 1, a very dangerous option. Just like defending the UCLA guard-downcut, X5 must get to the baseline side of 5 and he can bump 3 if 3 cuts on the baseline side of the pick, to buy time for X3 to recover to 3 (D-95).

guard-downcut, X5 must get to the baseline side of 5 and he can bump 3 if 3 cuts on the baseline side of the pick, to buy time for X3 to recover to 3 (D-95).

X5 must close back up on the baseline side of 5 quickly to prevent 1 from hitting 5 after 3 rubs off him. At this point 5 will step out to pick 1 (D-96). X1 should have gotten to the high side of 1 as soon as 1 caught the ball to fan him to the baseline and prevent the reverse pass. This puts X1 and X5 in perfect position to fan the pick and roll. X5 is in a position between the ball and the basket. If 1 tries to penetrate, X5 will trap with X1. X2 will play the pass out to the top, looking for a steal. X4 and X3 will jam in to form the baseline wall (D-97).

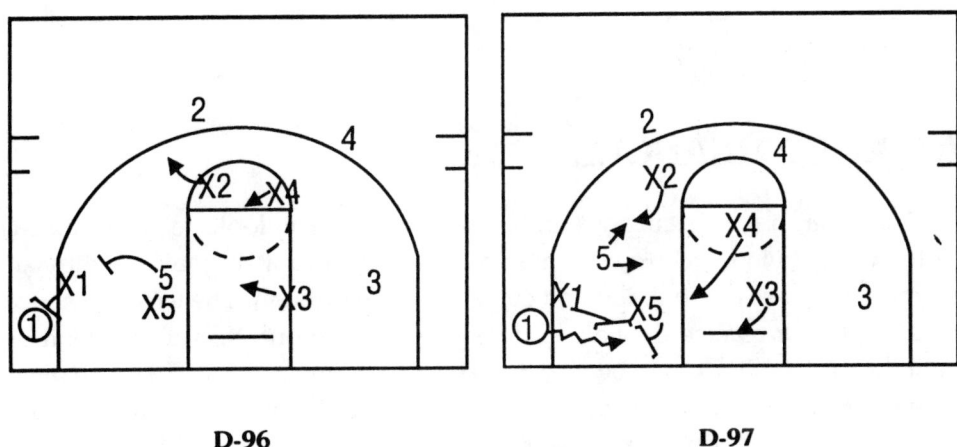

D-96   **D-97**

DEFENDING THE TURNOUT SERIES

Jack Ramsay, a master coach at many levels, popularized the turnout action among other contributions in his many years in the NBA. His champion Trailblazers were very good at utilizing turnout action in transition. Nearly every NBA team uses a form of the play more than fifteen years later. Whether in transition or as a set play for the regular offense, or from isolation, there are various options that can be utilized.

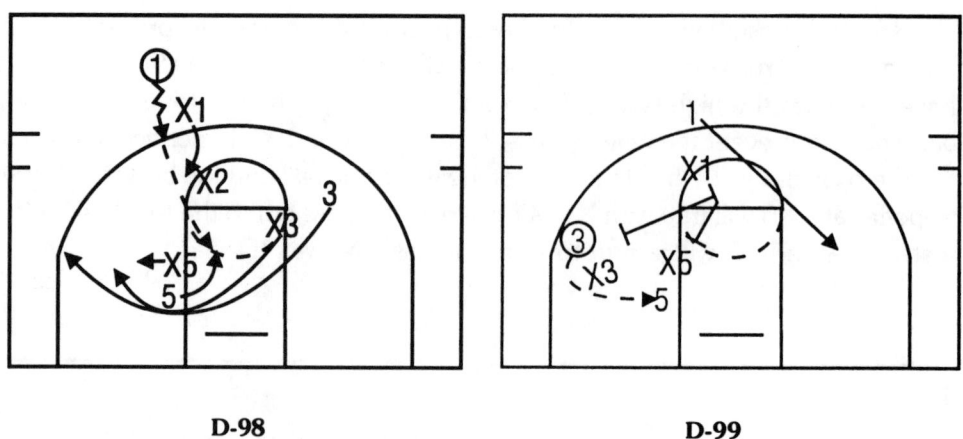

D-98   **D-99**

TURNOUT TRIANGLE OPTION

A shooter, player 3, cuts out under the post man and looks to catch the ball on the wing. As in D-98 player 1 may pass directly to 5 if X5 makes a mistake. Normally he passes to the wing and cuts diagonally through. The wing will shoot, drive, feed 5, or reverse the ball. In defending the turnout, X5 will stay high on 5 and try to give X3 room to be able to go over or under 5's pick. There are many possible options available on defense. X1 could trap the wing as soon as 1 cuts into the lane or X1 could wait to trap 5 in the low post, if the ball goes into him (D-99).

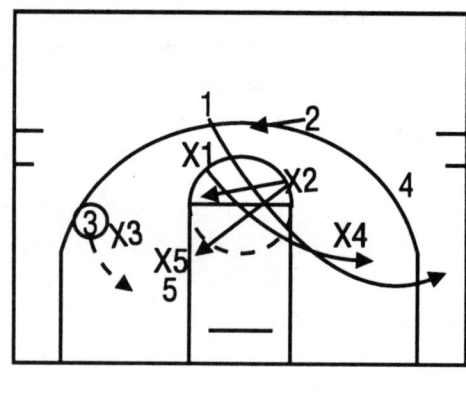

D-100

X2 could trap the low post or he could trap 3 on the wing after 1 has cut through (D-100). Naturally, the play can be defended straight up with help given only when it is needed.

LOW POST 1 ON 1 OPTION

If the wing passes to the low post, he will either drift for a kickout pass, cut through for a return pass or just clear out for 5's 1 on 1 move. In defending the play, X3 could trap from the wing when the pass goes in or trap off 3 after 3 cuts through the lane (D-101). The defense can trap with X2 as in D-100 or possibly with X4. Again, the defense could play 1 on 1 and wait to give help when absolutely necessarily.

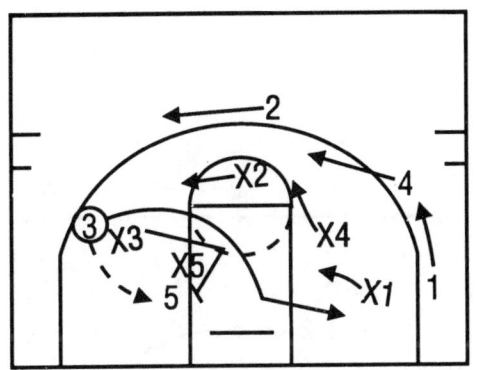

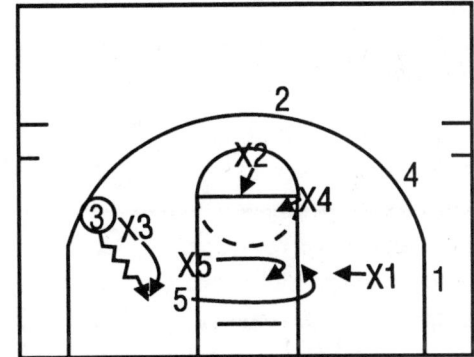

D-101   D-102

WING 1 ON 1 OPTION

Often times the offense will clear out to allow the wing player to go 1 on 1 as in D-102. There are several options to consider in attacking this action besides the obvious straight up man-to-man. The choices on defense include:

- Trap on the catch of 3 with X1 as mentioned; or on his first serious bounce with X2; or wait until the ballhandler/cutter is in the lane and then trap with the nearest man. The trapper can be told to come quickly or slowly. Regardless, the defense must be alert for a fake drive by the offense to "bait" the defense into committing to a trap to stretch the defense.
- The defense on 3 can force him to the outside or inside; play straight up tight; or drop in soft.

- The defense can trap from the nearest outside man (X2), or from the baseline (X5), or from the weakside (X4), or from the cutter (X1). Depending on the abilities of the players involved, the defense will usually select one or two options from the three bulleted above.

THE LOW POST CURL MOVE

Instead of turning out to the wing, the cutter can use the curl move. This requires the bump-the-curl technique on defense as shown in D-103. In defending the curl, X5 must be ready to put his body on 3, if 3 curls over 5. Player X3 must keep coming to get to 3 to release X5 so that X5 can close back up on 5.

There are some variations on this. X5 can play high and loose to allow X3 the choice to trail 3 as in D-103 or to short-cut between 5 and X5. X5 can put his body down on 5 (squeeze) and give X3 the same over or under option (D-104). Of course, if the ball goes inside, there are the various trapping options that are available.

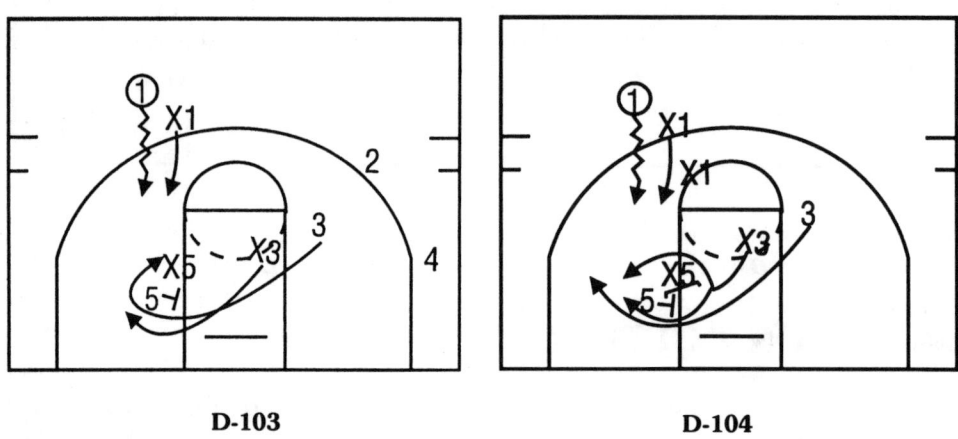

D-103   D-104

SUMMARY OF DEFENDING THE TWO- AND THREE-MAN EXERCISES

While the determination to play defense combined with the willingness to give up one's body physically are more important than technique, to be truly outstanding on defense an individual and team must combine intelligent technique with great desire.

This section on defending the 2- and 3-man exercises is critical to defensive success at both the individual and team levels. The better each individual understands different techniques in defending these plays, the more likely the team is to be able to put together a good overall defense.

All the major offenses involve the 2-man and 3-man actions described in this section, so when a player gets hot in an offense, knowledge of two or three ways to defend the basic offensive maneuvers can help a defender feel like he has a chance to equalize his assignment.

A FINAL WORD

It is my hope that high school and college players and coaches at various levels have benefitted from reviewing this book. While the most important determining factor in having successful defense for any player or coach will be the measure of his pure desire to get the job done, the knowledge of the various elements set forth in this book will be of great help. It represents an accumulation of information that has evolved over the years as the result of having worked with or against some of the best coaches and players who have ever been involved in the game.

While NBA basketball will always be considered a player's game because of the entertainment nature of the league and the necessary marketing of its great players, some of the best basketball minds in the history of the game have plied their trade in the NBA. Although credit may never be granted the pro coach like it is the college coach, every collegiate coach (including this one) who has ever entered the NBA ranks has at some point been overwhelmed by the depth of knowledge necessary to set up an NBA offense or defense. The NBA players are so good offensively that scouting reports, film study and developing new techniques to try to slow down the great players is a full time job for coaches and players alike.

Drills for Defense

The best drills for a team are those that are devised specifically and intelligently by the coach of that team. They will be drills that fit exactly into the framework of the concepts he is teaching, designed for maximum carryover and in a context that is logical to the players. The wise coach will be able to explain through these drills not only how to execute the various elements, but in the process will try to explain the more difficult concept of when to execute them.

The master coach will spend as much time in trying to figure out the best way to teach as he will what to teach. Good teaching demands ongoing curiosity. Great teaching requires finding simpler ways to impart the information.

The drills presented here are some that we have used to help get our points across, but each week we would often find a little different way to present a point. Therefore, these items are presented only for starters. Each good coach will find his own way to teach, which will be better than any drill book can demonstrate.

TRANSITION DEFENSE DRILLS

- **1-on-1 zig-zag.** D-1 shows X1 turning the ball by putting his body in front of the ball, making sure to force the ball to cross the halfcourt line in the outside lane. One line of players can begin at each end, being sure not to cross the imaginary vertical halfcourt line to avoid collisions. The offense will not wait for the defender to catch up if he beats him in the backcourt. At the halfcourt line the offensive player passes the ball to a coach or manager and gets it back to go a live, hard 1-1 in the front court.
- **2-on-2 contain.** D-2 shows the man guarding the inbounds passer getting into the 41 and going to the halfcourt, making sure to keep the ball out of the middle. The same can be done with 31 and 21. The players go 2-on-2 live after using the pass to the coach or manager as in the 1-on-1 drill. Mix in using this drill from a rebound.
- **4 on 4 contain.** Two more players are added. The back man becomes the safety and the other inside man becomes the sprinter. The ball is jammed, the outlet is covered, and they play 4 on 4 after the ball gets into the front court.

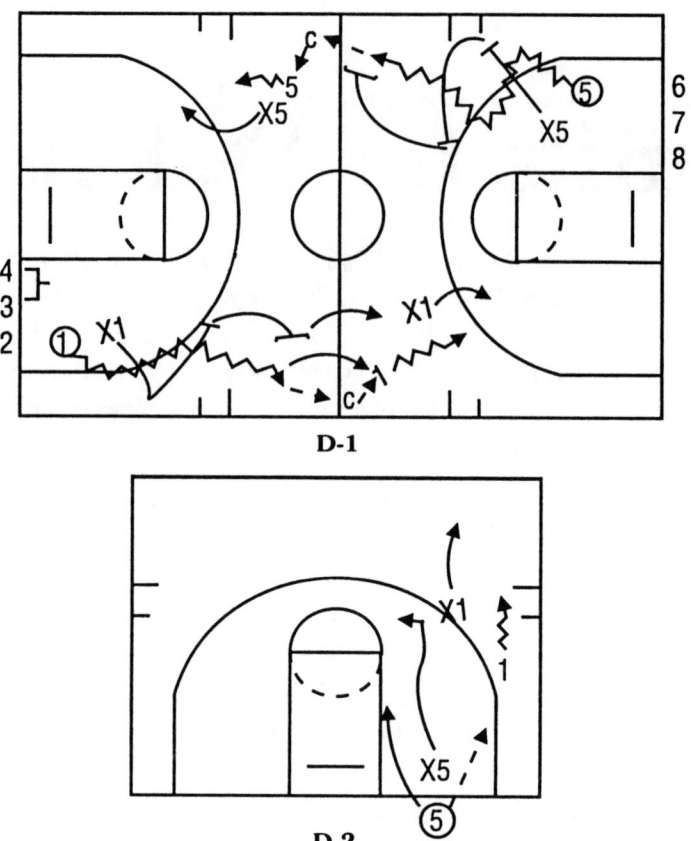

D-1

D-2

- **5-on-5 transition.** One of the most important drills involves having five offensive players pass the ball twice and then one player shoot the ball. The shot is contested only with hand pressure — it is not to be blocked. The defense executes the proper blockouts as monitored by a coach. The offense gets to the 2-2-1 for defensive transition. If the shot goes in, the defensive signaller (normally the point guard) calls out the defense and everyone adjusts. If the shot misses, the 41 defense against the missed shot is executed and is monitored by a coach. The ball is moved to the other end and is played live on the other end. If the new offensive team scores or misses, the new defense responds accordingly. The ball becomes dead and the drill starts over once the play is ended on the original end. It's only up and down the court once, then the drill is started over for more effective teaching. After three repetitions, the teams change defensive and offensive positions on the original end. Later, it is possible to allow up and back two times or even three times before the play is stopped.

Note: This controlled work must be done 2-2, 4-4, and 5-5, but the controlled aspect of this is what full court transition teaching is all about. The team learns all the points about rebounding and transition offense and defense. When teams make mistakes, a good way to correct is to stop the action and line up everyone just where they were when the error was made. Then let them finish the play (either from an offensive or defensive standpoint) in a better way.

- **Transition vs. the numbers.** One coach takes a pool of 5 players and lines them up at the halfcourt line while five defensive players take position on the other end. A coach or player throws up a shot and the five defenders get the ball and attack the other end. As the shot goes up, the coach with the pool of players calls out 1, 2, 3, 4 or 5 player's names. If he calls out 2 names, then those two quickly get back to defend the goal against the fast break. The other three men must run from the halfcourt line to the top of the free throw circle and then catch up with the offense to try to stop the transition attack. They try to work to contain the break and to get big men inside and smaller men out in an effort to stop any easy shots. After one try, the drill begins again on the opposite end. Go three or five times and change the men in the pool.

HALFCOURT DEFENSIVE DRILLING

- All work at halfcourt with 1-on-1, 2-on-2, 3-on-3, 4-on 4 and 5-on-5 must be done to emphasize the various points of teaching needed: overplays for fan and funnel, pick and roll, backpicks, crosspicks, downpicks, etc. The coach can have three or four stations where the players can rotate after three to five minutes. At each station a coach will be teaching one aspect of defense. A good game to use is to play 3-on-3 or 4-on-4 and tell the offense that they have to run one of the basic moves before they can shoot. This can be changed to two or three moves. For example, they may be told they have to execute a crosspick and a backpick before they can shoot. Or they may be told to run a downpick and a pick and roll before they can shoot.
- Once the pick and roll action is being used extensively by opponents, it is worth ten to fifteen minutes to drill different ways to defend it quite often. This is where the players can be allowed to call out their own coverage (from choices given by the coach) after they become adept at three or four coverages or more.
- **Switching game.** Play passing game offense and/or set offenses against defense at halfcourt and alternate between allowing the defense *no switch* (except for the emergency switch); having the defense *switch every screen* and cross, regardless of mismatch (work on trapping out the mismatches); and on *switching equals* and big in/little out.
- **Low post defense.** Work all the players on the team on 1-on-1 low post defense in groups of four. This drills defense and offense as well. Be sure to work every player and drill on the various aspects listed in the book such as the early contact, fronting, etc.

- **Triangle low post defense.** Set 3-on-3 or 4-on-4 with a low post man. Put the outside triangle points in the wing and corner (D-3) and then change it to wing and top in the 3-on-3 (D-4). Work on denying the reverse pass up to prevent the easy lock-and-seal pass to the low post. "Splitting the post" moves can be drilled with this.
- **"Miami" or 6-point drill.** Tates Locke used this kind of drill at Miami of Ohio many years ago. It more than likely evolved from Al Lobalbo's theories and today most coaches use some variation of it. D-3 and 4 show how the wing defender denies his man out to the defensive perimeter at 19, 21 or 23 feet while the coach has the ball out front. The offensive player fakes a backdoor cut by going one or two steps to the goal and the defender does not totally accept this fake in favor of denying him a second time at the defensive perimeter. Then the offensive man cuts to the goal. The defender swivels his head (some defensive coaches prefer to have the defender open to the ball) and stays in a good position to keep the ball out of the low post. Then the offensive man crosses the lane and breaks out to the other side in D-4. The coach moves from elbow to elbow or passes it to another coach. The defender denies the ball out to the perimeter on the new side. The drill can end here or it can end by letting the offense catch on the wing and play 1-on-1. Players should get a lot of repetitions per week on this drill.

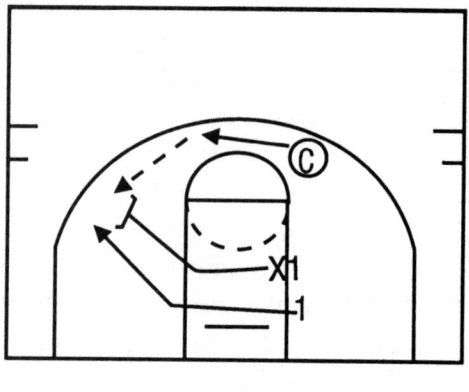

D-3   D-4

- **Bump the cutter drill.** D-5 and 6 show another fundamental drill that must be worked many times per week. Player 1 passes to the coach on the wing and cuts toward the low post and looks to post up. X1 executes the bump and release technique on the cutter and assumes a good post position on the man. The ball is passed into the corner to another coach. At that time the defender must get to the baseline side of the man. Player 1 gets so deep in the post that X1 is forced to front him and must yell out "front." Then 1 cuts through the lane and X1 goes with him but maintains his position, seeing the ball and guarding the man, the ball and the lane.

The ball is passed back up to the wing and at that time 1 cuts from the baseline to the ball. X1 must bump him away from the ball and maintain a denial position between the man and the ball. Player 1 then backcuts to the strong side block. X1 must open to the ball and feel the cutter as he cuts to the goal. Finally, he gets into a denial position once again in the post. The drill can end there or they can go 1-on-1 in the post.

This drill can be run in two parts as well. That is, the last part of the drill where 1 cuts from the weak side through the lane toward the ball, then backcuts to the strongside post can be called the "lane cutter" drill.

- **Rebound drill.** Put players in a line in front of the goal at two or more goals (D-7). The coach shoots up a shot and the first man must turn and block out the second man and get the rebound. He passes the outlet pass back to the coach under pressure by the man who did not get the rebound and that man goes to the end of the line. The coach tosses up another shot. If X1 gets three rebounds in a row, he gets to go to the end of the line or to another station. This drill can be expanded to two or three lines and the number of rebounds can vary from two to three or four. If you make it too many, it can last too long. Still, it is good to stay tough and let the players know they cannot get anywhere if they do not rebound.

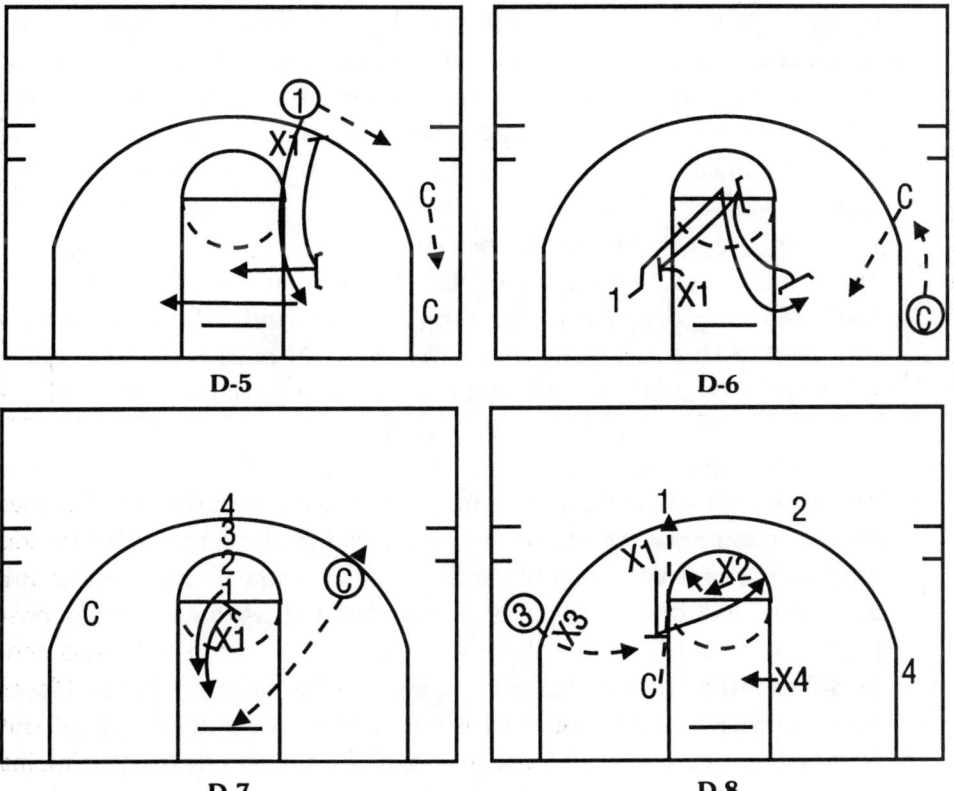

D-5   D-6

D-7   D-8

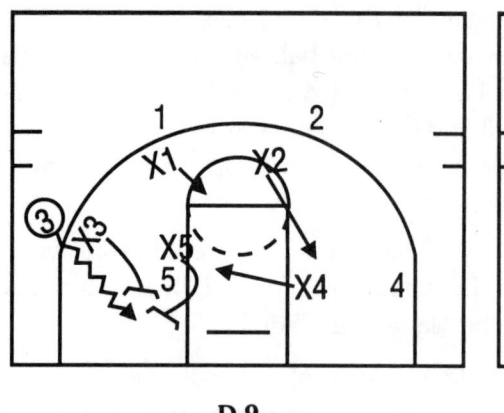

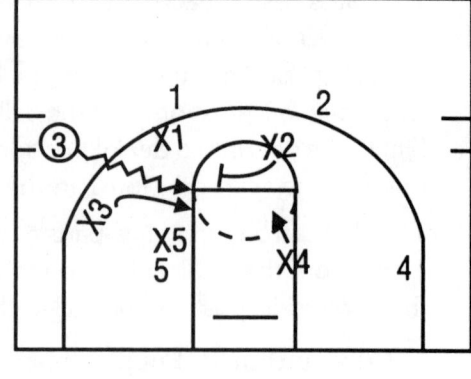

D-9   D-10

ROTATIONS DRILLS

- **4 on 4 with the coach.** Put the coach in the low post. Four offensive players spread out with two out front and two on the wings as in D-8. The ball will be passed to the coach from the wing and the coach will call out where the trap will come from (area 1, 2, 3, or 4). After drilling the basics this way, the coach can send a cutter through when the trap is made. Do a wing cutter and then do a cutter from the front. Insist on the proper execution of traps, rotations, getting to the zone spots, talking to hand off cutters, etc.

- **Expand the rotations drill** to include all five offensive and defensive players after a few practices. Again, the coach must call out the options to be used in the traps. As a team gains in proficiency, use variations like "live man," live off of a particular man, and finally the "5," where they are on their own. Be sure to work all players at all spots since players may be anywhere when a trap occurs.

- **Drill the traps in the high, wing, corner and elbow areas and emphasize the rotations.** Note that you can have a halfcourt game whereby the offense is not allowed to shoot until there has been a trap, in order to give both the offense and the defense this experience.

- **Build the baseline wall.** Put the ball on the wing and place the rest of the players in general positions spread out on the court (D-9). Then have the wing man drive the ball to the basket and work on the techniques of building the wall. Work with the low post filled and with it open. Be sure to put players in different positions. One team goes five times and they rotate.

- **Middle penetration drill.** Do the same as in the baseline rotation, except have the ballhandler penetrate the middle. Work on the front men from both the strong side and weak side plus the back men reacting to the penetration (D-10).

MASTERS PRESS

DEAR VALUED CUSTOMER,

Masters Press is dedicated to bringing you timely and authoritative books for your personal and professional library. As a leading publisher of sports and fitness books, our goal is to provide you with easily accessible information on topics that interest you written by the most qualified authors. You can assist us in this endeavor by checking the box next to your particular areas of interest.

We appreciate your comments and will use the information to provide you with an expanded and more comprehensive selection of titles.

Thank you very much for taking the time to provide us with this helpful information.

Cordially,
Masters Press

Areas of interest in which you'd like to see Masters Press publish books:

☐ COACHING BOOKS
   Which sports? What level of competition?

☐ INSTRUCTIONAL/DRILL BOOKS
   Which sports? What level of competition?

☐ FITNESS/EXERCISE BOOKS
   ☐ Strength—Weight Training
   ☐ Body Building
   ☐ Other

☐ REFERENCE BOOKS
   what kinds?

☐ BOOKS ON OTHER
   Games, Hobbies
   or Activities

Are you more likely to read a book or watch a video-tape to get the sports information you are looking for?

I'm interested in the following sports as a participant:

I'm interested in the following sports as an observer:

Please feel free to offer any comments or suggestions to help us shape our publishing plan for the future.

Name _____ Age _____

Address _____

City _____ State _____ Zip _____

Daytime phone number _____

BUSINESS REPLY MAIL

FIRST CLASS MAIL   PERMIT NO. 1317   INDIANAPOLIS IN

POSTAGE WILL BE PAID BY ADDRESSEE

MASTERS PRESS

2647 WATERFRONT PKY EAST DR

INDIANAPOLIS IN 46209-1418

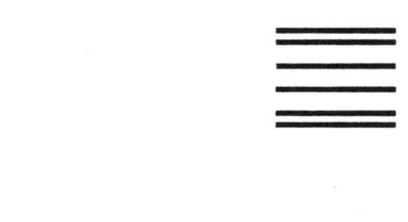